Holocaust Representations in History

Perspectives on the Holocaust

A series of books designed to help students further their understanding of key topics within the field of Holocaust studies.

Published:
Holocaust Representations in History, Daniel H. Magilow and Lisa Silverman

Forthcoming:
Postwar Germany and the Holocaust, Caroline Sharples (2015)
Sites of Holocaust Memory, Janet Ward (2016)
Anti-Semitism and the Holocaust, Beth A. Griech-Polelle (2016)
The Holocaust in Eastern Europe, Waitman W. Beorn (2017)

Holocaust Representations in History

An Introduction

DANIEL H. MAGILOW AND LISA SILVERMAN

Bloomsbury Academic
An imprint of Bloomsbury Publishing Plc

B L O O M S B U R Y
LONDON · OXFORD · NEW YORK · NEW DELHI · SYDNEY

Bloomsbury Academic
An imprint of Bloomsbury Publishing Plc

50 Bedford Square
London
WC1B 3DP
UK

1385 Broadway
New York
NY 10018
USA

www.bloomsbury.com

BLOOMSBURY and the Diana logo are trademarks of Bloomsbury Publishing Plc

First published 2015
Reprinted by Bloomsbury Academic 2015

British Library Cataloguing-in-Publication Data
A catalogue record for this book is available from the British Library.

ISBN: HB: 978-1-4725-1030-3
PB: 978-1-4725-0684-9
ePDF: 978-1-4725-1300-7
ePUB: 978-1-4725-1242-0

Library of Congress Cataloging-in-Publication Data
Magilow, Daniel H., 1973 – author.
Holocaust representations in history: an introduction/Daniel H. Magilow and Lisa Silverman.
pages cm
Includes bibliographical references and index.
ISBN 978-1-4725-1030-3 (hardback) — ISBN 978-1-4725-0684-9 (paperback) — ISBN 978-1-4725-1300-7 (epdf)
1. Holocaust, Jewish (1939–1945)—Historiography. 2. Holocaust, Jewish (1939–1945)—Influence. I. Silverman, Lisa, 1969– author. II. Title.
D804.348.M34 2015
940.53'18072—dc23
2014024671

Series: Perspectives on the Holocaust

Typeset by RefineCatch Limited, Bungay, Suffolk
Printed and bound in Great Britain

To Saul Kagan (z"l) and Susan Magilow,
who introduced us to the importance of Holocaust history,
memory, and representation.

Contents

List of Illustrations ix

Acknowledgments x

Holocaust Representations in History: An Introduction 1

PART ONE The 1940s and 1950s 11

1   The Boy in the Warsaw Ghetto (photograph, 1943):
     What do iconic photographs tell us about the
     Holocaust? 13

2   *Nazi Concentration Camps* (documentary film, 1945):
     Can the Holocaust be adequately represented on
     film? 23

3   *Yizker-bukh Khelm* (memorial book, 1954): How did Jews talk
     about the Holocaust in its aftermath? 33

4   *The Diary of Anne Frank* (drama, 1955): What is the
     Americanization of the Holocaust? 43

5   *Night* (memoir, 1956/1958): What does it mean to be a
     Holocaust survivor? 53

PART TWO The 1960s and 1970s 61

6   *Eichmann in Jerusalem* (book, 1963): What role do trials
     play in how we remember the Holocaust? 63

7   *The Deputy* (drama, 1963): What role did the Catholic Church
     play in the Holocaust? 73

8   *Il portiere di notte* (*The Night Porter*) (film, 1974): What is the
     ongoing appeal of the Holocaust and Nazism? 83

9   *Holocaust: The Story of the Family Weiss* (television, 1978):
     Do representations for mass audiences trivialize the
     Holocaust? 93

PART THREE The 1980s and 1990s 101

10 *Shoah* (film, 1985): What is the role of witness testimony in
     representations of the Holocaust? 103
11 *Maus: A Survivor's Tale* (graphic novel, 1986–1991): How is the
     memory of the Holocaust transmitted across generations? 113
12 United States Holocaust Memorial Museum (museum, 1993):
     How do countries outside Germany commemorate the
     Holocaust? 123
13 *Fragments: Memories of a Wartime Childhood* (fiction, 1996):
     What does it mean to lie about the Holocaust? 133

PART FOUR The 2000s and Beyond 141

14 The Children's Holocaust Memorial (memorial, 2001):
     How is the Holocaust used to teach about diversity? 143
15 *Mirroring Evil: Nazi Imagery/Recent Art* (museum exhibition,
     2002): Has the memory of the Holocaust become too
     commercial? 153
16 Memorial to the Murdered Jews of Europe (memorial, 2005):
     Is there an end to Holocaust memory? 163

Notes 173
Further Reading 195
Index 211

List of Illustrations

Cover German prisoners of war forced to watch atrocity films

1	The Boy in the Warsaw Ghetto	12
2	A British army cameraman films at the newly liberated Bergen-Belsen concentration camp	22
3	A representative page from the *Yizker-bukh Khelm*	32
4	Susan Strasberg, who played the title role in the Broadway play *The Diary of Anne Frank*	42
5	Elie Wiesel at a wreath-laying ceremony in Birkenau in 1979	52
6	Adolf Eichmann on trial in Jerusalem	62
7	Protestors disrupt a performance of Rolf Hochhuth's *The Deputy*	72
8	Lucia Atherton (Charlotte Rampling) entertains SS-men in *The Night Porter*	82
9	Inga Helms Weiss (Meryl Streep) laments the loss of her husband in *Holocaust: The Story of the Family Weiss*	92
10	Director Claude Lanzmann interviews Polish villagers in *Shoah*	102
11	A page from Art Spiegelman's *Maus* on a Budapest subway train	112
12	Visitors at the United States Holocaust Memorial Museum	122
13	Binjamin Wilkomirski, author of *Fragments: Memories of a Wartime Childhood*	132
14	The Children's Holocaust Memorial in Whitwell, Tennessee	142
15	Zbigniew Libera's *LEGO Concentration Camp* on display at *Mirroring Evil: Nazi Imagery/Recent Art*	152
16	Peter Eisenman's *Memorial to the Murdered Jews of Europe* in Berlin	162

Acknowledgments

The authors would like to thank several individuals and institutions for assisting with various aspects of this book. The Department of Modern Foreign Languages and Literatures, the Humanities Center, and the Office of Research and Engagement at the University of Tennessee, Knoxville assisted this project with publication subvention. Thanks go out to Megan Bryson, Doug Canfield, Georg Essl, Eric D. Gedenk, Maria Stehle, and Rebecca Steinitz for their assistance with drafts and photographs. Nancy Hartman and Judy Cohen at the United States Holocaust Memorial Museum offered assistance in locating images in the Museum's photo archives. Nevertheless, the views or opinions expressed in this book and the contexts in which the images are used, do not necessarily reflect the views or policy of, nor imply approval or endorsement by, the United States Holocaust Memorial Museum.

Holocaust Representations in History:

An Introduction

The Holocaust is not simply a label for the twentieth century's best-known genocide. It has become a household word, a "master moral paradigm," in one scholar's phrasing, unparalleled in its enormity and scope and, whether appropriately or not, the point of comparison for all other major disasters.[1] Interest in the Holocaust has grown tremendously among students and scholars over the last few decades, in parallel with new media that have made it possible to access its history at the click of a button. But interpreting the Holocaust has never been a straightforward endeavor. Like every complex set of historical events, the Holocaust has never consisted of a simple set of recognizable and agreed-upon facts. To begin with, there are controversies about its origins, the motivations of the Nazis and the ordinary people who supported them, the extent to which Jews resisted or cooperated, and how persecution varied among people of different genders, among many other topics.[2] But even as people argue these specific points, there is the greater challenge to interpretation: that our knowledge of the Holocaust comes from *representations*, the term at the heart of this book.

Holocaust representations are the documents, testimonies, photographs, memoirs, novels, interviews, dramas, artworks, films, monuments, and other symbolic depictions, created at the time and after the fact, whose subject matter is the Holocaust. For those of us who were not there—and today that includes all but a dwindling few of us—representations are the way we access the Holocaust. To effectively unpack a Holocaust representation, we need to ask specific crucial questions, including: Who made it? Where, when, why, and under what circumstances? What audiences did it initially target, and how have these audiences evolved? Has the representation itself changed over time and, if so, how? What popular and scholarly discussions have developed around these representations? *Holocaust Representations in History: An Introduction* aims to supply students, their instructors, and general readers with the background and analytical tools they need, both to begin answering these questions and to pose new ones. It is intended as an introductory companion to the classroom study of Holocaust representations across a wide range of media. Each chapter's task is to condense and clarify the complex debates around these works and thereby situate them within their historical and geographic contexts. Although the chapters follow a chronological arc (see below), each is self-contained and thus the book need not necessarily be read from cover to cover. Yet this book is intended only to complement, not replace, the readings of primary texts. To this end, individual works are summarized only to the extent that doing so helps one understand their significance.

This book is not intended to serve as a history of the Holocaust, nor even as a history of the representation of the Holocaust. Rather, it is an attempt to model a responsible intellectual engagement with representations of the Holocaust. If, as one commentator argues, the representation of the Holocaust "now constitutes a language of its own, which is in wide circulation across all levels of our culture and is used and misused in manifold ways," this book provides the etymology and grammar of that language, so that students can better understand its use and misuse.[3] Its goal is not to impart definitive lessons, but rather to help students begin to pose their own questions about the broader meanings, ethical significance, and continued relevance of the Holocaust.

Learning to think critically about Holocaust representations, going beyond the platitudes that such a sensitive and horrifying subject invariably generates, is a vital undertaking. And its importance increases daily. In just a few years, there will be no one alive who actually witnessed the Holocaust: no perpetrators, bystanders, victims, killers, survivors, enablers, or liberators.[4] The Holocaust will become like any other long-past historical event, which we can only learn about and remember by reading, watching, and engaging with its representations, be they photographs, films, and diaries of the time, or dramas, graphic novels, memorials, and museums created decades later. If representations are to become our only access, we need to understand how and why they work the way they do.

Scholars have long noted that a combination of historical and ethical limits shape every attempt to represent the past events of the Holocaust, whether works of art, memorials, or history books.[5] This book argues that thinking critically about how these limits developed and changed over time is just as crucial to understanding these representations as is the analysis of the content of any particular work. To approach this challenge, this book uses selected case studies to examine key debates, questions, and controversies in the history of Holocaust representation. Proceeding chronologically from the 1940s to the present, each chapter introduces analytical tools and conceptual frameworks that both apply to the representations it addresses and can—and should—be applied to cultural materials that fall outside its immediate purview. Synthesizing recent scholarship, these analyses emphasize each Holocaust representation's specific historical and cultural significance and show how the issues it raises have informed broader theoretical, historical, political, and artistic debates in the United States, Europe, and beyond. Defining the six component words of the title *Holocaust Representations in History: An Introduction* further explains this book's goals and approach.

Holocaust

We use the term "Holocaust" to refer to the State-sponsored genocide of European Jewry perpetrated by Nazi Germany and its collaborators. Since the late1950s, this term has become the most well-known designation in English-language contexts, but it is only one of several names that have been given to this set of events, and it is a controversial one at that.[6] As scholar James E. Young notes, even the names that we assign to this genocide "automatically figure and contextualize [its] events, locating them within the continua of particular historical, literary, and interpretive traditions."[7] The Nazi bureaucrats who coordinated the logistics of murder used bureaucratic euphemisms such as *Evakuierung* (evacuation), *Umsiedlung* (resettlement), or *Endlösung der Judenfrage* (the final solution of the Jewish question) to describe their efforts. This last phrase quickly betrays its ideological prejudices by implying that Jews are a problem to be definitively solved. Indeed, "the final solution" suggests that the Nazis saw their actions not as catastrophic, but as valuable and necessary. Yet its vague, bureaucratic evasiveness also suggests that these perpetrators wanted to keep their (criminal) actions under wraps.

The terms that victims prefer are biased in their own ways. Yiddish speakers, a group that today largely corresponds to devout Orthodox Jews, refer to these events as *khurbn* (destruction) or *khurbn eyrope* (European destruction). *Khurbn* derives from the Hebrew *churban*, which originally referred to the destruction of the Second Temple in Jerusalem in 70 CE, the paradigmatic catastrophe of Jewish history that is commemorated annually on the holiday Tisha B'Av. By linking the twentieth-century catastrophe to such a significant predecessor, *khurbn* frames the modern genocide as part of a much longer history of Jewish persecution and historical identity. In short, the names people ascribe to this particular act of State-sponsored mass murder embody their assumptions, whatever their standpoints.[8]

Even the most familiar English-language designation, Holocaust, rests on assumptions that some find deeply offensive. Yad Vashem, The Holocaust Martyrs' and Heroes' Remembrance Authority in Israel, defines Holocaust thus:

(in Hebrew, *sho'ah*), the name used in English to refer to the systematic destruction of European Jewry at the hands of the Nazis during World War II. The word *Holocaust* comes from the Greek word *holokauston*, which is a translation of the Hebrew word *olah*. During Biblical times, an *olah* was a type of sacrifice to God that was totally consumed or burnt by fire. Over time, the word holocaust came to be used with reference to large-scale slaughter or destruction.[9]

Etymologically, then, the term Holocaust would seem to imply that six million Jews died for a reason, or even that their deaths were a necessary sacrifice. For many audiences, this language of offerings, sacrifice, martyrdom, and dying for a higher purpose evokes redemptive Christian imagery. Indeed, scholars have long noted that consciously or not, the Holocaust and its representations are often approached through confessional lenses, often those of non-Jews. As David G. Roskies has written, "the most private of Jewish concerns [the genocide of Jews] becomes part of the public domain, external perceptions replace inner realities, and borrowed words and archetypes are enlisted to explain the meaning of the destruction not only to Gentiles but even to Jews."[10] While the desire to give some meaning—any meaning—to the senseless slaughter of millions is perhaps understandable, the complex etymology of the term "Holocaust" suggests that redeeming the Holocaust is a religious and theological project, not a purely historical one. And even if this word origin remains obscure to most audiences, many scholars prefer *sho'ah* or *shoah* (Hebrew for "catastrophe") for its specifically Jewish associations. This book uses Holocaust because it has become the most common term, but it is nevertheless important to acknowledge its origins, especially in the face of the representations that try to redeem the Holocaust and find some intrinsic value in mass murder.

Another controversy in defining the Holocaust has to do with its victims. During the planning phases of the United States Holocaust Memorial Museum (USHMM), intense debates broke out over the extent to which the Holocaust should be defined (and thus exhibited) as specifically Jewish or if the definition should also include other victimized groups.[11] In the end, the museum defined the Holocaust as "the systematic, bureaucratic, state-sponsored persecution and murder of approximately six million Jews by the Nazi regime and its collaborators," and then extended its definition with the following sentences: "During the era of the Holocaust, German authorities also targeted other groups because of their perceived 'racial inferiority': Roma (Gypsies), the disabled, and some of the Slavic peoples (Poles, Russians, and others). Other groups were persecuted on political, ideological, and behavioral grounds, among them Communists, Socialists, Jehovah's Witnesses, and homosexuals."[12] Yad Vashem, however, stakes its ground more narrowly: "Although the term is sometimes used with reference to the murder of other groups by the Nazis, strictly speaking, those groups do not belong under the heading of the Holocaust, nor are they included in the generally accepted statistic of six million victims of the Holocaust." These differences reveal the powerful political legacy of the Holocaust. The USHMM's definition reflects the American self-image of the United States as a haven for all persecuted peoples, while Israel's self-understanding is closely tied to the notion that it exists to protect Jews from further catastrophes. In the ramifications of these varying names and definitions of a single event, we see the workings of representation at the most basic levels of our undertaking.

Representations

"Representations" is an umbrella term for signs or symbols that stand in for something else.[13] In the simplest sense, the word "apple" is a representation of a red fruit, just as Da Vinci's *Mona Lisa* is a representation of a noblewoman during the Italian Renaissance, and Holocaust representations are representations that in some way reference the genocide defined above. However, representation is often used as a synonym for art, in the sense of highly valued cultural products. Indeed, many of the cultural materials addressed in the following chapters—dramas, memoirs, films, photographs, and memorials, to name a few—are precisely the kinds of representations studied in university courses on "Holocaust Art and Literature." This book focuses on representations, instead of art and literature, because the latter terms raise value judgments about what kinds of representations qualify as art or literature. These distinctions have been a defining element of Western tradition since classical antiquity, and the belief that exposing young people to great works of art ennobles them, broadens their horizons, and frees them from prejudice and ignorance has long guided the project of a liberal arts education.

To appreciate why this idea might not be entirely valid, one need only look at the first page of the minutes of the January 20, 1942 meeting at the Wannsee Villa outside Berlin, where German bureaucrats planned the logistics of their "final solution." Half of the participants have the title "Dr." in front of their names, signifying their attainment of the pinnacle of a university education. This example may be extreme, but it reminds us that being educated at one of Germany's world-class research universities was not enough to prevent these men from becoming war criminals. Moreover, one of the most frequently cited quotations in the study of Holocaust representations further challenges the notion that art ennobles people. In 1951, the German philosopher Theodor W. Adorno famously wrote, in the essay "Cultural Criticism and Society," that "To write poetry after Auschwitz is barbaric."[14] This declaration is sometimes read as a ban on representing the Holocaust at all, a so-called *Bilderverbot* (image ban, a German word that evokes the biblical prohibition on making graven images). In this interpretation, "poetry" serves as a metaphor for all types of representation; Adorno is claiming that any attempt to represent the Holocaust, whatever the medium, will fail to do it justice. But it is also possible to interpret Adorno as speaking directly to the difference between art and representation. As scholar Gene Ray notes, in designating "poetry after Auschwitz" as a form of barbarism, Adorno is asserting that, "Auschwitz was the irreversible and unanswerable repudiation of culture's traditional claim to ennoble and improve humanity."[15] Ray understands Adorno to be arguing not that the Holocaust cannot or should not be represented, but rather that the historical calamity of the Holocaust, perpetrated by one of the most cultured nations in the world, forces representation to surrender its lofty claims to making people better. To be sure, however, the study of Holocaust representations can still accomplish much: it can broaden historical understanding; heighten critical sensitivities to how representations communicate, both intentionally and unintentionally; and familiarize us with a discourse of trauma and suffering that, for better or worse, has become a staple of everyday culture and politics.

If we follow this second reading of Adorno, however, we must acknowledge that the study of Holocaust representations cannot be an intrinsically edifying project. For this reason, this book takes as its subject not Holocaust art, but Holocaust representations, both those that adhere to the unwritten rules of Holocaust representation that have emerged over the decades and those that violate them. In 1987, the Holocaust scholar Terrence Des Pres listed three of these rules that have effectively created the category of Holocaust art:

1   The Holocaust shall be represented, in its totality, as a unique event, as a special case and kingdom of its own, above or below or apart from history.

2   Representations of the Holocaust shall be as accurate and faithful as possible to the facts and conditions of the event, without change or manipulation for any reason—artistic reasons included.

3   The Holocaust shall be approached as a solemn or even a sacred event, with a seriousness admitting no response that might obscure its enormity or dishonor its dead.[16]

Des Pres's ironically biblical tone, evoking the dictates of the Ten Commandments, Leviticus, and Deuteronomy, conveys the extent to which these rules have become entrenched clichés, as pious realism has become the dominant paradigm of Holocaust art. But while there are certainly many examples of such Holocaust representations that merit attention in an introduction to the subject, it is equally important not to dismiss tacky, insensitive, or even humorous Holocaust representations out of an irrational fear that they will open the floodgates for Holocaust denial or irreparably "undermine its gravity" and devalue the meaning of genocide.[17] When situated within their intellectual and historical frameworks, even Holocaust representations that violate unwritten rules and taboos become useful for illuminating those very boundaries and how they came into place. For this reason, *Holocaust Representations in History: An Introduction* incorporates both canonical works of Holocaust representation and works that have been attacked—perhaps even legitimately so—as insulting trash.

In History

The third and fourth words of this book's title speak to its method and organization. Each of the chapters below offers a case study that analyzes a specific Holocaust representation and situates that representation within the historical contexts in which it was created. These analyses also consider how those contexts have changed, particularly as landmark representations and events have modified public opinions toward the Holocaust, and as new technologies (first television and later the Internet) have made it possible to disseminate Holocaust representations to wider audiences. Several conceptual frameworks provide the scaffolding for the following chapters.

The first and most visible organizational structure of this book is a four-part chronological division of the history of Holocaust representations. Grouping the chapters according to time, rather than by genre or country of origin underscores the fact that general social, political, and other non-Holocaust-related events greatly influenced the development of a variety of Holocaust representations over time. At the same time, it also emphasizes that earlier representations, especially those that found international audiences and/or generated much controversy, necessarily influenced later ones. For example, the popular American drama *The Diary of Anne Frank* (1955) echoes earlier documentaries of the immediate postwar period featuring concentration camps by downplaying specific references to Jews and including a redemptive message. It is only in more recent decades that Holocaust representations—including art, film, literature, and drama—have explicitly challenged this standard narrative. And the widely viewed American television miniseries *Holocaust* (1978) affected not only how the Holocaust was depicted on German television, for example, but also laid the groundwork for public debate on how the Holocaust should be remembered, leading ultimately to national memorial projects such as the *Memorial to the Murdered Jews of Europe* in Berlin (2005).

But if these representations can't be separated from time, then they also cannot be separated from place. Even if the chapters are not grouped according to country, each one is nevertheless mindful that national narratives form a crucial aspect of how Holocaust representations are developed and interpreted. Certainly all nations exercise selective memory when it comes to the Holocaust, choosing to highlight some events and de-emphasize others depending on the country's role in the Holocaust in the past and its political needs in the present. The context and reception of a work that originated in Germany, for example, where the exclusion of Jews from public life formed the first steps in the Nazis' eventual destruction of European Jewish life, will necessarily differ from that of one from the United States, home to many of Europe's Jewish refugees.

Furthermore, memory is not only political, but also personal. Each chapter also acknowledges that Holocaust representations are deeply influenced by individual circumstances. The authors of each representation range from those who experienced the Holocaust and its effects as children and as adults, as men and as women, as Jews and as Christians. They include survivors of concentration camps, refugees from Europe, and those who never had a direct connection to its events and those who were born decades after the Holocaust ended. To be sure, the background of any author or artist can be construed as an important part of interpreting their art, but in the case of the Holocaust, given its gravity, their roles take on special significance. Such a notion forms the foundation for the discussions of the backgrounds of each author.

Part One considers representations created during the genocide and its immediate aftermath in the 1940s and 1950s, when many of the key features of Holocaust representation coalesced, including the idea of the Holocaust as the worst atrocity imaginable and the emergence of Holocaust types such as the child victim (Anne Frank) and the survivor (Elie Wiesel). Part Two moves to the 1960s and 1970s, a period of growth in public awareness of the Holocaust that runs from the highly publicized trial of Adolf Eichmann (1961) and Hannah Arendt's book about the trial, *Eichmann in Jerusalem* (1963), to the television miniseries *Holocaust: The Story of the Family Weiss* (1978). These events helped to establish the Holocaust as a topic of interest for mainstream audiences and sparked widespread soul searching about responsibility for the genocide. Part Three addresses the memory boom of the 1980s and 1990s, when the sheer volume of Holocaust representations spiked dramatically. In 1993, the dedication of the United States Holocaust Memorial Museum and the popular success of Steven Spielberg's *Schindler's List* epitomized the era when Holocaust memory truly went mainstream.[18] The final section considers the twenty-first century, examining some of the more imaginative turns Holocaust representation has taken, as the final living links to the genocide disappear and new technologies expand the possibilities for dealing with that loss. Interviews with survivors are being turned into interactive holograms,[19] and it is now possible to visit the USHMM virtually, via the online world Second Life, to learn about the Holocaust and interact with other visitors. As these new and controversial methods of representing the Holocaust appear, we need to be able to interpret them. The final chapter introduces readers to Berlin's controversial Memorial to the Murdered Jews of Europe and considers how we might interpret its implications for the future of Holocaust memory and representation.

Each of these four sections includes case studies of Holocaust representations that are considered key to the history of the subject. Interwoven among these familiar images, texts, and places, however, are less well-known representations, whose inclusion in this book forms its second organizing structure. 1950s Yiddish memorial books (yizkor books), 1970s Nazisploitation films, Binjamin Wilkomirski's 1995 invented Holocaust memoir *Fragments*, and early twenty-first century memorials and art exhibitions such as the Children's Holocaust Memorial in Whitwell, Tennessee, and *Mirroring Evil: Nazi Imagery/Recent Art* all problematize the canonical tradition of Holocaust representation by violating Des Pres's rules or otherwise undermining audience expectations. We include them in this book to undermine the notion of a clean, linear, comprehensive account of Holocaust representation and to point instead to the many unpredictable vectors of Holocaust memory. These Holocaust representations tend not to appear on course reading lists for a variety of reasons: they have not been available in English translation (yizkor books), they border on pornography (Nazisploitation), they take significant liberties with historical facts (*Fragments* and the Children's Holocaust Memorial), they are intentionally offensive (*Mirroring Evil*), or they simply are not a priority when so many other Holocaust representations obey the rules. Yet precisely because they are so jarring, these representations offer valuable opportunities to challenge dominant accounts. For many years, to take one example, most scholars considered the 1950s to be a silent period in the history of Holocaust representations. Texts like yizkor books reveal that survivors were not silent; they simply spoke of their traumas within smaller circles, to fellow Jews, not mass audiences. Similarly, an invented Holocaust memoir such as *Fragments* can illuminate the tremendous fascination with Holocaust survivors in the 1980s and 1990s and the extent to which Holocaust memoirs, whether truthful or not, rely on clichés and reinforce reader expectations. Situating such works alongside canonical works offers an integrated approach to the study of Holocaust representation.

An Introduction

A third organizing structure of this book relates to the pedagogical mission embodied in its title's final words. Structuring a short book as a series of chronologically organized case studies in which influential works are interspersed with less canonical representations has the unavoidable consequence of excluding many important and interesting examples. One might legitimately ask about the absence of Paul Celan's poem "Todesfuge" ("Death Fugue"), Ruth Klüger's memoir *Weiter leben: eine Jugend (Still Alive: A Holocaust Girlhood Remembered)*, Holocaust music, and any number of important feature films. But compiling a comprehensive survey of Holocaust representations is not the primary goal of this book; rather, our goal is to develop a nuanced set of approaches that can be expanded, accordion-like, to encompass different kinds of media and additional Holocaust representations, especially those not included in this book.

To acknowledge the gaps in coverage and, at the same time, provide tools for exploring representations and topics not included in the book, each chapter opens with a leading question. These broadly conceived questions can be used to guide additional research or writing assignments. Chapter 1, for instance, asks "What do iconic photographs tell us about the Holocaust?" and offers an answer, in the form of a thesis, with regard to one often-reproduced Holocaust photograph. Students can easily ask this question of other well-known atrocity photographs. Similarly, Chapter 12 asks "How do countries outside Germany commemorate the Holocaust?" Its response focuses on the United States Holocaust Memorial Museum in Washington, DC, but the same questions might be asked of Holocaust museums in other countries, such as Israel's Yad Vashem, or of the new museums of Jewish history that have recently opened in Berlin and Warsaw.

Ultimately, this book is not just an instruction manual. Rather, it is a provocation. It seeks to encourage its readers to adopt critical postures in the face of often-disturbing material and to rise beyond the purely emotional responses or silent postures of reverential awe that mainstream Holocaust representations can inspire. By modeling the sorts of fundamental questions students can ask of Holocaust representations and then showing, by way of example, how answering them requires solid, argumentative claims, *Holocaust Representations in History: An Introduction* will introduce a new generation to original ways of understanding this material and showing why it still matters.

PART ONE

The 1940s and 1950s

This famous photograph from the Spring of 1943 of a boy in the Warsaw Ghetto shows Jews captured by German troops being marched off for deportation. The original German caption reads: Mit Gewalt aus Bunkern hervorgeholt *(Pulled from bunkers by force)*. This now-familiar image originally appeared in a secret German bureaucratic report documenting the successful suppression of the Warsaw Ghetto Uprising.

National Archives and Records Administration, College Park

1

The Boy in the Warsaw Ghetto (photograph, 1943):

What Do Iconic Photographs Tell Us About the Holocaust?

"The Boy in the Warsaw Ghetto" is one of the most recognizable photographs ever taken.[1] The image shows a crowd made up largely of women and children being marched away at gunpoint, the first step in a journey that will no doubt end in a Nazi death camp. At the front of this group stands a young boy in dark knee socks, shorts, coat, and hat. Slightly apart from the others, he holds his hands in the air under the watchful gaze of the stone-faced SS soldier behind him. The look on the boy's face is one of sheer terror and desperation, and it's hard to imagine what a small child possibly could have done to merit such treatment. As a signature image of the Holocaust, this photograph appears so frequently that it is familiar even to those who know little about the genocide of Europe's Jews.

"The Boy in the Warsaw Ghetto" is emotionally devastating. Its political and visual asymmetry—heavily armed, uniformed German soldiers standing guard over dirty, unarmed, raggedly dressed civilians—invites us to ask how Nazi Germany could ever have been so threatened by Jewish civilians that they felt the need to exterminate all of them, even small children. But it is precisely because of this emotional, political and visual power that the photograph has come to symbolize the evils of National Socialism and the horror of the Holocaust, as if it conveys the very essence of the murder of millions of Jews. The photograph has influenced photojournalism as well: from Vietnam to Afghanistan to Darfur, few subsequent conflicts have passed without generating at least one shocking photograph of a young child needlessly victimized by adult violence.

Its wide circulation and resounding influence mark "The Boy in the Warsaw Ghetto" as an iconic image.[2] Originally used to refer to religious figures such as Jesus, Mary, and the saints, iconic images symbolize something much larger than themselves (an image of Jesus on the Cross, for instance, symbolizes Christianity). In so doing, they stand in for—or at least appear to stand in for—broader histories and stories that are distilled into a single visual representation. One finds examples of iconic imagery across a wide range of human endeavors: the American soldiers raising the flag at Iwo Jima, the *Mona Lisa*, the Nike Swoosh, and the six-pointed Jewish star are all iconic images that elicit specific responses with clear political, artistic, commercial or religious meanings. Yet in spite of their familiarity, or perhaps precisely because of it, it is easy to forget the origins of these iconic images. This is particularly the case with iconic photographs, which become so popular that those origins disappear, and the photographs themselves become significant less for what they actually depict than for what posterity decides they depicted.[3]

While "The Boy in the Warsaw Ghetto" is often used to symbolize the Holocaust in its entirety, if we examine its specific contexts—where, when, and why it was taken; whom it depicts; to what ends it has been used—we can better understand the problematic effect of investing an image of a single moment of the Holocaust with so much explanatory power about a larger and more complex history. Once we unpack the photograph's controversial history, it becomes more difficult to let "The Boy in the Warsaw Ghetto" simply symbolize pure evil or innocent children in an adult world gone mad.

The history of the photograph

While we know that "The Boy in the Warsaw Ghetto" was taken in the ruins of the Warsaw Ghetto in late April or early May 1943 and first appeared in a Nazi report, other basic questions about the image's origins remain unresolved, including who took the photograph and the identities of many of the people it depicts, even the boy himself. Still, to understand the dangers of relying on an iconic photograph to understand a complex history, it is essential to know as much as possible about both the photograph's broader historical context and the specific circumstances of its creation. Although those who see a photograph outside of its original context often lack these details, they are nevertheless essential to a thorough and accurate reading of the image.

World War II began almost four years before the photograph was taken. Soon after the Germans invaded and occupied Poland on September 1, 1939, they implemented their plans to transform Eastern Europe into a future racial utopia. Under this project, racially pure Aryan Germans would settle the land,

and Slavs, notably Poles, Ukrainians, and Russians, would become their slaves. Jews had no place in this new racial order. Although the overwhelming majority of Europe's Jews were law-abiding and productive members of European societies, Nazi ideology held them responsible for all kinds of economic and social problems, from world financial crises to the spread of Soviet Communism, and were determined to remove them from the region. After the quick success of their initial military operations, German occupation authorities turned to the Jews, either murdering them on the spot or removing them from their homes and concentrating them in squalid urban ghettos, from which they were eventually deported to the east, the common euphemism for sending them to the extermination camps where many more were murdered.

In October 1940, the Jews of Warsaw, Poland's capital, were ordered to move to the Muranów district, just west of the city center. On the night of November 15, 1940, the Germans sealed off the Warsaw Ghetto, cynically claiming that it needed to be quarantined because of disease, when in fact their own policies had made the Ghetto dirty and unhygienic. Jews struggled against starvation and disease in this overcrowded prison, and many died. Some toiled in factories and shops that made goods for the German war effort in return for meager rations.[4] Others, however, started underground soup kitchens, orphanages, and other forms of communal self-help.[5]

The situation for children like the boy in the photograph was particularly grim. To Nazi Germany, Jewish children represented a future for Judaism and Jews simply by existing. In the racist Nazi worldview, it made no sense to exterminate Jewish parents while allowing their children to replenish the population. Thus children were generally not spared their parents' fates. Those too young to work faced immediate selection for gas chambers at death camps. Of all Jewish children alive in Europe in 1939, only 11 percent survived the war and one and a half million in total were murdered.[6]

Within the Warsaw Ghetto, the situation was especially dire. According to one estimate, as many as 80 percent of the approximately one hundred thousand children in the overcrowded ghetto needed some sort of assistance.[7] Jewish community organizations did what they could to alleviate the misery, organizing schools, day care, and cultural opportunities such as libraries and theater performances, but faced with growing numbers of the needy, their efforts could not go far enough. The depths of the despair are chilling: desperate parents abandoned their children on the streets or starved to death and left them orphans. Freezing children begged for bread crusts and filled the nights with their cries.

In the summer of 1942, the Germans began to liquidate the Ghetto, sending approximately 265,000 residents to Treblinka to be murdered. But unlike so many other episodes of the Holocaust where the Germans faced limited or no resistance, the remaining Jews of the Warsaw Ghetto, despite their many political and religious differences, were determined not to give up without a fight. Sporadic acts of resistance started in January 1943, and the final battle of the Warsaw Ghetto Uprising began on April 19, 1943, the eve of Passover, the Jewish holiday that celebrates the Jews' release from bondage in ancient Egypt. Warsaw's Jews used whatever weapons they could muster to resist German attempts to empty the ghetto, but for all of their bravery, they simply lacked the resources and numbers necessary to wage an effective campaign against the overwhelming strength of the better-trained and better-armed Germans. Within the next month, as people like those in the iconic photograph retreated to hidden underground bunkers and sewers, the Germans successfully contained the rebellion. After several weeks of intense fighting, German soldiers under the command of SS-Gruppenführer und Generalleutnant der Waffen-SS (SS-Group leader and lieutenant general of the Waffen-SS) Jürgen Stroop suppressed the Warsaw Ghetto Uprising. On May 16, 1943, they blew up the Great Synagogue on Tłomackie Street to symbolize the completion of their gruesome task.

Though Stroop's troops ultimately succeeded in their mission, the Jews had put up significant resistance and several hundred German soldiers had lost their lives. As a result, Stroop needed to save face and demonstrate his competence to his own superiors. To this end, he compiled a 125-page, leather-bound report entitled *Es gibt keinen jüdischen Wohnbezirk in Warschau mehr!* (The Jewish Quarter of Warsaw is No More!). The Stroop Report, as it is now known, contains 78 pages of text, consisting largely of Stroop's daily communiqués, which were forwarded by his direct supervisor, Friedrich Wilhelm Krüger, the Höherer SS- und Polizeiführer (Higher SS and Police Leader) in Kraków, to Heinrich Himmler, Reichsführer SS (Head of the SS) in Berlin. It also includes a cumulative tally of the number of Jews captured and killed.[8] The Stroop Report documents the clearing of the Warsaw Ghetto in meticulous detail. A representative communiqué from April 27, 1943 reads: "For today's operation, I formed 24 raiding parties with the same task as on several days of last week; they had to search the former Ghetto in smaller groups. These search parties pulled 780 Jews out of bunkers and shot 115 Jews who resisted. This operation was terminated about 1500 hrs; some of the parties had to continue to operate because they had found more bunkers."[9]

After this narrative of extermination appears a 53-page appendix or *Bildbericht* (report in images) of photographs glued onto thick paper. "The Boy in the Warsaw Ghetto" first appeared in this last section of the Stroop Report. To viewers today, the images in the appendix unambiguously symbolize atrocity, but their captions provide a jarringly positive spin. Typical captions of photographs showing German soldiers destroying buildings, extracting hiding Jews from bunkers, searching and interrogating prisoners, and marching them off to the train station, most likely to their deaths in the Treblinka extermination camp, read "Jewish traitors," "Jews are marched away," and "Destruction of a block of buildings." The Germans appear confident, powerful, and in charge, while the Jews look haggard, desperate, and defeated. The captions regularly describe Jews as *Banditen* (bandits) or as biologically degenerate: the caption of a photo that includes a naked man whose posture is contorted by severe scoliosis reads "dregs of humanity." "The Boy in the Warsaw Ghetto" first appeared immediately after this photograph. Its original caption, written in the same neat calligraphic script as all the others, says "*Mit Gewalt aus Bunkern hervorgeholt*" (forcibly taken from bunkers). To Stroop, these captured Jews were not innocent women and children, but biologically degenerate bandits, fully deserving of their treatment. He presented this photograph, like the others, as evidence of his successful operations against them in the Warsaw Ghetto.

Doubts and certainties

Only three copies of the Stroop Report were produced, and its intended viewership was no more than a few top German officials, yet soon after World War II, "The Boy in the Warsaw Ghetto" transcended this original context to become an iconic photograph. During the postwar trials of Nazi war criminals in Nuremberg, American prosecutors introduced the full Stroop Report as a prosecution exhibit. Journalists reporting on the trials recognized the photograph's rhetorical power, and *The New York Times* published it on December 26, 1945, describing it matter-of-factly as being one picture "among several hundred introduced at war crimes trials in Nuremberg" from "a report of an SS commander charged with the destruction of the city's Ghetto and the removal of Jews to concentration camps."[10] The next day, however, the *Times* printed a description of the photograph that implicitly encouraged readers to understand it as a broader metaphor for Nazi cruelty:

> The luckier of the ghetto's inhabitants died in battle, taking some Germans with them. But not all were lucky. There was a little boy, perhaps 10 years old. A woman, glancing back over her shoulder at the supermen with their readied rifles, may have been this boy's mother. There was a little girl with a pale, sweet face. There was a bareheaded old man. They came out into the streets, the children with their little hands raised in imitation of their elders, for the supermen didn't mind killing children.[11]

On the basis of this and similar media reports, the image soon came to symbolize the entirety of the Holocaust. In subsequent decades, books, magazines, educational materials, and, eventually, websites and other media have reproduced the image alongside discussions of events that took place in ghettos, camps, trains, cities, and villages all over Europe over a span of several years. Yet if one irony of the photograph's subsequent history is that it has been associated with events that have nothing to do with it, another is that we still do not know some basic information about the picture itself.

To begin, it is not even clear who took the photograph. Several different photographers contributed images to the Stroop Report. Stroop's own assistant Karl Kaleske said that members of the German *Sicherheitsdienst* (security police) took it, though that claim does not identify the individual photographer. Others attribute it to Albert Cusian, a member of a German military unit known as a *Propaganda Kompanie* (a PK, or propaganda company). Propaganda companies traveled with military units and shot photographs and film that were used in magazines and newsreels. As a PK photographer, Cusian took many pictures of street scenes and business activities in the Ghetto, often downplaying the horrible conditions of daily existence.[12]

The most likely candidate, however, appears to be Franz Konrad, an SS-Obersturmbannführer (lieutenant colonel). Nicknamed *Der Warschauer Ghettokönig* (the king of the Warsaw Ghetto) for his cruelty, Konrad was in charge of confiscating Jewish property in the Warsaw Ghetto and transporting it back to Germany.[13] At his war crimes trial in 1951, Konrad claimed, implausibly, that he had taken the photograph as part of a secret report that would implicate Stroop in the murder of Jews. Konrad also used photography as part of his defense, responding to one accusation of murder with the simple statement *"Ich war nicht aktiv. Ich habe fotografiert"* (I didn't take part. I was taking photographs). Konrad's attempts to clear his name failed, and on March 6, 1952, he was hanged as a convicted war criminal, but he remains the most likely candidate, though in all likelihood, the photographer's identity will never be known for sure.

Controversy also surrounds the identities of the Jews in the photograph, especially the identity of the boy himself. As we have seen, the captions in the Stroop Report were generic, focusing on the Jews as a degraded category—"traitors" or "dregs of humanity"—and providing no help in definitively identifying individuals. Still, multiple people have claimed to be the boy in the photograph, including Artur Dąb Siemiątek, Levi Zeilinwarger, Israel Rondel, and the most persistent claimant, Tsvi Nussbaum.[14] Each man's story includes historical details that do not correspond to the photograph and its history, and none have proven conclusively to be the boy. Controversy also surrounds the identities of the women and children behind the boy.

The only person in the photograph who has been definitively identified is Josef Blösche, the soldier in the background with the submachine gun.[15] Blösche was an ethnic German born in 1912 in the Sudetenland, the border region of Czechoslovakia that Germany annexed in October 1938. In late 1939, he was drafted into the German military. He first trained and served as a border guard, and then, after Germany invaded the Soviet Union in 1941, he joined Einsatzgruppe B (Task Force B), one of the mobile killing units that exterminated Jews and alleged Soviet sympathizers in newly conquered regions. Soon thereafter, Blösche was posted to the Warsaw Ghetto as a member of the *Sicherheitsdienst*. There he earned a reputation as a brutal sadist, murderer, and rapist. Ghetto residents nicknamed him "Frankenstein."

Blösche's infamous role as the soldier in "The Boy in the Warsaw Ghetto" only became known in 1967, when East German secret police followed up a tip and arrested him. For over a quarter century he had eluded arrest and lived a peaceful rural life. Immediately after the war, in 1945, Blösche was sent to a Soviet labor camp as a prisoner of war. In 1946, he was transferred to a coal mine in Czechoslovakia, where an industrial accident left his face grotesquely disfigured. After a lengthy recovery, he returned to the new East Germany in 1947, settling in the quiet village of Urbach in Thuringia. There he married a war widow, fathered two children, and worked in a local potash mine.[16] After his arrest, Blösche confessed that he was the man in the photograph. He also appeared in several other images in the Stroop Report, so it was not difficult to corroborate this claim, even with his facial deformities. On July 29, 1969, Blösche was executed by firing squad. Ironically, if the child's anonymity turns him into more of a symbol, knowing the actual cruel story of the man holding the gun makes him worse than any symbolic interpretation. It not only reinforces the point that this is a photograph rooted in a specific time and place. It also highlights the fact that we know much more about Nazi perpetrators—because they left reports—than we do about their victims.

Tempering the influence of iconic images

Once we know the back story of "The Boy in the Warsaw Ghetto"—the Warsaw Ghetto Uprising, the Stroop Report, Franz Konrad, Tsvi Nussbaum, and Josef Blösche—it becomes obvious that the photograph cannot be read as an image that captures the entirety of Holocaust. While the photograph may appear alongside pictures of *Kristallnacht*, Auschwitz, Anne Frank, and other iconic Holocaust images, it is important to remember that each one of these images represents a discrete moment within a much larger complex of events. "The Boy in the Warsaw Ghetto" emerged from a specific context and tells a specific history, some of which will likely remain forever unknown.

Ultimately, then, iconic photographs do not tell us about the Holocaust, or at least, they do not tell us about the Holocaust writ large. Rather, they depict specific events, perpetrators, and victims about which we may or may not have essential and nuanced information. In the case of "The Boy in the Warsaw Ghetto," a photograph that has long been read as a sign of brutal German power and weak Jewish victimization actually registers the end of one of the most inspiring episodes of Jewish resistance in the entire Holocaust. Although the women and children are being herded off to their likely deaths, they are thin, raggedy, tired, and scared because they and their community have been fighting so hard for so long. And yet, they have lost their battle, reminding us that it is as dangerous to over-read an image in a counterintuitive direction as it is to over-read it in a predictable direction. To be sure, the image records a brave moment of resistance, and so it is appropriate to see the Jews it depicts as more than just victims. But it is also important to keep in mind that the resistance failed, an equally important component of what the photograph actually depicts. Thus, even if turning a photograph into an iconic image almost inevitably sacrifices historical accuracy to symbolic generalization, it is important to remember that doing so does deep injustice to the specificity of lived experience.

In a frame from the British atrocity film The True Glory, *a British Army Film and Photographic Unit cameraman and photographer, Sgt. Mike Lewis, is caught on camera as he films the burial of the dead following the liberation of the concentration camp at Bergen–Belsen in Germany in April 1945.*

Imperial War Museum

2

Nazi Concentration Camps (documentary film, 1945):

Can the Holocaust Be Adequately Represented on Film?

Given the ubiquity of television and the Internet, the omnipresence of war and violence on the news, and the popularity of horror movies, we have long since become accustomed to film images of death, destruction, and gore. It's hard now to imagine how an hour-long, black and white documentary film depicting newly liberated Nazi concentration camps would have shocked its viewers. But in a *New York Times* article entitled "War-Crimes Court sees Horror Films" (November 30, 1945), about the showing of *Nazi Concentration Camps* at the Nuremberg Trials, a reporter described that shock:

> the showing of the film taken at twelve such camps, with horror pooled on horror and mounting in dreadfulness as it went along, was almost more than anyone could bear. There were mutters of "Oh God—Oh God!" and "Why can't we shoot the swine now?" from the audience of mainly American, British, French, and Soviet soldiers, officers and correspondents. The tribunal itself was so moved that, when the film ended and the light came on, the judges walked out rigidly and the president of the court forgot to announce the adjournment until tomorrow morning.[1]

Despite the eye-catching headline and the reporter's insistence on the film's horrific nature—in the article's first paragraph he describes it as a "one-hour nightmare in motion pictures"—the article has no description of the film's actual content. Instead, it focuses on the topic discussed at the trial that day, which was the Nazi annexation of Austria in 1938 and their violations of the Treaty of Versailles. Only toward the end does the article report on viewer reactions to the film, contrasting the distressed audience's emotional outbursts with the dispassionate faces of the accused Nazi officials who were compelled to watch, under special lighting set up to show their reactions in the otherwise darkened room. According to the reporter, they sat through the film "with less expression than the spectators watching a dull newsreel." The comparison between the deeply moved audience and the stoic Nazis underscored the central claim of the film itself: that the Nazi leaders accused of these indescribable crimes were monstrous individuals (see Chapter 6 for an account of Hannah Arendt's refutation of this claim in her controversial report on the trial of Adolf Eichmann, 16 years later).

Nazi Concentration Camps was one of a small number of black and white documentaries produced in the immediate postwar period. Others include *The Nazi Plan*, which was commissioned by the United States and produced by 20th Century Fox. It included footage from German propaganda films made between 1918 and 1945, and was shown at the Nuremberg Trial to instruct the tribunal about the development of National Socialism, *The Nazi Supreme Court Trial of the Anti-Hitler Plot, Sept. 1944–Jan. 1945*, which presented a shortened version of those trial proceedings; *Nuremberg*, which contained a record of the trials and German atrocities; and *Death Mills*, which was directed by Billy Wilder and shown to German audiences as part of the efforts of the Allied Forces to make Germans confront the crimes committed by the Nazis, as well as to discourage rebellion against the occupying forces.[2] All were created by established directors of mainstream feature films, who already knew how to craft visual material into gripping dramatic form.[3] While the core material of the films was footage from the war, the concentration camps, and the trials, in some cases the directors drew upon and even included clips from Leni Riefenstahl's famous 1935 Nazi propaganda film *Triumph of the Will*, as well as German newsreels (without attribution). Their visual images and editing also referenced tropes of contemporary horror films.

The fundamental purpose of these films, as with most Holocaust representations, was to document crimes and atrocities so unprecedented in scope and method that many of their victims feared no one would believe they really happened. As some of the earliest attempts at visual representation of Nazi crimes, it is not surprising that these films have profoundly influenced subsequent Holocaust documentaries, feature films, photographs and art, helping to establish what we might call a visual lexicon of Holocaust representation that includes emaciated concentration camp prisoners, charred corpses in crematoria, bulldozers pushing piles of bodies into mass graves, and other familiar images. Indeed, according to Anton Kaes, they established standards for representations of the Holocaust that "have by now become so conventionalized that they determine what is a 'correct' representation of the period and what is not."[4] But iconic as these shocking images have become, their foundational use in these films forces us to confront a key problem in the study of Holocaust representation: the naïve acceptance of "documentary" representations as the unvarnished truth.

One critical limitation of these "atrocity films," as they were commonly known, is their lack of Jews. The films were conceived for very specific legal and political purposes that had to do with increasing awareness of what the Nazis did, not whom they did it to; these purposes did not include documenting the genocide of the Jews of Europe. Although the films do include images of Jewish victims, they rarely, if ever, specifically mention Jews, an omission echoed by many representations of the Holocaust in television, film, and drama to come. *The Diary of Anne Frank*, for example, ends before its protagonist actually falls victim to the Holocaust, which made the dramatic rendering of her diary all the more palatable to general audiences, who cared about atrocities, but not necessarily about Jews (see Chapter 4). One of the initial ironies of these films, then, is that they have become foundational, authoritative images of the Holocaust, yet they omit a crucial, even central, element of Nazi ideology, strategy, and criminality. Decades later, most Holocaust representations deal directly and specifically with the destruction of European Jewry, yet they continue to be influenced by these early black and white atrocity films, which were designed to shock and horrify as much as to inform and enlighten. A close examination of *Nazi Concentration Camps* illuminates the elements of this visual legacy and its relationship to Jews.

Film as eyewitness

The making of *Nazi Concentration Camps* is deeply intertwined with the Trial of the Major War Criminals before the International Military Tribunal in Nuremberg, Germany, the first and best-known of several trials held by the Allied Forces at Nuremberg to bring Nazi leaders to justice. In the first trial, which began in November 1945, 21 Nazi leaders, including Hermann Göring, Reichsmarshall, and Rudolf Hess, Hitler's deputy, were accused of crimes against peace, crimes against humanity, and war crimes, along with "engaging in a common plan or conspiracy" to perpetrate these crimes. The tribunal also attempted to have entire groups of perpetrators, such as the SS (*Schutzstaffel*) and Gestapo, declared "criminal organizations," so courts could try their members in other courtrooms in the future. According to Supreme Court Justice Robert H. Jackson, who served as chief U.S. prosecutor, the trials encompassed the largest magnitude of litigation ever attempted; some regard his opening statement as one of the greatest courtroom addresses ever given.[5]

Although the Nuremberg Trials have a momentous reputation and legacy, numerous accounts confirm that their day-to-day proceedings were often tedious. The first trial lasted almost a year, from the reading of the initial indictment on November 21, 1945 to the International Military Tribunal's final judgment on October 1, 1946. The prosecution built its case on thousands of pages of documentary evidence, which the Allies believed to be more reliable than eyewitness testimony. The Tribunal's rules required many of these texts to be read aloud to the court, and some that addressed multiple charges had to be read twice. The court called over 90 witnesses, some of whom gave testimony that observers described as repetitive, rambling and even irrelevant.[6] In this context, the film's powerful and immediate images of liberated concentration camps must have been a dramatic contrast.

Although photographs of crime scenes had been admissible trial evidence since 1915, the use of film in a courtroom, without corroborating witnesses, was unprecedented. Given the magnitude and scope of this extraordinary trial, however, the International Military Tribunal declared that the court would not be bound by the usual rules of evidence.[7] But while this declaration allowed important evidence to be introduced, it also raised concerns that the proceedings would be considered a show trial rather than a serious legal proceeding, its outcome preordained in favor of the military victors. The use of film as supposedly irrefutable documentary evidence of Nazi crimes was intended to support both the status of the courtroom as a fair tribunal and the testimony of those whose descriptions of the atrocities they had witnessed might not otherwise be believed.[8] The director of *Nazi Concentration Camps* was able to draw upon photographs and films that had already been taken specifically for this second purpose. Throughout 1945, Dwight D. Eisenhower, the Supreme Commander of the Allied Expeditionary Forces, had sent American soldiers and German civilians to the newly liberated camps to create photographic and film records of their horrors. As General Eisenhower put it, "The things I saw beggar description . . . The visual evidence and the verbal testimony of starvation, cruelty and bestiality were so overpowering . . . I made the visit deliberately, in order to be in a position to give first hand evidence of these things if ever, in the future, there develops a tendency to charge these allegations to propaganda."[9]

Nazi Concentration Camps was first shown on November 29, 1945, just over a week into the trial. Its gripping images include piles of dead bodies and skeletal remains that Allied forces found upon liberating the camps, emaciated former prisoners, and the gruesome by-products of the Nazi killing machine, like shrunken heads and lampshades purportedly made of human skin. To be sure, the film does not depict any actual crimes being committed, and it was not likely that any of those accused at Nuremberg—Nazi top brass who generally worked in government offices in Berlin—directly murdered or tortured the actual victims shown in the film. But in showing audiences the horrific evidence of crimes that had clearly occurred, *Nazi Concentration Camps* pushed the bar for how people understood and visualized what had happened, and in doing so became a foundational influence on the subsequent presentation and reception of Holocaust representations.

Constructing the documentary record

It is crucial to note that although *Nazi Concentration Camps* makes use of images taken directly from the camps, it embeds those images within a carefully constructed framework. The film begins by showing the text of three statements by United States officials, two of which are sworn affidavits that are also read aloud. The first, from Justice Jackson, dated August 28, 1945, reads: "This is an official documentary report compiled from films made by military photographers serving with the Allied armies as they advanced into Germany. The films were made pursuant to an order issued by General Dwight D. Eisenhower, Supreme Commander, Allied Expeditionary Forces." The film's director, Lieutenant Colonel George C. Stevens of the U.S. Naval Reserve (who later won two Academy Awards for Best Director and directed the first screen adaptation of *The Diary of Anne Frank*), reads the next text aloud in a powerful voice. It is a sworn statement certifying that his official duties in the armed forces included photographing the concentration and prison camps. He testifies that military personnel under supervision compiled the images in the film, which constitute "true representations" of what they depict and have not been altered in any way. Stevens is followed by U.S. Navy Lieutenant E.R. Kellogg, who, in another sworn statement, asserts that before he joined the army, he was employed by 20th Century Fox as a director of photographic effects and is familiar with all photographic techniques. He also swears that the images in the film are "true copies of originals, held in the vault of the U.S. Army Signal Corps. Excerpts comprise 6,000 feet of film selected from 80,000 feet, all of which I have reviewed, all of which is similar in character to these excerpts."

According to Lawrence Douglas, this prologue highlights "a novel understanding of the documentary as a privileged witness independently competent to swear to the truth of its own images."[10] Beginning the film with these verbal assertions, as if the images cannot speak for themselves, also reveals the ambiguities surrounding the supposedly sharp line between truth and fiction when it comes to documentary photographs and film. On the one hand, such images are often considered to most accurately represent the truth of a scene or event. On the other, people are generally—and increasingly—aware that they can be manipulated, even to the point of convincing someone of an untruth. The Allied prosecutors had to tread this line carefully with *Nazi Concentration Camps*. While there is little doubt that the film shows the actual post-liberation concentration camps, the insistence of these opening texts on its authentic—and by implication unmanipulated— nature obscures the fact that it—like the other atrocity films—was shot and edited by skilled filmmakers with feature (i.e., fiction) experience, precisely to arouse emotions of shock, horror, and disgust.

The film's visual imagery begins with a map of Germany and the surrounding countries that shows the locations of concentration camps. It is then divided into sections showing images at or near each camp, including Leipzig, Ohrdruf, Penig, and Buchenwald. Solemn voiceover narration provides descriptions of the camps and general facts about their prisoners, including the fact that more than 200 political prisoners were burned to death at Leipzig, which held Russian, Polish, Czech, and French inmates. Images of Penig show women prisoners sitting up on stretchers, clearly posed to smile for the camera, and attended by German nurses. The narrator notes, "The women are able to smile for the first time in years." But such smiles are juxtaposed against shocking images of emaciated and lesion-covered flesh: in one particularly unsettling scene, a woman on a rooftop lifts her skirt to show what the narrator calls gangrenous wounds. These living survivors are in turn contrasted with the dead bodies shown lying on the ground and, in the final scene, being bulldozed into a mass grave by British forces. Along with these human images, cameramen were apparently instructed to film material that would connect the camps to German industry, such as the manufacturer's name plates on incinerators and gas chambers.[11] If these images are carefully selected and arranged, *Nazi Concentration Camps* is also important historically for the way it frames the victims of the Nazi crimes it depicts. Although many of the inmates and dead bodies are Jews, the voiceover mentions Jews only once. This disjunction between images and words—and subtle manipulation of the facts, by omission—serves to downplay the genocide of the Jews and instead emphasize the Nazis' general war crimes, as per the overall intent of the International Military Tribunal's prosecution.[12]

Nazi Concentration Camps includes one brief mention and image of an actual German perpetrator, Josef Kramer, "former commandant of Belsen," but the film does not otherwise let Germans off the hook. Rather, it features narrated scenes showing German civilians from the city of Weimar walking to Buchenwald and being compelled to look at the evidence of the atrocities, thus implicating them in their horrors. According to British cinema entrepreneur Sidney Bernstein, forcing German civilians to tour the camps was part of a policy of "psychological warfare" intended to arouse their hatred of the Nazi party by exposing them to what had actually happened, as well as to discourage them from organizing resistance movements against the Allied occupation. It was also intended to make them realize that they could not avoid responsibility for their country's crimes "and thus to promote German acceptance of the justice of Allied occupation measures."[13] These scenes come from another Anglo-American film project, the *German Atrocity Project*, whose films were made primarily to be shown to German civilians and prisoners of war, though versions were also prepared for the neutral and liberated territories, Great Britain, and the United States.[14] En route to the camps, the Germans seem to be walking along happily, as if on a pleasure outing; the narrator emphasizes their smiling faces and cheerful outlook, which contrast dramatically with their horrified, shocked reactions when they see items in the camps, like shrunken heads of prisoners and a lampshade made of human skin and painted with obscene pictures. One visitor who has fainted is carried away, while an elderly woman appears to be so horrified that she needs assistance to walk away.

Understanding how the directors of *Nazi Concentration Camps* purposefully constructed the film to achieve a variety of goals helps us to view its opening statements of authenticity in a more critical light. But they also speak to a bigger insight: all representations of the Holocaust are mediated, no matter how "truthful" they may attempt—or claim—to be, and downplaying or denying this mediation risks distorting important information.

Viewing atrocities

American audiences were, to an extent, already primed for the horrific images in *Nazi Concentration Camps*. They had already seen newsreels from the war and accounts by photojournalists in magazines and newspapers. Since 1943, Hollywood studios had been producing anti-Nazi films like Fritz Lang's *Hangmen Also Die* (United Artists, 1943), about the massacre of over a thousand partisans and their relatives at Lidice, Czechoslovakia, in 1942, and Andre De Toth's *None Shall Escape* (MGM, 1944), a feature film that depicted the Holocaust before the war was even over.[15] Films from the camps began to be screened publicly as early as April 1945 (scenes from some of these earlier films were incorporated into both *Nazi Concentration Camps* and *Death Mills*).

Nevertheless, its prominent role at the Nuremberg Trials made *Nazi Concentration Camps* a powerful influence on future film representations of the Holocaust, particularly in their efforts to arouse shock and horror.[16] Even films that attempt to represent the Holocaust without terrifying their audiences must engage with this mode of representation by rejecting it. The deeply influential *Nuit et brouillard* (*Night and Fog*, 1955) attempts to subvert the directly shocking images of early Holocaust films with its combination of documentary images of the camps and scenes from fictional films, its montages of still and moving images, and its "haunting commentary," "discordant music," and cuts between color and black and white.[17] Yet as in *Nazi Concentration Camps*, although *Night and Fog* pictures Jewish victims, it uses the word Jewish only once. Created initially to commemorate the deportation of political prisoners by the French, it too was criticized for not addressing the genocide of the Jews.

Nazi Concentration Camps is, at best, an imperfect filmic representation of the Holocaust. But if film has the ability to present itself as less mediated— that is, closer to the truth—than other forms of Holocaust representation, then its viewers must acknowledge and enquire into the mediated nature of the information it conveys. Once we understand the specific mediations— intentions, origins, manipulations, juxtapositions—of a film's images, sound, and narrative, we can come closer to understanding the role it plays in representing its specific part of the Holocaust.

　יזכור בוך כעלם　

אָפּגעשטעלט די פאַרשלעפּטע יידן און זיי געצוווונגען אַריבער־
צוגיין צו די סאַדעטן. די רוסישע אַרמייער האָבן אָבער די מתנה
יידן ניט אַריבערגעלאָזט. האָבן צענדליגער יידן זיך געהאַנגען
אין בוג. די שוומערס זיינען זיי עס אין אַריבער אויף דער סאַ־
וועטישער זייט און זיינען פון קיינעם ניט פאַרהאַלטן געוואָרן.
די יידן, וואָס האָבן נישט געקאָנט שווימען, זיינען דערטרונקען
געוואָרן אין בוג... א פאַר הונדערט יידן, וועלכע זיינען געבליבן
אויף ברעג, זיינען דערנאָך דורך די דייטשן אויסגעפירט גע־
וואָרן ערגעץ אין א קאָנצענטראַציע־לאַגער...

אויסער דעם דערמאַנטן הערש וועלטשער (די אלמנה מיט
די יתומים זיינען שפּעטער אַנטלאָפן פון כעלם אויף האַלב־
זיינען דערנאָכשאַסן געוואָרן) בעת דער שחיטה אויף פאַלנגעדי־
קע פּאַטריאָ רעך יידן פון כעלם: דר. אָקס. דער פּאַסטאַגראַפּיסט
ראָזענבלאַט, די דריי ברידער לעווינשטיין — רייבע אייזן־סוחרים.
גאַמולקע, א גער. ליטוואַקאָוו פון פּוילישן מיליטער, און אַישע
שנויצער, אײַנבויימער פון א פּערפומערייע סקלאַד... זיינערע
טווים קערפּערס האָבן צו פּוילערים. וואָס האָבן זיי געקומען.
געמוען און דערנאָך אַריבערגעטראָגן די פאַרטומערמטע פאַמיליע.
די אַנדערע דערשאַסענע יידן זיינען, ווי שוין געזאָגט. באַגראַבן
געוואָרן אין ברידער־קברים צו 50 מאָן אין א קבר...

איך געלאָזן בעטן א ביסל וואַסער. די פויערים האָבן אָבער מורא
געהאַט מיר צו געבן א ביסל וואַסער... ענדלעך, האָט זאָט איין
פויער גענומען וואַסער און ער אַליין איז גענאַנגען מיר העלפן
ראַטעווען דעם פאַטער. איך און דער פויער האָבן אַרייגגעטראָגן
דעם גוטסטריק טאָטן צו א יידישן ישובניק. מען האָט דעם פאַ־
טער געפרוווט ראַטעווען, אָבער די נסיעה האָט אים ניט לאַנג גע־
דויערט. ער איז געשטאָרבן... איך בין געבליבן ביים פויער און
שפּעטער מיט אים געשיקט דאָס ברייוול צום יידן..."

אָט דאָס איז די שוידערלעכע דערצײלונג פון 16 יאָריק
יינגל. וואָס איז עפּ״י א גם גערמעטעוועט געוואָרן פון די נאַצי קוילן.
און וואָס האָט געשען מיט דער מתנה יידן? די אַנדערע גערעטע
וועטע האָבן דערצײלט: מער ווי העלפטן האָבן די דייטשן אַרויס
געשאָסן און דערמאָרדעט אויפן וועג. פיל זיינען געווארן פאַר־
ווונדעט און זיך צעלאָפן אין די אַרומיקע דערפער. קײן הרוביב־
שאָוו זיינען אָנגעקומען לעבעדיק ס״ה 300 כעלעמער יידן... דערט
האָט מען זיי א גאַנצן מעת־לעת געהאַלטן אין א שטאַל אָן עסן
און אָן טרינקען. דערנאָך האָבן די דייטשן אויך אין הרוביעשאָוו
אָראַנזשירט אַזא בלוטיק שפּיל אויסן מאַרק. געגומען די 300 כע־
לעמער און א פאַר הונדערט יידן פון הרוביעשאָווע און צוזאַמען זיי
אויפגעשלעפּט צום בוג. ביים ברעג זיך מיר האָבן די דייטשן

3

Yizker-bukh Khelm (memorial book, 1954):

How Did Jews Talk About the Holocaust in Its Aftermath?

Well into the twenty-first century, many scholars still believe that people, especially Jews, did not talk about the Holocaust between the end of World War II and the early 1960s.[1] As proof, they point to the comparative scarcity of Holocaust representations during this period: there were no blockbuster Holocaust films like *Schindler's List* and few books or survivor memoirs from major publishing houses. To the extent that they existed, Holocaust memorials drew few visitors. The rare Holocaust representations that attracted widespread attention, notably the first book, stage, and film versions of Anne Frank's *The Diary of a Young Girl*, downplayed Jewishness and tailored their content to appeal to non-Jewish audiences (see Chapter 4).[2] According to the "myth of silence,"[3] this reticence persisted until Adolf Eichmann's capture, trial, and execution (1960–1962) (see Chapter 6). At that point interest in the Holocaust began to grow, and then the 1978 television miniseries *Holocaust: The Story of the Family Weiss* opened the floodgates for a deluge of Holocaust books, films, artwork, memorials, and public discussion (see Chapter 9).

While this account of postwar silence contains some truth, it relies on unexamined assumptions about audience, specifically who the audiences for Holocaust representations were and how those audiences have changed over time. In other words, rather than asking whether people talked about the Holocaust between 1945 and 1962, we must instead ask who talked about the Holocaust with whom, why, and in what contexts. Approaching the debate on postwar silence through this more open frame reveals that significant discussions of the Holocaust did take place during this period, but within limited circles. These postwar Holocaust representations may not have commanded widespread popular attention, like their successors a generation later, but it simply is not accurate to assert that the Holocaust was not discussed in the 1950s.[4]

To investigate this vital question of the changing audiences for Holocaust representations, this chapter examines one early representation intended for a limited audience: the memory books known in Yiddish as *yizker-bikher* (yizkor books). Published in the years after the Holocaust by and for Jews from specific communities, yizkor books were intended to memorialize those who had perished in mass graves and gas chambers. The very existence of yizkor books reveals that intense, public discussion of the Holocaust did indeed take place in the postwar period, and the books themselves show how that discussion concerned itself not only with the latest, grim chapter of Jewish history, but with the longer history of Jews in Eastern Europe. But persistent anti-Semitism and a realigned postwar political climate meant that the audiences for this particular kind of Holocaust representation stayed small. Not everyone wanted to hear this discussion, and because it took place in Yiddish or Hebrew, many people could not even understand it. Yet it was an important discussion, because it emphasized the point that to understand the Holocaust's impact, we must understand its place within broader arcs of Jewish history.

The myth of silence and the question of audience

Before examining how yizkor books challenge the myth of silence, it is useful to revisit the postwar political context that produced this myth, even as it shaped—and perhaps muted—the Holocaust representations that did appear at the time. The argument that generally explains postwar silence begins in the immediate aftermath of World War II, when the atrocities that we now consider the Holocaust were seen not as a discrete genocide, but rather as one particularly gruesome aspect of wartime violence that affected people of many nations and ethnicities. Radical changes in postwar geopolitics also made it taboo to discuss the specifics of Jewish suffering with non-Jewish audiences. During World War II, the United States, Great Britain, France and the Soviet Union shared a common enemy in Nazi Germany. However, after a capitalist West Germany and socialist East Germany emerged from the ruins of their defeated nation, new fault lines emerged, with the Americans and their NATO allies on one side and the Soviet Union and, eventually, the Warsaw

Pact nations as their enemies on the other. During the ensuing Cold War, a period of intense political rivalry between the United States and the Soviet Union, downplaying German crimes in the interest of buttressing support for these new nations became politically expedient on both sides of the Iron Curtain, the political line between Western and Eastern Europe. West Germany was a particularly important ally for Americans and other Western Europeans, which made it less than desirable to criticize their past actions. Meanwhile, the Soviets and East Germans cynically—and inaccurately—claimed that, as communists, they too were victims of Nazi Germany, and that West Germany, not East Germany, thus bore the entire burden of German guilt.[5] At the same time, the Soviets and other Eastern European States maintained anti-Semitic policies and denounced Jews as anti-Soviet and pro-Zionist, making it politically unwise for Jews to draw attention to themselves by talking openly to non-Jews about their suffering—to say nothing of their rage or desire for vengeance.

Another argument about the myth of silence suggests that, across national contexts, Jews had good reasons to self-censor. In Europe, the United States, Israel, and elsewhere, many Holocaust survivors wanted only to rebuild their shattered lives and purposefully repressed the horrors of the recent past. But politics also conditioned the behavior of Holocaust survivors and other Jews. First in Jewish Palestine and then in the newly created State of Israel, the image of the Holocaust survivor was, in one scholar's phrasing, "hardly complimentary because Israeli society emphasized 'heroism and resistance,' and suppressed narratives of vulnerability and victimization."[6] Zionist caricatures represented Holocaust survivors as Yiddish-speaking, overly intellectual, indecisive, weak Jews who had for centuries allowed themselves to be victimized by gentile majorities in Europe and elsewhere.[7] They represented the opposite of the Zionist ideal and their experience of destruction, coupled with their apparent failure to resist, was downplayed in favor of stories of Jewish heroism.

In postwar America, attitudes were gradually liberalizing, but Jews were often still associated with the evils of unwelcome immigration and radical communism. In the politically conservative early 1950s, the media attention devoted to Julius and Ethel Rosenberg, American Jewish communists tried, convicted, and executed for passing nuclear secrets to the Soviets, only reinforced the stereotype of the Jewish Bolshevist. Before the Civil Rights movement, when American universities and professions still had Jewish quotas, such negative publicity only reminded Jews that it was in their interest to downplay their religious and ethnic identity by assimilating, playing up their status as Americans, and limiting their discussions of the Holocaust in mixed audiences.

Although these arguments about Cold War politics and postwar Jewish self-images help to explain the relative absence of Holocaust representations during this period, the existence of a wide range of cultural artifacts made exclusively by and for Jews during these same years cautions us against totalizing accounts of silence and self-censorship. In the succinct phrasing of historian Mark L. Smith, "The claim that Holocaust survivors were largely silent during the early postwar years neglects the internal culture of the Yiddish-speaking survivors."[8] The key word here is "internal." Around the world, Jews discussed and represented the Holocaust, but not necessarily in ways that non-Jews could easily access. Historian Laura Jokusch has written of the early efforts of Holocaust survivors "to chronicle, witness, and testify."[9] By assembling materials while memories were fresh, these efforts helped to establish important historical archives. In the displaced persons camps that housed Holocaust survivors immediately after the war, former concentration camp inmates organized theatrical performances that addressed their wartime experiences.[10] In texts that literary scholars would later describe as examples of *khurbn literatur* (Holocaust literature), writers such as Abraham Sutzkever and Mordecai Strigler explicitly addressed the fates of Jews during the war, but in Yiddish, the language of Eastern European Jews.[11] Along similar lines, Hasia R. Diner has argued that American Jews with varying personal connections to the Holocaust publicly commemorated and discussed it in a wide range of forms, including bulletins, magazines, newsletters, sermons, concerts, speeches, radio programs, and songbooks.[12] These postwar Holocaust representations are united by the fact that they were specifically created by and for Jews. Written in Jewish languages or presupposing insider knowledge of key aspects of Jewish history, religion, and culture, these representations did not appeal to mass audiences of gentiles, nor were they meant to.

Yizker-bikher: By and for Jews

Yizker-bikher (the plural form of *yizker-bukh*, also spelled *yisker-bukh*) are memorial books that commemorate towns and regions whose Jewish communities were destroyed during the Holocaust. The word "yizkor" ("remember" in Hebrew) is the first word of a prayer for the dead that Jews recite in synagogue four times a year. In their very name, yizkor books reference Jewish religious practice, suggesting a limited audience. Post-World War II yizkor books belong to a significantly older tradition of Jewish memorial texts that commemorate significant calamities in Jewish history. The first known yizkor book appeared in Nuremberg, Germany, in 1296, to memorialize Jews killed in the region over the previous 200 years, beginning with those murdered by Crusaders en route to Jerusalem in 1096.[13] It served the practical function of supplying Jewish mourners with specific names to include in their prayers. Yizkor books appeared after subsequent catastrophes, but the genre truly came into its own after World War II, when the unprecedented scale of the slaughter of Jews gave rise to hundreds of new titles.

These Holocaust memory books generally appeared under the auspices of *landsmanshaftn*, mutual aid societies for immigrant Jews from the same hometowns in Central and Eastern Europe. Many *landsmanshaftn* formed in the late nineteenth and early twentieth centuries to help new immigrants get their bearings after arrival in the United States, Palestine, Canada, Argentina, South Africa, Cuba, Brazil, and elsewhere. The resources available to individual *landsmanshaftn* varied, depending on the economic situations of their members. The production values, size and scope, press runs, and professionalism of their yizkor books varied accordingly, from amateur paper pamphlets published in displaced persons camps to deluxe, multi-volume editions edited by professional historians and published decades after the Holocaust.[14] Some volumes focus on individual small towns, while others cover entire regions or even countries. Such variations in form and content have made it difficult to establish either the limits of the genre or the exact number of yizkor books in existence. Using a broad definition, Yad Vashem classifies 1,421 titles in its collection as yizkor books. More conservative estimates suggest 700–800.[15] Individual titles were rarely published in more than a few hundred copies, given the limited size of their intended audiences.

Yizkor books were intended to spur memory and to provide a sort of textual gravestone for those who perished in mass graves and gas chambers.[16] Their necrologies (lists of deceased individuals to be remembered) suggest close familial or communal relationships between readers and the dead. The titles of many yizkor books feature the word *sefer* (tome), a word used by Orthodox Jews only in reference to books related to Torah study, which reinforces their specific grounding in Jewish religion and culture. Meanwhile, their contents embody the specific community they reference: the core materials of a yizkor book include a history of the town's Jewish community, essays on its prewar politics, biographic sketches of its residents, Holocaust testimonies, discussion of survivors' postwar lives, and, at the end, memorial dedications and a necrology.[17] Photographs, drawings, maps, and other visual elements further personalize the books, anchoring them to specific people and places, sometimes to the point of evoking a photo album or yearbook. Their readers were those most directly impacted by the Holocaust: survivors and the families of victims, known in Hebrew as the *she'erit hapletah* (surviving remnant).

The *Yizker-bukh Khelm*

While no single work exemplifies the yizkor book genre, the memory book for Chelm, Poland (Polish: Chełm, Yiddish: Khelm) is fairly typical of mid-1950s yizkor books. A detailed examination of the contents of the *Yizker-bukh Khelm* can provide us with a richer understanding of this particular kind of Holocaust representation as well as how Jewish communities talked about the Holocaust in the first decade after the war.[18] In 1939, Chelm was a *shtetl* (market town), with 18,000 Jews making up approximately 60 percent of its total population. Today, no Jews live in Chelm. The destruction of Chelm's Jewish community began early in World War II. On December 1, 1939, the Germans trucked hundreds of Jews to nearby Hrubieszów where they were forced onto a death march to the Soviet border. In October 1940, a ghetto was established for the remaining Jews, and in late 1941, it was sealed. Throughout 1942 and early 1943, the Germans deported waves of Chelm's Jews to death camps, usually Sobibór and Majdanek, virtually eradicating the population. About 200 Chelm Jews survived the Holocaust. Two yizkor books have been published to commemorate the town's once thriving Jewish community. In 1954, the Yiddish-language *Yizker-bukh Khelm* (translated within the book itself as *Commemoration Book Chelm*) appeared under the auspices of the Chelemer Landsmanschaft Society of Johannesburg, South Africa. In 1981, the Chelm Society in Israel and the U.S. published the Hebrew-language *Sefer ha-zikaron le-kehilat Chelm*.

The *Yizker-bukh Khelm* totals over 750 pages, a notable but not unprecedented length. It is divided into six sections: (1) History of the Jews in Chelm; (2) Men of Fame, Personalities, Types, and Characters; (3) Memoirs and Notes; (4) Destruction of Chelm; (5) *Chelemer landsmanshaftn*; and (6) yizkor (the necrology). Strikingly, the book does not discuss the town's fate during the Holocaust until page 505. Even though the Holocaust motivates its very existence, the *Yizker-bukh Khelm* is not exclusively fixated on death and destruction. To the contrary, it turns to the Holocaust only after fully chronicling local history and life. Its structure implicitly stresses that there is much more to Jewish history than the Holocaust. Focusing solely on Jewish death, as so often happened in the years after World War II, ignores the long, complex, and irreducible history of Jewish life in Eastern Europe.

To reinforce this point, the first section of the *Yizker-bukh Khelm* provides a diverse account of the town's prewar life, including its political parties and youth groups, library and theater, local artists and writers, and significance in Yiddish literature. The various contributions paint a rich and frequently nostalgic portrait of a nearly 600-year-old community. With a proud tone of civic boosterism, the preface emphasizes Chelm's history as a center for Torah study and adds, "In the field of Jewish industry, commerce and handicraft, as well as in the world of culture, Chelm played its great part."[19] Again emphasizing the town's significance, an essay entitled "The Myth of Chelm in Jewish Literature" considers the town's mythic status in Jewish folklore as a community of loveable fools. In the "Chelm stories" of Yiddish literature, the *khelemer khakhomim* (wise men of Chelm) perform absurd but humorous actions like trying to capture moonlight in buckets or push two mountains further apart to create more room. Additional essays create a rich mosaic of political diversity within Chelm's Jewish community, describing the roles of Jewish and Zionist political parties and youth groups. In the "Memoirs and Notes" section, the first-person reminiscences of former Chelm residents exemplify how yizkor books smooth over differences and produce positive memories. Contributions such as Faivel's Zygielbojm's "Chelm as I Remember it" and Rivka Szrojt's "Jews of My Town" fondly recount the town's celebrity status in Jewish literature even as they angrily lament episodes of anti-Semitism by the town's Polish residents.

The sketches of local personalities in the section "Men of Fame, Personalities, Types and Characters" complement these accounts of the town's social groups by focusing on individuals. Like a school yearbook, these stories, along with the personal memories and poems in "Memoirs and Notes," are meaningful to former Chelm residents and their families, but of limited interest to others. Short narrative sketches and captioned photographs commemorate individuals now obscure. Yet the original readers might very well have remembered neighbors such as Berl Askrad, "a well-known person in Chelm, known as an active communal worker who was represented in the most important communal organizations in Chelm. He was the synagogue warden of the *kehile* [religious governing body], councilman and alderman in the Chelm city council and was managing director of the Jewish public school."[20] These short biographical sketches disproportionately focus on men but do mention important local women, including Dora Dubkowska, a "famous singer [. . .] distinguished by her beautiful lyrical voice"[21] and Dr. Leah Fryd, "a gifted and extraordinarily capable woman," who provided medical care to Chelm's poor and indigent and "acquired a very good reputation in Chelm."[22] In his 1955 review of the *Yizker-bukh Khelm*, historian Jacob Shatzky denigrated the value of these sketches, noting that "all biographies are written in a bombastic style and contain errors." Yet Shatzky's subsequent comment is telling: "there is a lot of reverence in this style of writing but not much concrete biography."[23] Although he intended this comment as a criticism, Shatzky inadvertently emphasized the important therapeutic and memorial functions of yizkor books for their first readers. They helped survivors and victims cope with the destruction of their hometowns and put a generally positive spin on local history.

A distinguishing characteristic of yizkor books is their emotionally fraught tone. The *Yizkor-bukh Khelm* includes not only dispassionate, documentary essays, but also contemplative, nostalgic, angry, and even vengeful language. Such mixed emotional language is unsurprising, given the book's collective authorship and its appearance not fifteen years after the annihilation of their community. One author, for example, writes angrily of a Jewish collaborator who helped the Germans loot Chelm. An anonymous poem titled "Revenge, Revenge!" speaks of pain, rage, recurring nightmares and the final words of the narrator's father: seek vengeance.[24] Yet as scholars Jack Kugelmass and Jonathan Boyarin note, even these differences in content and tone are "subsumed within a positive image of the Jewish community."[25] The retrospective look back at Chelm ends up being a positive appraisal, more an obituary than any kind of critical history.

Following generic convention, the *Yizker-bukh Khelm* concludes with the "yizkor," the specific call to remember the dead. This section divides into two parts: a set of memorial dedications gathered from victims' families around the world and a list of the murdered. As they commemorate the departed, the dedications, short texts that often include photographs, again speak in a distinctly Jewish idiom. A dedication from Miriam Fligelman-Szteinberg recalls:

> My most beloved and dearest who perished as martyrs at the hands of the Hitlerists, may their names be erased. Father, Jakov Fligelman; mother, Cwia Fligelman; brothers, Josef, Shmuel-Shimkha; sisters, Frimet, Feyga. Your holy memory will remain forever. May these lines serve as a headstone for their holy souls as well as for our dear city, Chelm. May their souls be bound up in the bond of eternal life.[26]

The phrase "may their names be erased" is the translation of *yimakh shemo*, a Hebrew-Yiddish curse directed at enemies of the Jewish people. Originally applied to the biblical enemy Haman, here aimed at the "Hitlerists" (i.e. the Germans or Nazis), it has been recycled for new enemies over the centuries and places the Holocaust within a longer history of anti-Jewish persecution. We see here, once again, how the yizkor book represents the Holocaust through the lens of Jewish history and tailors it to a Jewish audience still coping with raw anguish.

Yizkor books and the future of Holocaust memory

The *Yizkor-bukh Khelm* commemorates a single *shtetl*. Yet as one book among a corpus of hundreds of yizkor books, it helps form a unique chapter in the history and memory of the Holocaust, one narrated by the survivors. Because not every destroyed community has a yizkor book, and because the nostalgia and grief of contributors shaped and often biased their accounts, yizkor books are an imperfect historical source that may offer little insight to a mass cultural audience. Yet for the communities that did create them, like the Jews of Chelm, they clearly played a powerful emotional and practical role in negotiating grief and perpetuating memories.

In recent years, interest in yizkor books has spiked, thanks in no small part to the Internet. Free online archives have made vast libraries of rare yizkor books instantly accessible in their original Hebrew and Yiddish and in translation. Digital reprints have made it possible to own facsimile copies of individual books. At the same time, social networking websites now replicate the role of *landsmanshaftn* by virtually circulating news about survivors and publishing memorial announcements. Yet technology alone does not explain the revived interest in yizkor books. These online archives and virtual *landsmanshaftn* are themselves responses to perceived needs. At a personal level, descendants of Holocaust survivors want to learn more about family genealogies and ancestral homelands. Meanwhile, scholars seek to understand the Holocaust in greater detail from the perspectives of its victims and to learn about the lives as well as the deaths of murdered Jews.

While yizkor books must be read with an eye to the personal and political biases of the grief-stricken people who made them, they play a significant role in the history of Holocaust representation. They offered and continue to offer a voice to those who ostensibly kept silent after the war. They are a powerful reminder of what has become a cliché: that there is a story for each of the six million Jews lost in the Holocaust. Even if they did not lead extraordinary lives or achieve postwar or posthumous fame, these people deserve to be remembered. Ultimately, the audiences for Holocaust memories are as diverse as these victims themselves: they have different needs that are met by different representations, and we cannot understand the full range of Holocaust representations without taking them into account, whether they be a handful of survivors from a small village reading a Yiddish memory book or tens of millions of people reading *Anne Frank: The Diary of a Young Girl*.

In this January 25, 1956 image, seventeen-year-old Susan Strasberg mounts a ladder and sees her name in lights over the Cort Theater (New York), where she appeared in the title role in The Diary of Anne Frank. *She shares the billing with Joseph Schildkraut, who played Otto Frank. Adapted by Frances Goodrich and Albert Hackett from the famous diary, the play contributed significantly to posterity's image of Anne Frank as an optimistic, saint-like figure of childhood innocence.*

Bettmann/Corbis

4

The Diary of Anne Frank (drama, 1955):

What is the Americanization of the Holocaust?

In the final scene of Frances Goodrich and Albert Hackett's play *The Diary of Anne Frank* (1955), Anne's father Otto, the only surviving member of the family, returns, just months after the war's end, to the Secret Annex where his family hid from the Nazis for two years. There, the Dutch friends who helped them hide give him his daughter's diary. Thumbing through its pages, Otto describes Anne's mood at Westerbork, the Dutch transit camp where the Franks were taken after German Security Police discovered their hiding place. "It seems strange to say this, that anyone could be happy in a concentration camp," Otto says. "But Anne was happy in the camp in Holland where they first took us. After two years of being shut up in these rooms, she could be . . . out in the sunshine and the fresh air that she loved."[1] He examines the diary and, as he reads a passage, the audience hears the voice of Anne Frank recite its most famous line: "In spite of everything, I still believe that people are really good at heart." Closing the diary, Otto says, "She puts me to shame," and the curtain falls.

Anne Frank's diary was first published in the Netherlands as *Het Achterhuis* (The Secret Annex) in 1947. In the United States, *Anne Frank: The Diary of a Young Girl* appeared in 1952, and the drama *The Diary of Anne Frank* premiered in 1955. The image of Anne Frank that emerged from these works has exerted a powerful hold on the popular imagination ever since. Seventy years after her death, Anne Frank remains a symbol of the innocent Holocaust victim who, despite her suffering, maintained her faith in humanity and hope for the future. In the play, her girlish enthusiasm and infectiously positive attitude encourage theater audiences to believe that good can overcome any catastrophe, even the Holocaust.

This saintly image is so entrenched that Anne Frank has become an instantly recognizable pop cultural icon, along the lines of Marilyn Monroe, Elvis Presley, James Dean, or Che Guevara. Today, Anne Frank-inspired representations can be found in all kinds of political and cultural contexts. Some are reverential: eleven saplings pruned from the chestnut tree Anne observed outside the Secret Annex are being replanted at symbolic locations in the United States, including Liberty Park, which overlooks the 9/11 memorial in New York, and Little Rock's Central High School, a hotbed of conflict over desegregation during the Civil Rights movement. Anne Frank also appears in high and low culture alike: in the title story of Nathan Englander's 2012 collection *What We Talk About When We Talk About Anne Frank*, a couple plays the "Anne Frank game" and wonders which of their friends would hide them were the Holocaust to happen again, while in the web comic "Anne Frank Conquers the Moon Nazis," Anne is reimagined as a superhero who fights Hitler in the future. Other appropriations are simply absurd: in April 2013, after visiting the Anne Frank House in Amsterdam, Canadian pop star Justin Bieber drew criticism for suggesting that, had she lived, Anne would have been his devoted fan. Scholars have described this diverse range of engagements with Anne's life and diary as "Anne Frank, the phenomenon."[2] While these appropriations testify to the powerful and ongoing fascination with Anne Frank and the Holocaust, we still need to ask how an ordinary German-Jewish girl hiding in wartime Amsterdam came to occupy such a prominent role in Holocaust representation.

Ironically, the historical evidence suggests that Anne Frank was a much more typical Holocaust victim than the unique paragon into which she has been transformed by posterity.[3] Anne was born in 1929 in Frankfurt, Germany to a family of assimilated Jews who, like 25,000 other Jews, took refuge in the Netherlands after the National Socialists took power.[4] In May 1940, however, Nazi Germany occupied the country, implemented strict anti-Jewish measures, and forced the Franks into hiding. Aided by a family friend, the Dutch gentile Miep Gies, they retreated into in a secret annex at 263 Prinsengracht in Amsterdam and remained there until early August 1944, when an informant tipped off authorities to their presence. But the Franks were not unique as Jews who went into hiding, and Anne's diary was just one of many composed in secret during the Holocaust.[5] In addition, details of the final seven months of Anne's life after her arrest suggest that her rosy outlook on life soon evaporated and that she responded to suffering in less than inspiring ways. In 1988, Dutch filmmaker Willy Lindwer interviewed survivors of Bergen–Belsen and his research revealed that although Anne and her sister Margot managed to stay together in the Bergen–Belsen concentration camp, they suffered tremendously, bickered with each other, grew thin from hunger, and died agonizing deaths from typhus, after which their bodies were likely dumped into anonymous graves.[6] And yet, a scrubbed image of the eternally optimistic Anne Frank remains the face of the Holocaust, particularly for young readers, who often first encounter the Holocaust through *Anne Frank: The Diary of a Young Girl*. Indeed, for many people, the diary remains their only exposure to the Holocaust.

To begin to understand how Anne Frank the victim became Anne Frank the phenomenon, it is necessary to revisit the complex publication history of her diary and the 1955 Goodrich/Hackett play, an early and influential adaptation that set the tone for many subsequent appropriations. Anne's transformation from anonymous Holocaust victim to cultural celebrity is due largely to what critics have called the "Americanization of the Holocaust," evident in the diary's editing and perpetuated in the play, which has powerfully influenced the production and consumption of Holocaust representations.[7] Americanization encompasses a variety of interrelated and sometimes contradictory phenomena that, in spite of the name, do not apply exclusively to the United States, though they point to America's powerful influence over how we have remembered the Holocaust.

Americanization refers to a certain way of presenting the history of the Holocaust such that its overwhelming horror becomes more palatable and more redeemable via its commercialization. The audience for these representations of the Holocaust is often, though not necessarily, American, but the term Americanization also reflects to how they represent values mainstream Americans have generally embraced, including individualism, tolerance, democracy, and anti-communism. The Americanization of Anne Frank reframes her significance and legacy to the point that, in Alvin H. Rosenfeld's apt phrasing, "The Anne Frank we remember is the Anne Frank we *want* to remember . . . the Anne who stands as a positive symbol of articulate innocence and transcendent optimism in a world of brutal and ultimately lethal adversity."[8] Americanization is an important concept in the study of Holocaust representations because of the powerful influence of the United States and Hollywood, in particular, on media around the world. Representations from other countries have certainly affected the shape of Holocaust memory, but film, drama, television, and other representations originating in the United States frequently find a broader audience and thus have a disproportionate influence. The story of Anne Frank's diary is an exemplary case study of this process.

The complex history of *Anne Frank: The Diary of a Young Girl*

Ironically, Anne Frank herself began what we can call the Americanization of Anne Frank, even though she never went near the United States. Few readers fully appreciate the extent to which Anne Frank's saintly image was first constructed in the editing of the diary, a process which she herself began. In 1986, the Netherlands Institute for War Documentation published a critical scholarly edition of the diary that revealed the artifice involved in its creation. The critical edition distinguishes between three versions of the diary: version A (the original text Anne wrote), version B (a revision of the first part of the original text, written by Anne in the spring of 1944), and version C (the published version, further edited by Otto Frank).

Anne had two inspirations for rewriting her original diary (some parts of which were later lost or destroyed). On May 11, 1944, she wrote that "my greatest wish is to become a journalist someday and later on a famous writer," and added "I want to publish a book entitled *Het Achterhuis* after the war."[9] Around the same time, a minister of the Dutch government in exile in London appealed to his countrymen, through the clandestine Radio Oranje, to keep letters, diaries, and other materials as proof that they had resisted the Nazi occupation.[10] Duly motivated, Anne rewrote her diary with an eye toward future publication. She understood that publication would require her to tone down or even eliminate many of the private thoughts and fantasies of version A, give her text an accessible literary form, and make its historical significance more evident. To these ends, Jeffrey Shandler writes, Anne "transformed her wide-ranging entries into a kind of suspense novel *à clef*, featuring continuing characters (with decodable pseudonyms), a running plot interspersed with suspenseful and comic episodes, a narrator offering reflections on the story she is relating, and background information on the larger context in which events inside the Annex take place."[11] She also added the famous salutation "Dear Kitty," which starts each entry in *Anne Frank: The Diary of a Young Girl*, taking the name Kitty from a series of popular Dutch young adult books, and thus giving the diary literary form as an imaginary friend to whom she confessed her secrets and true feelings.

When Otto Frank first published *Het Achterhuis* in the Netherlands in 1947, he was not simply telling a raw tale of wartime suffering; he was fulfilling his daughter's wish to be a published author. Before he submitted the book to publishers, Otto and the editors he hired made additional edits, correcting misspellings and grammar, and introduced more substantive changes resulting in what is now known as version C. "For the sake of propriety," scholar Gerrold van der Stroom writes, Otto "felt he had here and there to omit certain passages."[12] These passages included Anne's fascination with her changing pubescent body and budding sexuality, her complex self-identification as an assimilated German Jew in the Netherlands, her harshest statements about her mother and the state of her parents' marriage, and details of contemporary Dutch society and politics. One famous passage, restored decades later in the critical edition, dates from March 24, 1944, when Anne described her genitalia in extensive and graphic detail. This passage was considered inappropriate for the conservative sexual climate of the late 1940s and early 1950s, and still is by some readers today, like the Michigan parent who, in 2013, unsuccessfully protested the assignment of a restored version of the diary to seventh graders as pornographic and inappropriate.[13]

Other deleted passages expose Anne's sometimes difficult relationship with the seven other residents of the Annex: her mother, father, and sister; the three members of the van Pels family; and Fritz Pfeffer. Describing a disagreement brought on by the close quarters, Anne wrote in version A that Auguste van Pels was "an idiot of a woman!!!!" In late August and early September 1942, she complained repeatedly about her mother, saying things like, "Mummy gave me another frightful sermon this morning; I can't bear them." She ended another entry, "I've got to go and peel potatoes for the most rotten person in the world, that's a bit exaggerated, but only a little bit."[14] Yet another passage from version A, "Mummy always treats me like a baby, which I can't bear," made it into version C, but only after Otto changed "always" to "sometimes."[15] In the original diary, these passages appear among more positive depictions of life in hiding, revealing Anne as a normal teenager in an extraordinary situation, rather than a martyr with superhuman powers of patience, tolerance, and optimism.

Less intrusive edits in version C, such as spelling and grammar corrections and the translation of passages written in multiple languages into a single language, still make a significant difference. Anne lived in a historically specific situation. She was an exiled German Jew with German-speaking parents in a Dutch-speaking environment. Rendering her diary solely in English (or any other language) elides the fact that she lived in a multilingual environment. Together with the more substantive additions and omissions, these minor formal changes typify the editorial choices that helped Anne Frank transcend the specifics of her history to become a more general symbol of not only Holocaust victims but all victims of oppression. This trajectory intensified significantly after the book's American publication.

Meyer Levin, Otto Frank, Frances Goodrich, and Albert Hackett

The first American edition of *Anne Frank: The Diary of a Young Girl* appeared in 1952 and attracted rave reviews precisely for its universal message. Its most famous reviewer was Meyer Levin, a Jewish-American journalist and novelist who went on to play a critical and controversial role in popularizing the book in the United States and getting it adapted to the stage. Levin, one of the first

American war correspondents to see the atrocities at the newly liberated concentration camps, was, by his own description, obsessed with Anne Frank.[16] When he read a French translation of *Het Achterhuis* in 1950, he became fixated on Anne's story. He befriended Otto Frank, becoming an unpaid agent of sorts for the book. Although several publishing houses had already rejected it, Levin publicized the book in magazine articles and wrote letters to his contacts in the entertainment business in the hope of interesting American publishers in the diary. Given that the diary's reputation was already growing, independent of his efforts, Levin developed an overblown sense of his role in ultimately getting *Anne Frank: The Diary of a Young Girl* published in the United States. When Doubleday finally published the book in 1952, Levin wrote a glowing review for *The New York Times*, noting:

> There is anguish in the thought of how much creative power, how much sheer beauty of living, was cut off through genocide. But through her diary Anne goes on living. From Holland to France, to Italy, Spain. The Germans too have published her book. And now she comes to America. Surely she will be widely loved, for this wise and wonderful young girl brings back a poignant delight in the infinite human spirit.[17]

Lawrence Graver argues that this enthusiastic review "launched *Anne Frank: The Diary of a Young Girl* on its spectacular career in America," sparking significant sales and piquing the interest of potential producers who wanted to secure rights to adapt it to film, radio, television, and theater.[18]

Although Levin tirelessly advocated for the diary, Anne Frank biographer Francine Prose notes that one of the great ironies of his involvement was that, despite his good intentions and desire to avoid cheapening Anne's story, his bitter and public disagreements with Otto Frank did precisely that.[19] Much has been written about Levin's falling out with Otto over the development of the dramatic version of the published diary, titled *The Diary of Anne Frank*. As Otto's unofficial agent, Levin felt a sense of ownership over Anne's story. From the beginning of his relationship with Otto, he had expressed interest in adapting the story for the stage. Otto at first agreed to Levin's involvement in this project, but Broadway producers, the diary's publishers, and eventually Otto himself rejected Levin's drafts of a play based on the diary as "too dark" and "too Jewish" for the Broadway stage (many years of conflict and litigation ensued).[20] In light of conservative social attitudes in the United States in the 1950s and the complex (self)understanding of Jews vis-à-vis mainstream American culture after the Holocaust (see Chapter 3), "too Jewish" was also a code word for not commercially viable in the United States. This was a key turning point in the history of Holocaust representation, as the impetus to create a version of the play that Americans would like led to the version of

Anne Frank that has had so much influence on subsequent Holocaust representations, in the U.S. and around the world.

The desires of publishers and producers to create a commercially viable Anne Frank conveniently meshed with Otto's views about how to represent his daughter's diary on stage. Where Levin was convinced that Anne's story was first and foremost a Jewish story, which only a Jew could truly understand and properly adapt to the stage, Otto Frank disagreed. Convinced that his daughter's story had universal appeal, he wanted to make sure the adaptation was not, in scholar Edna Nahshon's phrasing, "too sectarian or too despairing."[21] Thus, Otto and the producers he was working with turned to the established (gentile) husband-and-wife playwright team of Frances Goodrich and Albert Hackett. The Goodrich/Hackett play took several years to complete, going through multiple rewrites and much internal drama, including plagiarism accusations from Levin. But the final version garnered critical and commercial success, winning a Pulitzer Prize and a Tony, and running for 717 performances.

One key source of the play's success was the way it further deemphasized the complexities of Anne's character, presenting her instead as a universal saintly figure, with whom audiences, including but not limited to Americans, would want to identify. Even the edited version of *Anne Frank: The Diary of a Young Girl* portrayed Anne as an intelligent and introspective young person who was sometimes conflicted about her body, her faith, and her family. But the Goodrich/Hackett play makes Anne into an optimistic, resilient, good-natured, and loveable girl next door, played by Susan Strasberg, an attractive American actress who didn't look stereotypically Jewish at all.

The Goodrich/Hackett play also tailors Anne Frank's story to the expectations of an American gentile audience. In Act I, Scene V, for instance, the residents of the Secret Annex celebrate Hanukkah, but they recite no prayers in Hebrew, and Anne distributes small, highly personalized presents, as if Hanukkah were simply a Jewish take on an American Christmas centered on gift giving and consumption. Similarly, the play stifles the complex reflections on Jewish identity in Anne's original diary. In her oft-quoted entry of April 11, 1944, she specifically lamented the suffering of Jews:

Who has inflicted this upon us? Who has made us Jews different from all other people? Who has allowed us to suffer so terribly up to now? It is God that has made us as we are, but it will be God, too, who will raise us up again. If we bear all this suffering and if there are still Jews left, when it is over, then Jews, instead of being doomed, will be held up as an example. Who knows, it might even be our religion from which the world and all peoples learn good, and for that reason and that reason only do we have to suffer now. We can never become just Netherlanders, or just English, or representatives of any country for that matter, we will always remain Jews, but we want to, too.[22]

While this diary entry shows Anne proudly identifying as Jewish, the Anne of the Goodrich/Hackett play avoids any overt statements of Jewish pride that, given lingering associations of Jews with communism and unwelcome immigration, might easily have been interpreted as anti-American by contemporary audiences. Instead, Anne's thoughts on victimhood take on a universal quality, notably in the oft-repeated line, "In spite of everything, I still believe that people are really good at heart." Yet even this line was more complicated in its original context. Anne's lengthy diary entry of July 15, 1944 reveals a more conflicted perspective: "That's the difficulty in these times," she wrote, "ideals, dreams and cherished hopes rise within us, only to meet the horrible truth and be shattered. It's really a wonder that I haven't dropped all my ideals, because they seem so absurd and impossible to carry out. Yet I keep them, because in spite of everything, I still believe that people are really good at heart."[23]

Beyond the drama

As we have seen, the image of Anne Frank that emerged in the 1950s, in particular through the Goodrich/Hackett play, was designed to appeal to mass American audiences. Although this representation differed in significant respects from the diary, the images it generated took hold of the world's cultural imagination and have not let go. Following closely on the heels of the successful play, the 1959 film adaptation further disseminated the angelic image of Anne Frank. Directed by George C. Stevens, who in 1945 made the atrocity film *Nazi Concentration Camps* (see Chapter 2), this adaptation featured another decidedly non-Semitic-looking actress, Millie Perkins, in its title role. Stevens's film further reinforced the image of Anne as an all-American girl and emphasized her story's melodramatic and romantic dimensions. As a dramatic score plays in the background, the trailer boasts, "Here is the thrill of her first kiss!" downplaying the Holocaust altogether; it further entices audiences by presenting two years in hiding as the stuff of a romantic thriller that will allow viewers to feel "The excitement of her first love!"

The Americanized image of Anne Frank produced by 1950s drama and film has persisted for decades. Otto Frank spent the rest of his life protecting his daughter's legacy, so it has only become truly possible to revisit this image since his death in 1980. The Netherlands Institute for War Documentation published the first critical edition of the diary in 1986. A 1997 revival of the play, starring Natalie Portman as Anne Frank, tried to accentuate Anne's

Jewish heritage, but still drew criticism for being "stuck in the 1950s."[24] More recently, a wide array of art projects has drawn attention to the constructed universality of Anne Frank's image and to those dimensions of the diary that popular editions suppressed or ignored. As part of *The Anne Frank Project* (1993), for instance, the feminist artist Ellen Rothenberg critiqued the ingrained sexism surrounding many Anne Frank representations by reproducing the diary passages about Anne's genitalia on a series of leather belts, explicitly drawing attention to Anne's body and her decidedly non-superhuman character. In 1999, artist Rachel Schreiber spray painted an iconic photograph of Anne Frank in public spaces around New York to draw attention to the extent to which Anne has become part of the fabric of modern life.

These revisions of Anne Frank's posthumous legacy are nevertheless exceptions to the rule. The saintly Anne Frank remains in the news and perpetuates further engagements with the diary. That image makes it possible to remember the Holocaust in ways that redeem its horror and ensure that the dead did not die in vain. Yet when we critically examine Anne's legacy and look at how the editing and adaptation of the diary changed its content, we encounter the uncomfortable question: what are people talking about when they talk about Anne Frank? Ultimately, it seems, talking about how we want to remember the Holocaust allows us to avoid close examination of its actual horrific events. This conceptually manageable framing of the past renders the Holocaust akin to a wound that can be healed and eventually overcome. Such a palatable version of horror is a chief legacy of the Americanization of the Holocaust.

Elie Wiesel (center) and other Holocaust survivors attend a wreath-laying ceremony at the memorial to the dead in Birkenau during the President's Commission on the Holocaust's fact-finding trip to Europe in the summer of 1979. The worldwide success of Wiesel's memoir Night *and his efforts to support Holocaust awareness made him a leading figure among Holocaust survivors.*

United States Holocaust Memorial Museum

5

Night (memoir, 1956/1958): What Does It Mean To Be a Holocaust Survivor?

In 1956, a relatively unknown Romanian journalist published an account of his Holocaust experiences in Yiddish. The 800-page memoir, titled *Un di velt hot geshvign* (And the world remained silent), appeared under the aegis of the Union of Polish Jews of Argentina, an organization formed in 1925, whose publishing house disseminated Yiddish works to Jews in Latin American countries.[1] During the 1950s, mainstream publishers had little interest in accounts of the Holocaust written by those who had experienced it, and the market for a lengthy memoir written in Yiddish was limited to say the least.[2] Nobody at the time would have guessed that a radically abridged translation of this story would become one of the most widely read Holocaust memoirs, or that its author, Eliezer "Elie" Wiesel, would become the authoritative voice of Holocaust memory and win a Nobel Peace Prize.

Two years later, Wiesel managed to publish his story in a more accessible form with a much wider potential audience, thanks to the intervention and support of French Catholic writer and Nobel laureate François Mauriac, whom Wiesel met in 1954 while on assignment for an Israeli newspaper. According to Wiesel, Mauriac first urged him to write the original story. Wiesel edited his Yiddish memoir, now titled *La Nuit (The Night, or Night)*, down to 127 pages, had it translated into French, and published it with the help of Mauriac. Like the original version, *La Nuit* tells the story of Wiesel's experiences during the Holocaust. Most of the book is devoted to his account of the pain, hunger, and humiliation he suffered in Auschwitz and Buchenwald. But this version was packaged for its French readership: it was shorter and much of its angry emotive language was excised. This version, translated into English in 1960 and eventually into dozens of languages, would sell millions of copies worldwide and become one of the definitive literary representations of the Holocaust.[3]

To understand the role of *Night* in fostering awareness of the Holocaust, it is important to trace its publication history and examine how it helped Wiesel become the most widely regarded moral authority on Holocaust memory. More than any other individual, Elie Wiesel has devoted himself to raising awareness of the attempted destruction of the Jewish people by the Nazis, in no small part by stressing its singularity. He was instrumental, for example, in popularizing the use of the term "Holocaust" to refer to this catastrophe.[4] Yet he also has worked tirelessly to convince broad audiences that this unique event was just one among many terrible crimes against humanity, whose repetition must be prevented in the future. For these efforts he was awarded the Nobel Peace Prize in 1986; announcing the prize, the Nobel Committee called him a "messenger to mankind."

While Wiesel's activities are incontrovertibly noble, his lofty reputation has surrounded his writings with an aura of reverence that renders it difficult to critique his work or assess its merits as one of a range of Holocaust representations. Nevertheless, it would be naïve to read Wiesel's (or any survivor's) Holocaust memoir as a mere record of what happened. A litany of unwritten but powerful rules governs both survivor accounts of the Holocaust and appropriate reader responses to them. Intentionally or not, survivor memoirs have traditionally adhered to specific narrative patterns and character types—many inspired by *Night*—to such an extent that pretenders have been able to pass off invented Holocaust stories as real (see Chapter 13). As Gary Weissman has pointed out, because *Night* often serves as an introduction to the Holocaust for many Americans, they learn that "the proper response to survivor memoirs is a kind of self-effacing reverence." Moreover, because of *Night*'s popularity, even those who have not read the book respond to its aura of reverence. Since Wiesel has become such an authoritative figure, readers and others accept his view of the Holocaust as a "sacred mystery" and an "event of intimidating, mystical religious magnitude" as an unquestionable given. As a result, Weissman argues, readers are compelled to approach all survivor memoirs with "awe, grief, or silence."[5]

To be sure, concentration camp survivors have created other iconic Holocaust representations, such as the works of Primo Levi, an Italian Jewish chemist, in particular his 1947 camp memoir *Se questo è un uomo* (translated as *Survival in Auschwitz*). However, Levi died in 1987, while Wiesel continues to be the most visible living representative of the Holocaust, a memorial personified, so to speak. As Cardinal Jean-Marie Lustiger, a French convert to Catholicism persecuted during World War II because he was born a Jew, points out, "It is not his literary oeuvre that has been celebrated, but that to which he himself and his writings bear witness: the fate of the Jewish people recognized as a sign of Peace for all men and women."[6] Here Lustiger articulates one key source of Wiesel's transformation into a moral authority: the desire of many Jews and non-Jews to understand the Holocaust as a meaningful event whose senseless violence can somehow be redeemed, an understanding Wiesel promotes. Both Wiesel's reputation and the popularity of *Night* reveal the unwritten rules for how audiences receive Holocaust representations, along with how those rules have shifted over time to fit the emotional and spiritual needs of different audiences. While we should not discredit or dishonor a Holocaust testimony without solid evidence that it has no historical basis, it is important to recognize these unwritten rules in order to critically analyze Holocaust memoirs. It is particularly important to approach iconic texts like *Night* critically, because the patterns they established have shaped how posterity remembers the Holocaust and venerates its survivors.

The men in the mirror

According to literary scholar Ruth R. Wisse, *Night* bore the influence of French literature even before it was translated from Yiddish into French. Wiesel's literary models, she notes, were French existentialists and other postwar influences "for whom individuality and individual conscience constituted the essence of art."[7] Thus, *Night* profoundly contrasted with most Yiddish memoirs of the war years, which tended to focus not on values, but rather on the specific identities of friends and relatives murdered in the Holocaust. Indeed, as Wisse notes, most Yiddish authors seemed to write about their experiences for the specific purpose of recalling the dead. In this sense, their writings were akin to yizkor books, which were published by and for Jews, to provide a testament to—and virtual gravestone for—those who perished anonymously in mass graves and gas chambers (see Chapter 3).

While the original *Un di velt hot geshvign* also resembles a yizkor book, with its bitter tone and details of Jewish life tailored to a knowledgeable audience, *Night* targeted a much broader readership and is first and foremost preoccupied with the relationship between the individual and God. *Night* begins in 1941, when Wiesel was thirteen years old and living with his parents and three sisters in the small Romanian town of Sighet. Although the war had begun two years earlier, Wiesel and his family initially felt few of its effects. Even after the first deportations, the town's residents were slow to suspect what might be in store for them. When the subsequent narrative shifts to Wiesel's imprisonment in the camps, the book's literary framework comes to the fore. The figure of poor, barefoot Moshe the Beadle, a foreign Jew who miraculously survives the first deportation, appears at the beginning of the story. Moshe returns to Sighet to warn the other Jews of their impending fate, but they do not believe his testimony and are subsequently deported themselves. His appearance thus also stands as a warning to readers, telling them they must believe the unbelievable horrors to which Wiesel testifies, or they too may be in danger. Moshe the Beadle was a real person, but Wiesel's depiction renders him a literary figure, the visionary fool, signaling the literary nature of the book.

In its emphasis on the importance of the witness who testifies to the experiences of Jews during the Holocaust, *Night* can be read as a literary analogue to the film *Shoah* (see Chapter 10). Unlike *Shoah*, however, Wiesel's text has strong religious overtones. Before the deportation, young Eliezer eagerly studies the Talmud and longs for an expert to introduce him to the mysticism of the kabbalah, settling for discussing it with Moshe the Beadle. But his ordeal in the camps causes him to question this faith, as revealed at first through ironic commentary: when his new shoes go unnoticed and therefore unconfiscated due to being caked in mud, he thanks God "for having created mud in His infinite and wonderful universe."[8] His emotions soon escalate to anger and the feeling that God has entirely abandoned him: "Why, but why should I bless Him? In every fiber I rebelled. Because he had had thousands of children burned in His pits? . . . My eyes were open and I was alone—terribly alone in a world without God and without man."[9]

The tension between Wiesel's feelings about God and the fact that he never truly abandons his faith forms the foundation of *Night*'s status as an iconic Holocaust representation. Even when Wiesel refuses to follow tradition and fast on Yom Kippur because he is angry with God, he still believes that God exists: "I no longer accepted God's silence. As I swallowed my bowl of soup, I saw in the gesture an act of rebellion and protest against Him."[10] As Cardinal Lustiger puts it, "Wiesel remained a man of faith, even when all evidence of God's presence was destroyed."[11] His ability to question God's presence and get angry but never become vengeful is one of the things that makes *Night* so compelling, for Jewish and non-Jewish readers alike. Even after liberation, Wiesel stresses the absence of vengeance: "And even when we were no longer hungry, there was still no one who thought of revenge. On the following day, some of the young men went to Weimar to get some potatoes and clothes—and to sleep with girls. But of revenge not a sign."[12]

Although this ethos of "turning the other cheek" has Christian overtones, many critics identify Wiesel, his principles, and his authoritative, ethical voice as quintessentially Jewish. Alvin H. Rosenfeld, for example, compares Wiesel to Primo Levi and Jean Améry, two other victims of Nazi persecution who wrote about their experiences in and after the camps. Although all three authors fear that people will not listen to their testimony, Wiesel alone claims that his deep faith in Judaism is what keeps him writing and testifying. As Rosenfeld notes, Wiesel "has located the source of this charge within Jewish religious traditions and identifies his vocation as a writer with the imperatives of Judaism itself."[13] According to Rosenfeld, Améry, who committed suicide in 1978, and Levi, whose 1987 death may have been suicide, were discouraged by their preoccupation with forcing Germany to face up to its acts, a desire he sees as secular. In contrast, Wiesel's major quarrel is not with the human perpetrators of the Holocaust, but with God. Like many other critics, Rosenfeld lauds Wiesel's affirmation of his Jewish faith and its direct connection to his determination to continue witnessing, no matter how discouraged he becomes.

Not all critics share this admiration. In her 1996 essay "Elie Wiesel and the Scandal of Jewish Rage," Naomi Seidman argues that the French version of *Night* was written specifically for a non-Jewish audience. As she notes, "The French reworking of *Un di velt hot geshvign* and Mauriac's framing of this text together suggest that *La Nuit*—read so consistently as authentically Jewish, autobiographical, direct—represents a compromise between Jewish expression and the capacities and desires of non-Jewish readers, Mauriac first among them."[14] Seidman claims that Wiesel was not happy with the limited reception of his Yiddish book. As many critics have noted, Mauriac, not Wiesel, got *Night* published in French. But to broaden the scope of his readership, Wiesel had to suppress his anger and take artistic license with some details of his experience. As Seidman puts it, "Wiesel found the audience he told his Yiddish readers he wanted. But only, as it turns out, by suppressing the very existence of this desire, by foregrounding the reticent and mournful Jew who will speak only when at the urging of the older Catholic writer."[15]

Seidman meticulously documents how the language of *Un di velt hot geshvign* articulates a strong sense of vengeance for what was done to the Jews, going so far as to distinguish between Wiesel's dual identities: the Yiddish survivor of *Un di velt hot geshvign*, who has no problem expressing his anger and desire for revenge against the Germans, and the French survivor of *La Nuit*, who panders to Christian audiences by turning the other cheek. In the original Yiddish version, she points out, Wiesel writes that the young liberated men go off to Weimar not merely to sleep with German girls, but, explicitly, to rape them. Wiesel also was forced to tone down his bitterness at the fact that a war criminal like Ilse Koch, whom he refers to as "the bestial sadist of Buchenwald" in the Yiddish version, is allowed to forget the past and "happily" raise her children.[16] As Seidman puts it, "the survivor who pointed an accusatory finger at Ilse Koch, then raising her children in the new postwar Germany, had been supplanted by the survivor haunted by metaphysics and silence."[17]

At the end of the French version, Wiesel leaves readers with the image of a survivor who, after liberation, confronts his face in the mirror and does nothing but stare back at himself: "From the depths of the mirror, a corpse gazed back at me."[18] But at the end of the Yiddish work, as Seidman points out, Wiesel is nothing like a passive victim, continuing, "Without knowing why, I raised a balled-up fist and smashed the mirror, breaking the image that lived within it. And then—I fainted. From that moment on my health began to improve."[19] Seidman seeks to show how Wiesel himself has been complicit in creating the palatable myth of the non-vengeful Jewish survivor, an image he has continued to promote since the publication of *Night*, in both interviews and his own writing. Indeed, she suggests, "It is only in later writings that Wiesel makes the further move of seeing this failure to take revenge as a sign of Jewish moral triumph—a nearly Christian turning of the other cheek— rather than the unfortunate result of cowardice or realism."[20] Ultimately, Wiesel is responsible for providing his non-Jewish audience with the image of a survivor who fulfills their desires: a Jewish survivor who exhibits no trace of revenge, not because he is cowardly or weak, but because he embraces the Christian value of turning the other cheek.

From victims to survivors

Although Wiesel entered the public eye after the publication of *Night*, he catapulted to international fame in 1986, the year he received the Nobel Peace Prize for his efforts on behalf of human rights.[21] Significantly, the growth of his reputation marks a turning point at which America signaled its readiness for a new spokesperson on the Holocaust. That role had been posthumously filled by Anne Frank, whose story was broadly disseminated in the 1950s through the book, drama, and film versions of her diary (see Chapter 4). Although Anne Frank remains a symbol of the innocent Holocaust victim who maintained her faith in humanity throughout her suffering, by the 1980s, there was widespread desire to move away from an emphasis on how victims suffered to how they were made stronger by overcoming suffering. Wiesel came to represent this survivor, as he articulately linked the crimes against the Jews to general crimes against humanity, touting the Holocaust as a unique event that could still teach universal lessons.

Anne Rothe outlines this shift in American culture from the victim paradigm to the survivor paradigm, noting that it was prefigured by a Holocaust discourse which accused all victims, including survivors, of failing to resist and passively accepting their fate. The negative terms used to depict both murdered and surviving victims framed them metaphorically as "weak losers" in the fight for survival of the fittest.[22] As the extent of the Holocaust was revealed, first through Anne Frank, then in accounts of the Eichmann trial (see Chapter 6), this view gradually shifted. Americans who lived through the Holocaust came to redefine themselves not as victims, but as survivors able to overcome suffering and become stronger as a result. As Rothe notes, this view recasts survival as the ultimate goal not only for Holocaust survivors, but for others trying to articulate their own pain in terms of the Holocaust, an attractive, yet dangerous move. Even as the Holocaust provides a compelling analogy, both individually and institutionally, appropriating the pain of others transforms victims into metaphors, allowing people (including teachers and students, see Chapter 14) to consider themselves "victims-by-proxy" and enabling victim fantasies that can become a highly problematic ethical game.[23]

American culture has recognized the limits of this appropriation of the survivor label, often through humor that may seem inappropriate but in fact offers a valid critique. Larry David's popular television sitcom *Curb Your Enthusiasm* aired an episode called "The Survivor" on March 7, 2004. As Rothe points out, this episode ridicules the American "cult of survival," mocks American trauma culture, and questions the role of discourse about the Holocaust in American culture. In the episode, a real Holocaust survivor is confronted by a contestant on the reality television program *Survivor*, and the two absurdly argue over who suffered more. As Rothe notes, this episode critiques the oversaturation of American culture with rote representations of Holocaust survivors and the ways these representations are misused as comparison points for overcoming difficulties that really do not compare.[24]

The problematic manipulation of the Holocaust is also evident in the trip Wiesel himself took with Oprah Winfrey to Auschwitz in January 2006, televised on two special episodes of Winfrey's television show in May of that year. As Jeffrey Shandler notes, the point of this visit was not so much to educate viewers about the history of the Holocaust, but rather to utilize the celebrity status of both Winfrey and Wiesel to transmit the "Holocaust's affective power and ethical challenges."[25] During the second episode, the show aired footage of Winfrey and Wiesel at Auschwitz, during which they spoke of the site's hallowed aura and moral significance. But on the first episode, the show featured winners of a national essay contest in which 50,000 high school students wrote about the relevance of Elie Wiesel's *Night*. The student essays related Wiesel's Holocaust experiences to their own personal suffering from crime-ridden neighborhoods, sexual abuse, and homelessness. The show also included a redemptive moment when a young Rwandan woman, who came to the United States after the Rwandan genocide, was reunited with her family.[26] Overall, the show affirmed the tradition of encouraging audiences to articulate the terms of their own sufferings via the figure of the Holocaust survivor.

Winfrey and Wiesel's visit to Auschwitz followed on the heels of a 2005 controversy in which Winfrey promoted James Frey's purported memoir *A Million Little Pieces*, later deemed to be fake, to bestseller status. This timing was not lost on many commentators. The Holocaust provided Winfrey with an opportunity to reestablish her credibility, for nobody could deny the truth of Wiesel's experiences without transgressing major social taboos. Wiesel himself undoubtedly viewed the trip as another chance to acquaint a broad audience with the moral lessons of the Holocaust. But he nevertheless, in this case and others, allowed his book and reputation to be used as a narrative of redemption and Jewish Nazi victims to be used as a metaphor for the suffering of others. In doing so, he has been complicit in eliding the terms of their actual suffering.

Demystifying the survivor

Elie Wiesel remains committed to the noble goal of fixing the memory of the Holocaust in our consciousness. As he has said, "Our deep conviction is that anyone who does not commit himself to active remembering is an accomplice of the executioner, for he betrays the dead by forgetting them and their testimony."[27] But his warning does not differentiate between remembering and appropriating, past and present; indeed, by foregrounding "remembering" and countering it with words like "accomplice" and "betrayal," he discourages the critical analysis of Holocaust representations. To be ethically responsible, as Alain Finkielkraut has noted, one needs to acknowledge that there is a gap in time between oneself and the person who suffered.[28] Thus *Night* itself is not problematic; the problem is the distortions that can result when readers are lulled into uncritical belief in *Night*'s aura of reality and embrace its narrative of witness and faith as the only acceptable story of the Holocaust. Primo Levi soberly reminded us that the only "true" witnesses of the Holocaust were those who died, and thus cannot testify to their experience; in his vision, the survivor is always already compromised. Indeed, to be a Holocaust survivor means that your story will always be partial, always open to appropriation, and inevitably shaped in some way by the unwritten rules of Holocaust representation. Readers thus have not just the right but the responsibility to read their stories critically; indeed, this is an essential step in honoring those silenced witnesses who could not tell their own stories.

PART TWO

The 1960s and 1970s

Former SS-Obersturmbannführer Adolf Eichmann takes notes on May 29, 1961 during his lengthy trial in Jerusalem. He was convicted and on May 31, 1962 hanged for his role in carrying out the Final Solution. The trial, which formed the subject of Hannah Arendt's book Eichmann in Jerusalem: A Report on the Banality of Evil, *helped draw attention to the Holocaust around the world.*

United States Holocaust Memorial Museum, courtesy of Israel Government Press Office

6

Eichmann in Jerusalem (book, 1963):

What Role Do Trials Play in How We Remember the Holocaust?

On May 23, 1960, Israeli Prime Minister David Ben-Gurion made a shocking announcement to the Knesset, Israel's parliament. Undercover operatives of Mossad, Israel's Central Bureau of Intelligence and Security, had captured the infamous Nazi war criminal Adolf Eichmann in Buenos Aires. A high-ranking administrator of the "Final Solution to the Jewish Question" was in custody in Israel awaiting trial. Eichmann's lengthy and historic trial for crimes against humanity and the Jewish people ended eighteen months after his capture with the only non-military death penalty sentence ever issued by the State of Israel. He was hanged on May 31, 1962.[1]

The first trials of Nazi war criminals had occurred fifteen years earlier in Nuremberg, but the Eichmann trial was a watershed event. Although accusations of crimes against the Jews certainly played a role at Nuremberg, they were not the International Military Tribunal's main focus. Rather, the prosecution sought to convict political and military leaders for perpetrating war crimes against people of many different nations and ethnicities. By contrast, Eichmann's trial not only framed the Nazi persecution and murder of European Jews as a distinct event, it also placed complicity at the center of the charges against the accused. Unlike other Nazi leaders tried for their actions during World War II, Eichmann may not have been personally responsible for any individual deaths. However, as a mid-level bureaucrat in the Gestapo's unassumingly named Department IVB4 or Jewish section, organizing and implementing the Nazi plan to destroy the Jewish people was his primary responsibility. This role was at the heart of the grave charges against him. The trial also helped expose the role of bureaucrats like him, the so-called *Schreibtischtäter* (desk perpetrators) who were also implicated in the deaths of Jews, not by killing people, but by carrying out tasks that made it possible for people to be killed, like making sure trains arrived at concentration camps on time.

The Eichmann trial was also the first time the testimony of Holocaust survivors played a crucial role in legal proceedings, with the goal of exposing and verifying not just a single act but an entire set of historical events. For many people, the trial, whether they followed it in the courtroom, on television, or in newspapers and magazines, served as their first exposure to eyewitness accounts of the atrocities visited upon the victims of Hitler's regime. Though footage from the documentary *Nazi Concentration Camps* was shown in a courtroom for the first time at Nuremberg (see Chapter 2), the Eichmann trial was the first trial held explicitly for the purpose of "doing justice to unprecedented crimes, clarifying a tortured history, and defining the terms of collective memory."[2] As such, it transcended its basic goal—judging a single Nazi operative—and became a transformative moment in how the Holocaust was understood, as well as how it would be remembered for decades thereafter. As late as 1959, Paul Benzaquin's account of one of the deadliest fires in American history was titled *Holocaust! The Shocking Story of the Boston Cocoanut Grove Fire*. After the Eichmann trial, however, the use and capitalization of the term Holocaust became indelibly connected with the genocide of Europe's Jews. From then on, the war crimes of the Nazis were seen less as violations committed in equal measure against many nations and peoples and more as a meticulously planned genocide of the Jews.

As important as the actual Eichmann trial was in shaping public understanding and memory of the Holocaust, however, it was Hannah Arendt's reporting from the trial, published first in *The New Yorker*, then as the book *Eichmann in Jerusalem: A Report on the Banality of Evil*, that made the trial accessible to a broad audience. It has continued to inform debates about the Holocaust and its implications for decades. By now, the flaws in Arendt's account, including factual errors, have become clear. Yet, despite its shortcomings, her reporting, with its philosophical musings and often sarcastic commentary, continues to be so well-known and influential that her ideas are essential to any discussion of the Eichmann trial.

A philosopher and reporter

Arendt's reporting on the trial cannot be separated from her own background as a German–Jewish refugee who fled to Paris in 1933, was imprisoned in the internment camp Gurs in 1940, and emigrated to the United States in 1941.

Born in Hanover in 1906, Arendt grew up in Königsberg and Berlin. By the time the Nazis came to power, she had already completed her studies in philosophy, most notably with Martin Heidegger in Marburg and Karl Jaspers in Heidelberg. As a student, Arendt had an affair with Heidegger, who was married at the time. Their liaison would become a sore point for her critics, given Heidegger's membership in the Nazi party and harassment of Jewish professors at the university in Freiburg where he became Rector. In 1929 Arendt married the Jewish writer and intellectual Günther Stern. They lived in Berlin, where she became politically active in the cause against Nazism and wrote a biography of Berlin salonnière Rahel Varnhagen (1771–1833), who wrote freely about the limitations imposed upon her as a German-Jewish woman.[3] Later attacks on Arendt's writing and accusations that she was a self-hating Jew stemmed from her ambivalence about her own Jewish self-identification, as well as her vociferous criticism of Jews, Israel, and Zionism. But it is important to remember that she faced anti-Semitism in Germany and supported Jews before, during, and after the war. As Jerome Kohn notes, "Hannah Arendt probably wrote more about Jewish affairs in general than about any other topic."[4]

By the time her reports on the Eichmann trial appeared in *The New Yorker* in 1963, Arendt was an American citizen who had lived in New York for 22 years. She had an established career as an influential writer and scholar, writing for *Aufbau*, a New York-based German–Jewish exile newspaper, as well as *Partisan Review, Commentary,* and *The Nation*. She also became a senior editor at Schocken books, a well-known German publisher, after it opened a branch in New York in 1945. Among her projects there was editing a German-language edition of Franz Kafka's *Diaries*.[5] Immersed in the New York intellectual scene, it is her rejection by many of her former supporters that stung her most. This point is emphasized in a recent popular iteration of her life, the biographical film *Hannah Arendt* (dir. Margarethe von Trotta, 2012) featuring Barbara Sukowa in the leading role, which focuses on Arendt's reporting on the Eichmann trial and the effects of the controversy surrounding it on her life. Although not emphasized in the film, the wave of controversy surrounding her reports represented a turning point for American Jewish intellectuals, who until that point only seldomly discussed the Holocaust in public. By challenging accepted views of angelic victims and monstrous perpetrators, Arendt's reporting catalyzed a public debate that signaled the willingness of American Jews to discuss anti-Semitism and the Holocaust in public life and the acceptance of those ideas by a wider public in the 1960s.[6]

Arendt's first references to the Holocaust in her work appear in *The Origins of Totalitarianism* (1951), where she analyzes Nazism and Stalinism. The book had a major impact, and in the next decade she received a prestigious Guggenheim Fellowship, lectured at Princeton and the University of Chicago, and wrote *The Human Condition* (1958), in which she set out her political philosophy. Subsequent publications included the essay collection *Between Past and Future* (1961) and *On Revolution* (1963), a study of the French and American Revolutions. However, none of these works dealt explicitly with the Holocaust or focused on Germany: even in *The Origins of Totalitarianism* she linked Nazism to other political developments and ideologies in Western Europe. Her reportage on the Eichmann trial, which remains her best-known work, was her first direct response to the Nazi effort to exterminate European Jews, an event from which she herself had narrowly escaped.[7]

By her own account, Arendt felt a personal responsibility to attend the trial; later, she would attest that as a Jew, a former Zionist, and a former German, writing about the trial helped bring her relief from a heavy burden.[8] She agreed to serve as a correspondent for *The New Yorker* and attended ten weeks of what turned into a four-month trial. The five articles she wrote, published in February and March 1963, sparked an intense debate between critics who labeled her a wicked writer of claptrap and half-truths and supporters who hailed her as the brilliant author of a masterpiece.[9]

Arendt heavily criticized the Israeli court, especially prosecutor Gideon Hausner, for grandstanding and distorting the trial's purpose. In her view, Eichmann's trial should have been a legal process to determine whether he was guilty or innocent of his alleged crimes. Instead, under Hausner's control, it came across as a contrived, theatrical performance, replete with witnesses picked from hundreds of Holocaust survivors for their abilities to effectively tell general tales of suffering rather than because they had any connection to Eichmann and his crimes. She saw her reporting as a corrective to what she viewed as these and other grave errors committed at the trial.[10] But two elements of her critique inspired the most outrage. The first was her characterization of Eichmann, whom she portrayed not as an evil demon driven by fanatical anti-Semitism, but as a mindless bureaucrat oblivious to the true implications of his acts. The other was her accusation that the Jewish Councils (groups of Jewish leaders forced by the Nazis to administer laws in the ghettos) acceded to Nazi demands to aid in the organization of their own destruction, and thus were to blame at least partially for their own fates. This accusation understandably caused an enormous outcry, particularly among Holocaust survivors, for whom implicating Jewish victims in their own persecution was intolerable.

Careful reading of her reports suggests that Arendt intended neither to minimize the harm done by Eichmann and other Nazis, nor to downplay the suffering of their victims, but rather to correct the court's refashioning of Holocaust victims as impossibly good and Holocaust perpetrators as uniformly demonic sadists. Although some people would later distort Arendt's claims beyond recognition, the "banality of evil" and the complicity of the Jewish councils are what many readers take away from her account of the courtroom proceedings. Still, no matter how controversial they consider her conclusions, anyone who writes seriously about the trial must invariably engage with her on these two key issues. When we look closely at these claims, we find that Arendt has been misread and that she herself misread her subject.

The banality of evil and the Jewish councils

Along with Adorno's pronouncement on the impossibility of poetry after Auschwitz (see Introduction), Arendt's "banality of evil" has become one of the ubiquitous phrases of Holocaust discourse, shorthand for the truism that the destruction of European Jewry was planned and carried out by mediocre bureaucrats like Eichmann, not unholy monsters. Interestingly, the phrase appears exactly once in Arendt's account, as she summarizes her view of Eichmann's role in the murder of Europe's Jews: "It was as though in those last minutes he was summing up the lessons that this long course in human wickedness had taught us—the lesson of the fearsome, word-and-thought-defying *banality of evil*."[11] She further explains his motivations: "One cannot extract any diabolical or demonic profundity from Eichmann. He *merely*, to put the matter colloquially, *never realized what he was doing*. It was sheer thoughtlessness—by no means identical with stupidity—that predisposed him to become one of the greatest criminals of that period."[12] Arendt wished to warn readers that viewing Eichmann as a perverted Other with whom they had nothing in common would inhibit their comprehension of his criminal nature and crimes. And to do this, she claimed, would be to fall for the courtroom drama and misrepresent the Holocaust.

Arendt's analysis was based on the sources she had on hand, namely, as a number of scholars have pointed out, her limited observations of Eichmann in the courtroom and her reading of Holocaust scholarship such as Raul Hilberg's seminal work, *The Destruction of the European Jews* (1961).[13] And, as Deborah Lipstadt argues, new sources to which Arendt did not have access, such as the full extent of Eichmann's journals, make it impossible for us to take her characterization of Eichmann at face value today: "In contrast to claims that would be made by Hannah Arendt that he did not really understand the enterprise in which he was involved, the memoir reveals a man who considered his Nazi leaders to be his 'idols' and who was fully committed to their goals."[14] Moreover, Bettina Stangneth points out that a series of 1960 interviews with Eichmann by Dutch Nazi collaborator Willem Sassen, which were not made available until 1979, reveal Eichmann socializing with friends and former Nazi colleagues in Argentina, underlining his commitment to anti-Semitic Nazi goals.[15]

Even if Arendt had had access to such materials, however, it is not clear that she would have definitively revised her view of Eichmann. Roger Berkowitz claims that Arendt had actually read enough of Eichmann's interviews, portions of which were published in *Life* magazine in 1960, as well as at least 70 pages of his 1956 memoir, to be able to judge his state of mind for herself. He concludes she was well aware of his anti-Semitic statements but believed that these reflected his boastfulness and ignorance rather than a deep-seated hatred of Jews that served as his main driving force. His first allegiance was, above all, to the Nazi movement, and as a "thoughtless" bureaucrat he was willing to do anything to serve it. As Berkowitz notes, "Arendt's point was that Eichmann—beyond being an anti-Semite, thrived upon the power and meaning he got from being a Nazi."[16]

Many have also sought to debunk Arendt's audacious criticism of the Jewish Councils. She was hardly the first to call into question the behavior of Jewish leaders placed in impossible positions by the Nazis, or to suggest that the process of killing might have been slowed, or more Jews might have been saved, had those leaders not complied with Nazi demands for things like names of deportees. The difference in her accusation, however, was her insistence that Jewish leaders had implicated themselves through their actions. She argues that "The whole truth was that if the Jewish people had really been unorganized and leaderless, there would have been chaos and plenty of misery but the total number of victims would hardly have been between four and a half and six million people,"[17] but this point has since been challenged by numerous scholars.[18]

However, her blurring of the boundaries between victims and perpetrators has itself been mischaracterized. Arendt was blamed for implying that Jewish victims of Nazi persecution were responsible for their own deaths because of their failure to resist. Yet it was she who actually criticized Hausner, the Israeli prosecutor, for implying that Jews contributed substantially to their own victimization. German-Jewish philosopher Gershom Scholem criticized Arendt in an open letter for her harsh comments, claiming that she was in no position to judge a situation she herself did not experience. Arendt countered that refusing to judge would be tantamount to discrediting both the law and history: "I have made my own position plain, and yet it is obvious that you did not understand it. I said that there was no possibility of resistance, but there existed the possibility of *doing nothing*. And in order to do nothing, one did not need to be a saint, one needed only to say: 'I am just a simple Jew, and I have no desire to play any other role.' "[19] In short, although Arendt's claims did not accord with standard Holocaust discourse at the time, in addressing these criticisms she anticipated debates about the role of Jewish resistance in the Holocaust that would later become the focus of significant historical inquiry.

Global impact

American audiences could watch the Eichmann trial on television, and they did, in great numbers. As Jeffrey Shandler has pointed out, these broadcasts were probably the first exposure American audiences had to the use of the word Holocaust to describe the Nazi persecution of European Jewry. However, Shandler also notes that although the televised trial may have been a turning point in the history of the Holocaust on television, it did not prove to be important in shaping Holocaust memory in the United States. It did, however, spur at least some American authors and playwrights, such as Arthur Miller and Sylvia Plath, to deal with its psychological effects and moral questions.[20] In the end, Arendt's account had a much more lasting impact on Americans than the televised trial, and Arendt herself continues to figure in popular culture well beyond the United States. German filmmaker Margarethe von Trotta's historical drama *Hannah Arendt* (2012) speaks to her continued relevance.

If Arendt received both support and criticism in the United States, her take on the trial was highly unpopular in Israel, not least because she criticized how the trial was used to promote Zionism. She faulted the judge and prosecutor for skewing the proceedings in service of supporting Israeli identity rather than administering justice. Few would dispute that the Israelis did indeed stage the Eichmann trial to teach history and shape collective memory. But not everyone agreed with Arendt's argument that a trial could not service justice and maintain such blatantly political goals at the same time. Still, her reporting influenced even her staunchest critics across the globe.

Art of trials

One of the most persistent debates in Holocaust representation is whether traumatic historical events like the Holocaust can be appropriately and adequately explored, either by art and literature or by fields like psychoanalysis and law. Susan Sontag addressed this challenge directly in 1964, using the example of the Eichmann trial:

> Among the unacknowledged art forms which have been devised or perfected in the modern era for this purpose are the psychoanalytic session, the parliamentary debate, the political rally, and the political trial. And as the supreme tragic event of modern times is the murder of six million European Jews, one of the most interesting and moving works of art of the past ten years is the trial of Adolf Eichmann in Jerusalem in 1961.[21]

Arendt undoubtedly would have disagreed with Sontag's radical contention that the trial should be lauded as a brilliant work of art. Indeed, she believed the opposite: that the sole goal of the Eichmann trial, like any other trial, should have been to "render justice, and nothing else."[22] Yet the significant afterlife of Arendt's rendering of the trial suggests that trials can do more than simply mete out justice, and reporting on trials can serve as more than a mere restatement of facts. Indeed, *Eichmann in Jerusalem* transformed subsequent representations and understandings of the Holocaust.

One striking example of Arendt's influence on later Holocaust representations is Eyal Sivan and Rony Brauman's controversial film *The Specialist*, based on *Eichmann in Jerusalem* and released in 1999, the same year the only Hebrew translation of the book to date appeared in Israel. The filmmakers began by viewing all 360 hours of videotape from the trial. They then edited selections into a two-hour film, overlaying them with sounds, images, and distortions to emphasize or amplify elements normally bracketed as unimportant, such as Eichmann wiping off his glasses. The film was received positively in some circles. Yet it caused controversy in others, including the Hebrew University in Jerusalem and the Steven Spielberg Jewish Film Archive, who felt that it distorted the historical record by editing survivor testimony and splicing scenes together. Such criticisms are characteristic of debates about the role of fact and fiction in Holocaust representations such as *Maus* (see Chapter 11). They also raise questions about whether Holocaust representations should be responsible for documenting events as they happened or allowed to highlight the very real distortions and errors that result from all accounts of past events, no matter how objective they purport to be.

As Darcy C. Buerkle notes, the filmmakers remain true to Arendt's portrayal of Eichmann, presenting him as boring, staid, and unremarkable. But the film also illuminates something implicit in her reporting: the trial's visual impact.[23] Buerkle notes that, as the first trial videotaped in its entirety, the Eichmann trial serves as a unique visual record of Holocaust representation. By restoring footage cut out of the transcript—such as interjections by members of the audience, Eichmann's twitching face and tics, and the disaffected demeanor of survivors as they testified—the directors could highlight pivotal emotional aspects of the process that Arendt reported on only parenthetically, including rhetorical references to emotion, as well as fainting, crying, and other bodily actions.[24] Buerkle argues that the film thus bucks the general trend toward minimizing unsanctioned emotions in visual representations of atrocity: "'Bracketing' affective eruption that is not sanctioned, choreographed, or, more specifically, sentimental and therefore fleeting has become symptomatic in contemporary consumption of atrocity images."[25]

Arendt's polemical statements overshadow the fact that the emotional testimony of the survivors formed the cornerstone of the trial and affected her deeply. She devoted little space to eyewitness testimonies in her account, and she was critical of some of the survivor testimony she did mention, such as survivor and author Ka-Tzetnik (see Chapter 8), who collapsed in the courtroom during his testimony. Yet Arendt's report on the trial, like the trial itself, was much more than a mere recounting of facts and events. Though she criticized some survivors, she noted that the ten-minute testimony of another, Zindel Grynzspan, packed the "needless destruction of twenty-seven years in less than twenty-four hours," after which, "one thought foolishly: Everyone, everyone should have his day in court."[26] Arendt did understand how central testimony was to the trial and how important it is for individuals to be able to tell their stories and be heard, which has been one of the fundamental roles trials have played in the Holocaust. But she objected to the use of testimony in the service of anything other than justice, and in so doing she pointed to the ways in which trials, like any other forum or representation, can be purposed to ends far beyond witnessing.

A group of young Catholic protestors disrupt a performance of Rolf Hochhuth's play The Deputy *on December 13, 1963 at the Theater De L'Athenee in Paris. The* Deputy, *which accused Pope Pius XII and the Vatican of failing to speak out against atrocities, helped spark a broader debate about the Catholic Church's role during the Holocaust. Protests like this one accompanied many early performances.*

Paris Match via Getty Images

7

The Deputy (drama, 1963):

What Role Did the Catholic Church Play in the Holocaust?

According to theater critic Eric Bentley, German playwright Rolf Hochhuth's play *Der Stellvertreter: ein christliches Trauerspiel* (*The Deputy: A Christian Tragic Drama*, 1963) provoked "the largest storm ever raised by a play in the whole history of the drama."[1] *The Deputy* tells the story of an idealistic young Catholic priest who urges the Vatican to protest the gassing of Jews in 1942 and meets only indifferent silence from Pope Pius XII (1939–1958). The play echoes history: Pius XII, who commanded tremendous political and moral influence in Nazi Germany, addresses the Nazi genocide only twice, most notably in his 1942 Christmas message, when he spoke only in generalities, never mentioning Jews specifically, opting only for vague verbiage about "ethnicity."[2] As the Germans rounded up the Jews of Rome on October 16, 1943, "under the Pope's very windows," to cite an official German phrase taken up by scholars, Pius XII did not publicly intervene.

Hochhuth made the terms of his political critique crystal clear by dedicating the play to two members of the clergy who acted when the Pope did not: "To the memory of two Catholic priests, Father Maximilian Kolbe, Inmate No. 16670 in Auschwitz [and] Provost Bernhard Lichtenberg of St. Hedwig's Cathedral, Berlin." Kolbe was a Polish Franciscan friar who voluntarily took the place of a condemned man at Auschwitz. Lichtenberg publicly protested anti-Jewish discrimination and Nazi euthanasia of the mentally ill and disabled. He prayed publicly for victims, refused to recant, was arrested, and died awaiting transport to Dachau. The fundamental thesis of *The Deputy* is that if the Catholic Church and Pius XII had followed the examples of Kolbe and Lichtenberg, untold Jewish lives could have been saved.

Hochhuth's deliberately provocative play garnered heated responses after its premiere in Berlin on February 20, 1963 and subsequent performances across Europe and North America. Rioters interrupted a performance in Paris in January 1964, and in Basel, Switzerland, 10,000 protestors marched silently in a torch-lit procession to the Basel City Theater.[3] The West German Chancellor Ludwig Erhard denounced Hochhuth and formally apologized to the Vatican on his behalf, though he had no interest in apologizing.[4] With the Eichmann trial (see Chapter 6) still fresh in the public's mind, The Deputy's accusation of papal indifference was a highly provocative act. Pius XII had only been dead for five years, and church officials, Catholic laity, and conservative groups alike accused Hochhuth of slander and, in particular, failing to understand the complex wartime situation into which the personally unassuming, non-confrontational Pope had been thrust.[5] American Jewish publications had raised the issue of the culpability of the Catholic Church in the Holocaust as early as 1947, but Hochhuth's play was the catalyst that mobilized intense debates about the Pope's actions, motivations, and legacy that persist even today.[6]

Criticism of the play's politics was not redeemed by praise for its artistic merits. Hochhuth's use of documentary theater—weaving historical events into the drama—may have strengthened The Deputy's incisive commentary, but the play itself lasted seven hours in its uncut version and, according to critics, had flat characters and stilted dialogue. Still, it was a momentous dramatic event. By accusing the Catholic Church of, at worst, active complicity with the Nazis, or, at best, callous indifference to the murder of Europe's Jews, The Deputy challenged longstanding taboos that had never been called into question so explicitly. Moreover, it dared to assert that responsibility for the Holocaust fell on people other than Hitler, Nazis, and Germans.[7] More broadly, The Deputy raised questions about the moral responsibility of bystanders (a term that only came into common use several decades later) in the face of injustice and genocide, a subject that received little attention in the first two decades after the end of World War II.[8] It thus stood out most from the most popular dramatic representation of the Holocaust to date, The Diary of Anne Frank (see Chapter 4).[9] As a stage performance, The Deputy could not reach the broad audiences that would later view the television miniseries Holocaust (see Chapter 9). But the effects of Hochhuth's play reached far beyond the theaters in which it was performed. Ultimately, The Deputy not only sparked the debate on the role of the Catholic Church in the Holocaust, but marked a turning point in Holocaust representations, as they extended their focus to the culpability of bystanders and the institutions they represented.

The Deputy: Documentary theater and moral accusations

The Deputy draws upon a mode of politicized drama known as documentary theater that was especially popular in Germany in the 1960s.[10] The characters, scenes, and action in documentary theater are based on documented historical facts, which make it a uniquely powerful artistic vehicle for Hochhuth's allegations of Vatican negligence. The characters and settings of *The Deputy* derive closely from real people, places, and events, and some of the dialogue comes verbatim from letters and other archival documents. Indeed, *The Deputy* is so long largely because of the sheer volume of its historical material. Hochhuth appended a 65-page essay to the script to substantiate his allegations of Church indifference, further highlighting the play's base in both historical fact and documentary theater. In it, he wrote, "[A]s far as possible I adhered to the facts. I allowed my imagination free play only to the extent that I had to transform the existing raw material of history into drama."[11] Unfortunately, for many contemporary critics, *The Deputy's* overtly documentary character compromised its status—or at least its quality—as art. Commenting on the "thick chunks of documentation which Hochhuth has piled into the play," literary critic Susan Sontag aptly noted that "Much of the play reads as an elaborate casebook in dramatic form. It is clogged with exposition."[12]

While its documentary frame gives *The Deputy* moral authority, the play also draws on less realistic theatrical traditions, notably the "alienation effects" pioneered by German playwright Bertolt Brecht to convince audiences that they were not merely invisible bystanders to the onstage action.[13] These effects are intended to create a sense of distance between the audience and the performance: a key example is the conspicuous superficiality of *The Deputy's* characters, which prevents audiences from identifying with them and believing they are real, which violates the traditions of Western drama. Thus, many scenes also feature psychologically undeveloped, unnamed figures, often identified only by their professions ("The Doctor," "The Cardinal," "A Manufacturer").[14] The script specifies that certain characters should be played by the same actor, like Pope Pius XII and a corrupt industrialist, underscoring the associations between them as a means of implicit critique. In stage directions that at times read as ironic critique, Hochhuth stressed that each character should be played in a non-realistic fashion: the actor who plays the Pope, for instance, "should consider that His Holiness is much less a person than an institution: grand gestures, lively movements of his extraordinarily beautiful hands, and smiling, aristocratic coldness, together with the icy glint of his eyes behind the gold-rimmed glasses—these should suffice."[15]

The Deputy does have some more fully developed characters, most significantly its two protagonists, SS Officer Kurt Gerstein and the idealistic young Italian priest Riccardo Fontana. The play's complex plot, which takes place in 1942 and 1943, follows Gerstein and Fontana as they desperately try and fail to persuade Pope Pius XII to speak out against German atrocities. Hochhuth's Gerstein is based on the real Kurt Gerstein, who witnessed the secret gassing of Jews at the Belzec and Treblinka extermination camps and felt compelled to inform the world. Fontana is a fictional composite of several real Catholic martyrs, including Maximilian Kolbe and Bernhard Lichtenberg. In the play, Fontana and Gerstein try repeatedly to convince Church officials, including the Pope himself, to leverage their moral authority, financial resources, and political influence to stop the genocide. Fontana's confrontations with Church authorities are interwoven with the persecution and eventual deportation of a Jewish family, the fictional Luccanis, whom he accompanies from Rome to Auschwitz. Hochhuth attempts to put a face on the victims through this family and Jacobson, a Jew hidden by Gerstein, who is also deported to Auschwitz.[16] As the screws tighten on Rome's Jews, Fontana's pleas for action grow increasingly desperate. Yet he continually runs up against the same excuses offered by the Catholic Church after the war to justify Pope Pius XII's wartime silence.

The Deputy's moral accusation against the Church climaxes in Act IV, when Pope Pius XII finally appears. Even after Fontana passionately implores him to act, the Pope stays silent, literally representing the Church's refusal to speak out on behalf of Jewish victims. When he eventually speaks, he is cold and distant, voicing vague platitudes. Ultimately, the Pope responds to Fontana's call for action by dictating an empty proclamation about the need for all men to "lay down their arms," avoiding any mention of Jews. While signing the proclamation, he inadvertently smears ink on himself, and at the end of the act, he washes it off, evoking Pontius Pilate's act of ritual absolution after Christ's crucifixion.[17]

While most of the play outlines the bureaucratic indifference that allowed the Holocaust to occur, the final act depicts Auschwitz, one of the first dramatizations of a concentration camp in the history of Holocaust representation.[18] Anticipating debates on how to represent the gas chambers that later preoccupied filmmakers such as Claude Lanzmann (see Chapter 10), Hochhuth steers a middle path between pure documentary and fictional abstraction. For all the historical evidence provided in *The Deputy*, the stage directions note, "No matter how closely we adhere to historical facts, the speech, scene and events on the stage will be altogether surrealistic."[19] Act V begins with characters on a train en route to Auschwitz, but the stage is darkened and only train wheels can be heard; there are "at first no other realistic effects, such as the murmur of voices, the crying of children, and so on that one would expect from a cattle car."[20] Then, three anonymous characters, an old man, a pregnant woman, and a girl, deliver monologues that bewail their fate and curse God.

Fontana, who has donned the yellow Star of David and accompanied the Jews to Auschwitz, tries to embody the moral fortitude lacking in the Vatican, effectively becoming the true "deputy" of God.[21] In a scene evoking famous literary encounters with the Devil, including Goethe's *Faust* and Milton's *Paradise Lost*, Fontana debates his faith with the cynical, nihilistic "Doctor," a cartoonishly evil SS officer identified by the stage directions and other characters as "the devil."[22] Based on Josef Mengele, Auschwitz's infamous "Angel of Death," and the skull-collecting Nazi academic and anatomist August Hirt, the diabolical Doctor temporarily spares Fontana's life but sends him to burn bodies at the crematorium, saying, condescendingly:

You'll have plenty to eat,
and a normal workday of about nine hours.
You can engage in studies there,
theological studies. Find out about God.[23]

These scenes transform Auschwitz into a moral laboratory for testing religious faith, a place to pose the usually rhetorical question of how and why God— and his earthly deputy, the Pope—can allow such suffering to take place.

When Gerstein arrives to try and save Fontana, Fontana, shaken to the core by what he has witnessed, implores him to save a Jew instead (Maximilian Kolbe, one of the characters Fontana is based on, sacrificed his life to save a condemned Polish prisoner). The plan falls apart when the ruse is exposed. At the play's melodramatic conclusion, Fontana is gunned down as he grabs for Gerstein's gun to shoot the Doctor. *The Deputy* ends with "the deliberate, refined voice of a well-bred elder statesman" reading aloud from a well-known letter dated October 28, 1943 from Ernst von Weizsäcker, Hitler's Ambassador to the Holy See, to the Foreign Office in Berlin. Writing just days after the deportations of Rome's Jews, von Weizsäcker reported that Pius XII "has not allowed himself to be carried away into making any demonstrative statements against the deportations of the Jews."[24]

The Vatican responds and the debate broadens

Historian Michael R. Marrus notes that the issues raised by *The Deputy* are historical as well as religious.[25] *The Deputy* caused waves not just in the theater, but in the field of Holocaust history, where it sparked scholarly investigations into the role of the Catholic Church during the genocide. In response to the question of whether Pius XII's silence was an act of political expediency, Church defenders argued that the Pope feared that speaking out would allow the Soviet Union to win the war and expand its sphere of influence westward, a prospect that became increasingly likely after Germany's defeat at Stalingrad in early 1943. Historian Michael Phayer dubbed Pius XII "the First Cold Warrior," underscoring the extent to which the Pope believed that, for all of their evils, Nazi Germany and Fascist Italy nevertheless represented a bulwark against atheist communism.[26] Neither Hitler's Germany nor Mussolini's Italy was particularly friendly to the Vatican, but, unlike Stalin's Soviet Union, they tolerated the Catholic Church. In response to these political explanations for Pius XII's silence, critics point to his instrumental role, before he became Pope, in negotiating with the German Reich to guarantee rights for the Church, as well as his alleged pro-fascist and anti-Semitic sympathies.[27]

The Deputy also spurred significant historical debate over the question of whether public protest by the Vatican would have incurred German retribution. In June 1963, just weeks before he was elected Pope Paul VI, Cardinal Montini, the Archbishop of Milan, addressed this issue in a letter about The Deputy to the Catholic magazine The Tablet. Cardinal Montini argued that if Pius XII had publicly condemned the deportations of Roman Jews, he "would have been guilty of unleashing on the already tormented world still greater calamities involving innumerable innocent victims, let alone himself."[28] A few weeks later, Hochhuth responded with evidence of two Roman Jews who were released from a deportation train because of unofficial protests by Pius XII. Hochhuth also cited several examples in which protests by Catholic priests and Vatican representatives in Germany, Slovakia, and Hungary helped save lives and, importantly, did not provoke harsh German retaliation.[29] His examples raised the counterpoint to Cardinal Montini's arguments: perhaps Nazi Germany's genocidal policies could have been stemmed if bystanders, particularly those with significant moral, political, and economic authority like the Vatican, had acted.

While Hochhuth's play catalyzed a major international debate over the Catholic Church's role in the Holocaust, in the months before the drama's debut, the Vatican was already internally confronting—or being forced to confront—its legacy of anti-Judaism. On October 11, 1962, Pope John XXIII opened the Second Vatican Council, a lengthy series of internal discussions that reevaluated and eventually changed many longstanding Church policies. On October 28, 1965, Pope Paul VI issued the declaration Nostra Aetate (In Our Time), in which the Catholic Church officially renounced deicide. This belief that Jews killed Jesus and their descendants remained collectively responsible for his death had been a central tenet of Catholic theology for centuries. The uproar around The Deputy surely contributed to the Church's acknowledgment that it needed to adapt its theology to the modern world, but the Eichmann trial, the Frankfurt Auschwitz trials, and increasing public awareness of the Holocaust in general also helped change attitudes.

The Deputy drew so much attention to the Catholic Church's wartime (in)activity that the Vatican decided to take extraordinary measures. Typically, the Catholic Church does not make its archives on contemporary events accessible until decades after the fact. But in 1964, Pope Paul VI convened an international task force of scholars, all of them priests, who culled the archives to produce eleven volumes of documents about the Church's wartime activities.[30] As historian Susan Zuccotti notes, however, this project left many scholars deeply unsatisfied, for the documents released were highly selective and "basically defensive in nature, intending to show the best of the Vatican's efforts, to refute charges of indifference and inaction."[31] The Vatican may possess archival materials that can definitively exonerate—or implicate—Pius XII, but it still refuses to open the archives. The result, historian Kevin P. Spicer has noted, is that for many Christians and Jews alike, Pius XII "stands for the indifference of the Church toward the murder of six million Jews and, in that context, represents both theologically and ideologically nearly two millennia of Christian anti-Semitism that led to the Holocaust."[32]

It is important to note, however, that the Catholic Church was not the only religious institution guilty of indifference. In an essay about *The Deputy*, Hannah Arendt suggested that if Hochhuth had written a play about German Protestant churches during the Holocaust, they "would fare hardly better, and possibly even worse" than the Catholics and Pius XII.[33] Subsequent scholarship has borne out Arendt's claim by examining, for instance, the emergence of the "German Christians," a movement that sought to bring German Protestantism in line with Nazi political and racial ideologies.[34] But just as Catholicism has its Maximilian Kolbes and Bernhard Lichtenbergs, the ranks of German Protestantism include courageous figures like anti-Nazi dissidents Dietrich Bonhoeffer and Martin Niemöller. The scholarly task at hand, ultimately, is to consider specific wartime actions of individuals, from ordinary clergy to the Pope, within the context of official Church policies and mitigating external factors. This will remain a difficult task, for it requires that historians scrutinize religious institutions to which millions of worshippers loyally pledge allegiance and separate cherished beliefs and convenient myths from documented fact.

The legacy of *The Deputy*

The Deputy raised broad questions of lasting historical and ethical significance about the wartime activities of the Catholic Church.[35] These discussions raged with particular intensity in 1963 and 1964, but they are still ongoing. In the early 2000s, for instance, a new wave of scholarship offered damning appraisals of Pius XII, to which the Church's defenders in turn responded vigorously.[36] As new documents come to light, historians continue to debate the role of the Pope and the Church in the Holocaust.

But *The Deputy* has a still broader reach. As Sidra Ezrahi notes, the play was produced at a crucial historical moment, when the conscience of the entire world was, metaphorically speaking, on trial. According to Ezrahi, *The Deputy*'s audience was meant to see the Pope not merely as a man who failed, but, in his position as the highest spiritual Christian authority, as the "embodiment of the failure of the spirit of every human being to rise to the burden placed upon it in those dark times."[37] The question, then, was not just about the responsibility of the Pope, but about the responsibility of all bystanders in the Holocaust. In raising this question, *The Deputy* paved the way for subsequent writers, artists, filmmakers, and playwrights to take on a range of issues regarding the complicity of bystanders in the Holocaust. Even if it was not able to definitively establish the complicity of the Catholic Church in the Holocaust, Rolf Hochhuth's *The Deputy* helped put the question of complicity firmly in the forefront of public thinking and showed the power of representation to inspire institutional soul searching.

In a famous scene from Liliana Cavani's Il portiere di notte (The Night Porter, 1974) *modeled on the biblical story of Salome, Lucia Atherton (played by Charlotte Rampling) sings the cabaret song "Wenn ich mir was wünschen dürfte" (If I could wish for something) as she entertains SS-men at a concentration camp.* The Night Porter *was an important example of 1970s* sadiconazista *films that represented Nazism as sexy and fascinating.*

Screen shot from Il portiere di notte, *Criterion Collection*

8

Il portiere di notte (*The Night Porter*) (film, 1974):

What is the Ongoing Appeal of the Holocaust and Nazism?

In the history of Holocaust memory and representation, the years between the Eichmann trial (1961, see Chapter 6) and the television miniseries *Holocaust: The Story of the Family Weiss* (1978, see Chapter 9) tend to receive short shrift. They are seen as a transitional period when Holocaust awareness grew steadily even as public attention around the world remained fixated on contemporary political, economic, and social upheavals, including the Vietnam War, the Civil Rights movement, student revolts, decolonization in Africa, Women's Liberation, the oil crisis, the Arab–Israeli conflict, and Watergate. During these years, under the influence of Raul Hilberg's landmark *The Destruction of the European Jews* (1961) and the increase in scholarship that followed, it became a matter of general agreement that the Holocaust was not just a side effect of World War II, but a distinctive genocide against the Jews.[1] Concurrently, an increasing number of Holocaust representations appeared in popular books, films, and television.[2] Yet even as awareness about the crimes of the Holocaust deepened, attitudes towards the Nazi past diverged. On the one hand, powerful authoritarian and neo-fascist governments took control in Italy and South America, and the Holocaust denial movement emerged in Europe and the United States. On the other hand, Jews found themselves once more under attack during the Six-Day War (1967), the Yom Kippur War (1973), and the Munich Olympics (1972). These spikes in anti-Jewish and anti-Israeli sentiment renewed many Holocaust survivors' fears, as they felt history might be repeating itself.

No single representation or event defines this period in Holocaust memory, yet its popular images of the Holocaust, Nazis, and World War II merit attention because they highlight a shift in Holocaust representation that remains relevant today. In a famous 1975 essay, public intellectual and essayist Susan Sontag highlighted the tendency, especially noticeable in popular culture, to evoke desire for fascism by uncritically mimicking the artistic strategies the Nazis used in their own propaganda. In "Fascinating Fascism," Sontag argued that the images—of power, order, unity, and submission to authority—used by propagandists to attract the German masses to the Nazi Party and Hitler became increasingly visible in popular culture of the 1970s, often in ways that whitewashed history. The implications of Sontag's argument are significant: though Nazi Germany no longer exists as a political entity, the attitudes and impulses that made it possible still persist today.

Liliana Cavani's *Il portiere di notte* (*The Night Porter*, 1974) is an instructive example of 1970s fascinating fascism. *The Night Porter* is the most famous of the Italian *sadiconazista* (sadism with Nazis) films, which, like North American Nazi exploitation or Nazisploitation films, were sexually explicit films about World War II and the Holocaust.[3] Unlike Nazisploitation films, *Sadiconazista* films were frequently the work of reputable and politically engaged filmmakers, with high production values and genuine artistic aspirations.[4] However, they were so graphic, sexually explicit, and provocative that many countries censored them for obscenity. In *Salò, o le 120 giornate di Sodoma* (*Salò, or the 120 Days of Sodom*, 1975), for instance, Pier Paolo Pasolini used torture, rape, sodomy, coprophagy (eating of feces), and other explicit acts to symbolize the political crimes of fascism. Though the movie was banned in many countries for decades, many critics still praised Pasolini for his provocative artistic gesture, and it appeared on lists of best films of the twentieth century.[5] By simultaneously attracting and repulsing viewers with images of fascism, *The Night Porter* and other *sadiconazista* films explored the complicated relationship we maintain with the Nazi past.

The controversy around *The Night Porter*

A brief plot summary of *The Night Porter* makes it clear why it—and the *sadiconazista* cycle—sparked such intense debate. The film tells the story of a sadomasochistic love affair between Holocaust survivor Lucia Atherton (Charlotte Rampling) and former SS officer Maximilian Altdorfer (Dirk Bogarde). Through a series of flashbacks, viewers learn that Max met Lucia when she was a young prisoner at a concentration camp, where he exercised complete physical, emotional, and sexual power over her. Lucia survived the war and married an American symphony conductor. In 1957, she accompanies her husband to Vienna during a concert tour; there she reencounters Max, who works as the night porter at her hotel. Toiling anonymously on the night shift allows Max to, in his own words, keep "quiet as a church mouse" and conceal his past crimes. However, when Max's former SS colleagues recognize Lucia as a witness to their crimes, they decide to kill her. To protect his former lover, but also to reclaim her and reignite their steamy love affair, Max imprisons the increasingly willing Lucia in his apartment. There they recreate the power dynamics of their concentration camp relationship, reverting to their sadomasochistic ways with chains, broken glass, and kinky role play. Hunger eventually forces them to leave their apartment-prison, at which point the former SS men assassinate them on a bridge over the Danube.

Many of the most influential American film critics expressed outrage that a film would dare to depict the relationship between a Nazi and a concentration camp prisoner as one of sexual pleasure produced through violence. Writing in *The New York Times*, Vincent Canby skewered *The Night Porter* as "romantic pornography" and, more bluntly, "a piece of junk."[6] Roger Ebert described the film as "a despicable attempt to titillate us by exploiting memories of persecution and suffering." He summarized the relationship between Max and Lucia in a tone of disgust: "Chains and broken glass and slaps on the face are their aphrodisiacs, and they make love mostly on the floor."[7] Yet even as American reviewers denounced the film and Italian authorities indicted Cavani and her producer on obscenity charges, others interpreted *The Night Porter* more sympathetically, rejecting the notion that it implicated Holocaust victims in their own persecution or suggested that victims in some way enjoyed their experiences.[8] Writing in the journal *Film Quarterly*, feminist film critic Teresa de Lauretis argued that Canby, Ebert, and other American critics had missed the point. *The Night Porter*, she suggested, does not use a male–female relationship with a radical power imbalance as an analogy for the Holocaust; rather, she argued, the film uses the radical differences in power between Holocaust perpetrators and victims as a lens for understanding the power imbalances in gender relationships in "our contemporary, post-Nazi society."[9] Like Sontag, de Lauretis saw *The Night Porter* as a sign that the dynamics of the Holocaust retained a powerful hold on the cultural imagination.

Critics like de Lauretis attributed the vitriol of mainstream American movie critics in part to a marketing campaign that misrepresented the film's complex dynamics of gender, power, and ideology and focused on Charlotte Rampling's sex appeal. Its now-iconic movie poster promotes *The Night Porter* as a sex film with an image from a key flashback scene that references the biblical story of Salome. In the scene, Lucia performs an erotic cabaret act for the SS officers, clad as a sexy Nazi, wearing only tight pants, suspenders, an officer's cap, and arm-length black gloves with which she provocatively covers her breasts. Salome danced for her father, King Herod, on his birthday, and Herod, pleased by the erotic performance, offered Salome anything she wished. Salome's mother Herodias advised her daughter to ask for the head of John the Baptist, who had denounced her marriage to Herod as incestuous. In *The Night Porter*, Max stands for Herod and rewards his "little girl," as he incestuously calls Lucia, for her lascivious performance with a present. When Lucia opens the box, she finds the decapitated head of another prisoner whom Max has executed because he is tormenting her. The Salome scene thus links the absolute power over life and death that the Nazis represent in the popular imagination with taboo sexuality and forbidden desires. The figure of Lucia as Nazi seductress also evokes Marlene Dietrich's *femme fatale* nightclub singer in Josef von Sternberg's classic *The Blue Angel* (1930), an allusion to the sexual decadence of interwar Germany decried by the Nazi party.

Its graphic scenes of sadomasochistic sex and gruesome violence led *The Night Porter*'s detractors to lump it together with Nazisploitation, another genre of sexually explicit films that developed in tandem with the *sadiconazista* cycle. Nazisploitation films were part of a wave of exploitation films in the late 1960s and 1970s, so named because they used exploitative marketing practices to entice viewers into movie theaters.[10] With their low production values, gratuitously excessive scenes of sex and violence, and provocative titles such as *Love Camp 7* (1969), *The Black Gestapo* (1975), and, most famously, *Ilsa, She Wolf of the SS* (1975), Nazisploitation films pushed the boundaries of taste well beyond their limits. Crassly commercial, they closely resembled both pornography and horror movies, appealing to emotions of sexual desire, fear, and disgust.[11] Their clichéd settings and stereotypical characters with bad German accents helped to create stark moral dichotomies between evil Nazis and their helpless victims. Although their characters were fictional, they drew upon sensationalized media accounts of actual sadistic and hypersexualized Nazis, most notably Dr. Josef Mengele, the cruel medical experimenter of Auschwitz, and Ilse Koch, the sadistic, sexually predatory wife of the commandant of Buchenwald, who purportedly had the skin of dead prisoners made into lampshades.[12] The advertising posters for *Ilsa, She Wolf of the SS* present the title character as the desirable Nazi, powerful, threatening, and sexually attractive with her high boots, riding crop, confident forward-facing pose, and prominently exposed cleavage. The sensationalist tagline reads, "The most dreaded Nazi of them all! She committed crimes so terrible . . . even the SS feared her!"

These films were not the only Holocaust representations that trafficked in explicit sexual fantasies. In Israel in the 1950s and 1960s, Auschwitz survivor Yehiel Dinur published popular semi-pornographic novels about sexual exploitation in concentration camps that included forced prostitution and pedophilia. Known better by his pen name Ka-Tzetnik 135633 (Concentration Camp Inmate 135633), Dinur was a significant figure in Israeli culture. His books were part of Israeli school curricula for many years, and he testified at the Eichmann trial and famously fainted during his testimony (see Chapter 6). Israeli director Ari Libsker's 2007 documentary *Stalagim* (*Stalags*) exposed a 1960s sensationalist pornographic genre of Israeli pulp fiction known as "Stalag fiction" that went beyond Ka-Tzetnik 135633. Anticipating the appeal of Nazisploitation and *sadiconazista* films, and written under British and American pseudonyms, these controversial books reimagined concentration camps (*stalags*) through scenes of sadomasochistic acts between prisoners and their sexy female Nazi overseers. In books with lurid titles such as *I Was Colonel Schultz's Private Bitch*, defeating Nazis literally called for conquering them sexually.[13]

If some wrote off *The Night Porter* as one more example of tasteless Holocaust pornography, others rejected this criticism as close-minded American puritanism and failure to understand an art film attempting to wrestle with the ongoing appeal of fascism. Today, despite its controversial combination of sex and genocide, or perhaps precisely because of it, *The Night Porter* has become something of a classic of Holocaust cinema. In 2000, it was reissued on DVD as part of the prestigious Criterion Collection, a highly regarded series of films by acknowledged masters of cinema. Standard histories of Holocaust cinema include *The Night Porter*, even as they generally ignore Nazisploitation. As film scholar Annette Insdorf has argued, *The Night Porter* remains important because it is not simply about the time in which it is set. Rather, the film "depicts not only the political continuity between the Holocaust and 1957 Austria, where Nazism is alive and well, but the psychological grip of a past that locks characters into repetition compulsion."[14] In other words, *The Night Porter* addresses both the fascinating hold fascism exerted in its own time, and the appeal of authoritarian politics several decades later.

Fascism, still fascinating

Critics may have debated the merits of *sadiconazista* films like *The Night Porter* and dismissed the lower-budget Nazisploitation films as tasteless junk, but both sub-genres are manifestations of a spike in sexualized Holocaust, Nazi, and World War II imagery in the 1960s and 1970s. The sheer volume of Nazi imagery in books and films of the time, especially in popular culture, bespoke an ongoing fascination, even when those cultural products ostensibly attacked the Third Reich and its genocidal policies. The interesting questions, then, are what this spike indicates about the contemporary state of Holocaust memory and how these representations influenced later works. At the time, writers and intellectuals sought to explain what the sexy Nazis, in both their trashy and arty incarnations, said about public understanding of National

Socialism and the Holocaust thirty years after the fact. Several critics offered versions of Sontag's taboo-breaking claim that the attraction of Nazism, for millions of Germans and their collaborators in other countries, was erotic and thus something to which anyone anywhere could be susceptible.

In "Fascinating Fascism," Sontag cited *The Night Porter* as an example of how the images, clothing, and paraphernalia of Nazism, such as boots, whips, uniforms, and leather, had become closely associated with deviant sexuality. "In pornographic literature, films, and gadgetry throughout the world," Sontag wrote, "the SS has become a reference of sexual adventurism."[15] She argued that Nazi Germany, a society that officially denounced deviant sexuality, had become such a powerful reservoir of erotic images because it represented an idea already prevalent in popular culture: that power and order are attractive, even sexy. In *Reflections of Nazism: An Essay on Kitsch and Death*, first published in French in 1982, historian Saul Friedländer echoed Sontag's claims by locating Nazism's power in its "emotions, images, and phantasms." Identifying a resurgence of these symbols in a variety of films across the political spectrum, he argued that the power of mythic storylines, powerful and desirable Nazi figures, and grandiose and explicit imagery causes viewers to suspend their ability to think critically and let themselves be seduced into the fascist political program.[16] In this context, *The Night Porter* is a film about the erotic charge of Nazi power. Sontag and Friedländer's interpretations of *The Night Porter* and similar films and representations confront the comfortable myth, subscribed to by many people in the liberal democracies of Europe and North America, that the past is past and they never would have elected Hitler or become Nazis. That self-delusion persists even in films where Nazi villains get their comeuppance.

Nazisploitation and *sadiconazista* films also helped blur the boundaries between subsequent exploitative and mainstream representations of Nazis, as their imagery, tropes, and strategies migrated into popular cinema.[17] Before he made *Schindler's List*, Steven Spielberg created the character of Dr. Elsa Schneider, an Austrian archaeologist and Nazi secret agent in *Indiana Jones and the Last Crusade* (1989). Played by the blond, blue-eyed actress and model Alison Doody, the treacherous *femme fatale* Elsa shares her name and appearance with *Ilsa, She Wolf of the SS*.[18] Yet the film that most powerfully instantiates the "fascinating fascism" argument, taking it beyond the sphere of World War II and Holocaust movies, is George Lucas's science fiction blockbuster *Star Wars* (1977), one of the most successful films ever. Nazi imagery and symbolism permeate *Star Wars*, even though it is set "a long time ago in a galaxy far far away." The Empire (a translation of *Reich*) has in Darth Vader an evil, charismatic, Hitler-like authority figure whose officers dress conspicuously like SS officers and whose troops are obedient, automaton-like storm troopers. The medal ceremony at the film's triumphal conclusion borrows directly from the most famous Nazi propaganda film, Leni Riefenstahl's *Triumph of the Will* (1935) (Lucas explicitly praised Riefenstahl as "the most modern filmmaker."[19]) As Luke Skywalker, Han Solo, and Chewbacca slowly approach the podium through an aisle formed by orderly rows of uniformed rebel forces, they directly echo the scene from *Triumph of the Will* in which Hitler ascends to the podium at a Nazi Party rally in Nuremberg after a long walk through tightly arranged ranks of the obedient Nazi faithful. Like *The Night Porter*, *Star Wars* deployed artistic strategies that appeal to the emotions using images of power and order in fantastical contexts, much as Nazism did. This is not to say that we fall for the attraction unilaterally: the deviant sexuality of *The Night Porter* is both repulsive and appealing, just as the Nazi-like Darth Vader is a ruthlessly evil character whom audiences love to hate. But the two films thus reveal how we can still be susceptible to that which we denounce.

Neo-Nazisploitation

The original Nazisploitation and *sadiconazista* cycles petered out by the early 1980s, but in recent years, they have enjoyed a renaissance of sorts. The Nazi imagery, fantastical storylines, and explicit sexuality that embody fascinating fascism have reemerged across a wide range of films, including mainstream Hollywood productions, European art films, and independent science fiction and horror cult films. In Paul Verhoeven's *Zwartboek* (*Black Book*, 2006), the Jewish female lead entertains Nazi officers with her cabaret singing and survives because of a sexual relationship with a Nazi protector, like Lucia in *The Night Porter*.[20] In *The Reader* (2008), a film based on German author Bernhard Schlink's international bestseller, Kate Winslet plays Hanna Schmitz, a 36-year-old former concentration camp guard whose story begins when she lures a 15-year-old boy into her bed.[21] Yet far from offending critics with their sexual explicitness, these films garnered significant accolades, as if the Nazi past had been completely mastered and contemporary audiences were now safely inoculated against ever engaging in fascist behaviors: *Black Book* was shortlisted for a Best Foreign Film Oscar and Winslet won Best Actress in 2008.

While these films subtly reflect the influence of Nazisploitation and *sadiconazista*, a concurrent wave of what we might call neo-Nazisploitation cinema more actively acknowledges and even pays homage to the original 1970s films. These movies detach Nazis from their historical origins and turn them into universal symbols of evil, building on a growing tendency in the 1970s to adapt Holocaust and World War II themes to familiar genres such as spy films, war movies, and science fiction. In the 1970s, these representations similarly coded Nazism as powerful, fascinating, mysterious and sexy, even as they criticized it. In *The Odessa File* (1974), a film based on Frederick Forsyth's 1972 novel that imagined the hunt for Nazi war criminals as an espionage thriller, a powerful secret conspiracy of former SS officers protects each other from the law and eliminates their enemies. Another novel adaptation, *The Boys from Brazil* (1978), envisioned a conspiracy devised by Dr. Josef Mengele, the notorious medical experimenter of Auschwitz, to clone Hitler and resurrect Nazi Germany.

The neo-Nazisploitation films resuscitate fantastical Nazi plots and character types and refit them to suit contemporary trends and technologies. In tandem with the current cultural fascination with zombies, for instance, Nazi zombie movies, including *Horrors of War* (2006), *Død Snø* (*Dead Snow*, 2009), and *Frankenstein's Army* (2013), have emerged as a distinct film sub-genre. The most well-known example of neo-Nazisploitation, Quentin Tarantino's *Inglourious Basterds* (2009), mimics 1970s exploitation films with its story of an undercover spy mission to blow up a movie theater during the premiere of a Nazi propaganda movie. While its title copies the 1978 war film *Quel maledetto treno blindato* (translated as *The Inglorious Bastards*), the key characters in *Inglourious Basterds* evoke and caricature Nazisploitation character types: blond, blue-eyed German actress and model Diane Kruger plays double agent Bridget von Hammersmark, Christoph Waltz is the calculating Nazi villain Colonel Hans Landa (nicknamed the Jew Hunter), and Mélanie Laurent is Shosanna Dreyfus, a Jew who escapes Landa's clutches and hides under the distinctly non-Jewish name Emmanuelle Mimieux, an allusion to the soft porn *Emmanuelle* films of the 1970s.

Yet there is a significant difference between the neo-Nazisploitation films and their cinematic precursors. Where *The Night Porter* and *Ilsa, She Wolf of the SS* were offered, if not necessarily received, as serious or at least not ironic films, *Inglourious Basterds*, Nazi zombie films, and other examples of neo-Nazisploitation are grounded in irony and self-consciousness, particularly about the tawdriness of the originals. Although they reproduce the campy sensibilities of 1970s exploitation cinema, they do so playfully and with higher production values. With its ludicrous plot about Nazis who escape Europe in 1945, establish a colony on the dark side of the moon, and plot an attack on Earth, *Iron Sky* (2012) extends well into the realm of the fantastic. Yet where Nazisploitation films played in seedy Times Square grindhouses, the continually evolving belief that the past had been successfully overcome made it possible for *Iron Sky* to premiere at the prestigious Berlinale film festival, while *Inglourious Basterds* earned eight Academy Award nominations.

The popularity of neo-exploitation films and their tendency to position themselves as ironic commentary on the trashy films of the 1970s suggest that contemporary audiences perceive themselves as having grown immune to the appeal of fascinating fascism—just as earlier audiences believed that they would not have been susceptible to the Nazis. Yet to believe that it is possible to consume Nazi imagery with no possibility of falling sway to its power is to fail to heed Susan Sontag's warning. New media may have made Nazi imagery more widespread, but ubiquity does not necessarily declaw the power of its symbolism. Were she alive today, Sontag might argue that Nazism has simply found new ways to enchant, new ways to make fascism fascinating.

Meryl Streep playing Inga Helms Weiss, a German gentile in the television mini-series Holocaust: The Story of the Family Weiss, *first broadcast on NBC in April 1978. Inga tries in vain to secure the release of her Jewish husband from the Theresienstadt camp. Viewed by millions,* Holocaust *played a vital role in catalyzing worldwide public interest in the Holocaust in the late 1970s, even as its critics accused it of trivialization.*

NBC via Getty Images

9

Holocaust: The Story of the Family Weiss (television, 1978):

Do Representations for Mass Audiences Trivialize the Holocaust?

It's hard not to dismiss *Holocaust: The Story of the Family Weiss* as pure kitsch. Written, directed, and scored, respectively, by New Yorkers Gerald Green, Marvin Chomsky, and Morton Gould, this American television miniseries was clearly designed to tug shamelessly at heartstrings. Trumpets wail over the first few seconds of the opening credits, then violins take over as the fiery beams of a small, isolated wooden synagogue verge upon collapse. The camera cuts to a group of impoverished women uselessly stretching their arms toward the burning structure, restrained by a wall of uniformed Nazis. The shiny round helmets of the soldiers contrast sharply with the women's rumpled kerchiefs, exemplifying the narrative's reductive message and suggesting that the history of the Holocaust can be reduced to a made-for-television story of love and murder, replete with Hollywood stars, historical gaffes, and commercial interruptions.

Holocaust warped facts, figures, and events by mixing them with fiction, creating a historical soap opera, rather than grappling with the nature of modern evil. In an essay published in *The New York Times*, Elie Wiesel lamented that the fictionalization of the Holocaust in a television show trivialized the deaths of millions of Jews.[1] Yet the extensively promoted, high-budget production had an undeniable impact. For the first time, audiences on a massive scale learned about the Holocaust up front and personal, through the experiences of victims, perpetrators, and bystanders, albeit fictionalized ones. When it first aired in the United States over four consecutive evenings in April 1978, *Holocaust* reached an audience estimated at 120 million; today, it has been seen by over 500 million viewers worldwide. In the era before videos and DVRs, viewers experienced the show collectively, many of them with their families; it thus fostered further discussion of the Holocaust not only in the public sphere, but inside the home. Regardless of the show's flaws, television gave *Holocaust* a vast reach, and its enormous success influenced how millions of people worldwide learned about the destruction of European Jewry.

A tale of mixed marriage

Because the social repercussions of *Holocaust* far outweighed its artistic merits, even those who acknowledge its significance tend to dismiss the details of its story. But representing the history of the Holocaust through the prism of an interfaith German–Jewish marriage was a significant move. As the opening credits end, the cheerful blare of an oompah band replaces the wailing violins, and viewers enter a fancy backyard wedding in 1935 Berlin, two years after the Nazi rise to power. A waiter in a bow tie carries a double-tiered wedding cake to the table of newlyweds Karl Weiss (James Woods) and Inge Helms (Meryl Streep). After the couple carefully cuts into the cake, Karl's brother Rudi calls for him to kiss the bride. When Karl bashfully explains that he's not used to kissing in public, Inge declares that she will fix that. To enthusiastic applause, she eagerly pulls her reluctant husband toward her for a passionate kiss. This seemingly playful reversal of gender norms establishes Inge as the more active partner in the relationship and underscores Karl's weakness and Rudi's forcefulness, the first signs of Jewish stereotypes that their respective fates of Nazi victim (Karl) and Zionist hero (Rudi) will bear out.

The reception is festive and seemingly good-natured, as the members of the Weiss and Helms families mingle, among them Karl's uncle Moses Weiss, visiting from Warsaw, and Inge's brother Hans, wearing his German infantry uniform. However, conversations about politics, class differences, and cultural preferences reveal the tensions simmering just below the polite façades and indicate the strength of the boundaries that separate Jewish and non-Jewish Germans, even at this moment of cultural fusion. It turns out that that Karl's parents, although both Jewish, have their own intercultural marriage of sorts: Josef is originally from Poland, while Berta's family has long lived in Germany, a geographical difference that also figures differences of class and religious observance. Josef jokingly refers to his wife as the "real" German, but also apologizes to his brother Moses for the wedding not being Jewish enough, assuring him with a smile that at least they still attend synagogue on the High

Holidays (Rosh Hashanah and Yom Kippur). His balancing act suggests that his own marriage is the first step toward his children, raised as acculturated Jews, marrying out. This progression would certainly be familiar to many American Jews; in a later interview, *Holocaust* producer Robert Berger noted the importance of telling the story of the Holocaust through the lens of a Jewish family trying to assimilate, which American audiences would be able to relate to as part of the American experience.[2] Ironically, using intermarriage as the symbolic apex of assimilation from which German Jews ultimately fall to their destruction suggests that cultural mixing has dangerous consequences and implicates Jews as agents in their own doomed future.

Holocaust focuses on four families, sharply contrasting Karl and Inge's mixed marriage with the Jewish Weiss family, the Christian Helms family, and the Christian Dorfs. In the scene after the wedding, another seemingly simple Jewish–Christian interaction, Marta Dorf and her husband Erik, an unemployed lawyer, pay a visit to Josef Weiss, Marta's doctor: in 1935, Marta appears perfectly happy to be treated by a Jewish doctor, and she and her husband are admittedly neutral on the subject of Jews. Soon, however, the couple will become rabid anti-Semites, as Erik rises to power as an assistant to Nazi leader Reinhard Heydrich (although Erik is a fictional character, he is modeled after SS officer Otto Ohlendorf). The story's narrative arc parallels the rise of the Dorfs and the fall of the prominent Weisses, who face the gradual restriction of their freedoms, exclusion from society, and eventually deportation and death. The only one who survives is Rudi, who fights in the resistance, becomes a Zionist, and is transformed into a triumphant Jewish hero who manages to survive against incredible odds.

Designed to reach the broadest audience possible, *Holocaust* is neither subtle nor sophisticated in eliciting emotional reactions from its audience. Still, although the miniseries makes no pretense of representing the Holocaust objectively, intellectually or even with complete accuracy, it takes its mission sufficiently seriously to intersperse newsreel footage of historical events and weave significant events like *Kristallnacht* and the Wannsee Conference into its story, showing how they affected the lives of its fictional families. Notably, *Holocaust* depicts the events from the perspective of both Jewish victims and non-Jewish perpetrators and bystanders, and, in contrast to films, novels, and television shows that focus solely on Auschwitz, it also includes depictions of the massacres at Babi Yar and the murders of Eastern European Jews by the *Einsatzgruppen* (Nazi Germany's mobile killing units).

While these efforts to present a multifaceted story are admirable, at the heart of *Holocaust* lies the predictable parallel between Rudi, who is transformed from an acculturated Jew into a Zionist hero after escaping from Sobibór extermination camp where his wife dies at the hands of the Nazis, and Erik, who is transformed from an ineffectual lawyer into a mastermind of evil. Ultimately, both Rudi and Erik have the opportunity to kill an enemy at close range, and both hesitate before doing so; while Erik later relishes the power of killing, Rudi becomes reflective and regretful, signaling the blatant evil of the one and the humanity of the other. When Inge tells Karl, shortly before he is deported to Auschwitz, that "No matter what happens, love conquers all," words she heard his mother say to his father shortly before he was deported, *Holocaust* anchors itself firmly in the realm of sentimental melodrama. Yet in presenting a triumphant narrative that reinforces the paradigm of innocent and/or heroic Jews pitted against evil Germans, *Holocaust* does no more—and no less—than what many more sophisticated dramas do, and its wider reach makes its effect worthy of consideration.

Television's turning point

Holocaust did not earn its reputation as a watershed moment in Holocaust representation in America for being the first major television representation of the Holocaust. That occurred in 1961, with the widespread television coverage of the Eichmann trial. Rather, as Jeffrey Shandler points out, the airing of *Holocaust* changed things in two ways. For one, it was the first film representation to single out Jews as the ultimate victims of the Holocaust, rather than as one of many groups victimized during World War II. Second, it raised the question of whether television was an appropriate medium for transmitting the history of the destruction of Europe's Jews.

Summarizing the history of film and television representations of the Holocaust, Shandler notes that American audiences saw newsreels about the liberation of concentration camps as early as 1945 (see Chapter 2). Although these films forced viewers to bear witness to horror, they also carried a redemptive message. Their documentary footage was accompanied by musical scores and titles, making them, to some extent, the first instances of war turned into theater. By 1978, audiences had been exposed to several decades of morally charged Holocaust dramas, and during the 1960s and 1970s, as television became a more significant mass media form, Holocaust topics became frequent, even routine, presences on a wide range of programs. Still, from news documentaries to science fiction shows, the Holocaust became, as Shandler puts it, "a point of entry into more general issues—the limits of justice, the consequences of intolerance, or the nature of evil," rather than a Jewish story.[3] These universalizing themes set the stage for the development of the Holocaust into a master moral paradigm for American culture, not only on television, but also beyond.

In this context, the 1978 airing of *Holocaust* represents a specifically American embrace of the story of Europe's Jews. Although many of those

Jews had come to the United States after the war, the increasing comfort with Jewish self-identification in America and the growing power of Israel grounded this powerful shift in how the Holocaust was represented. *Holocaust* also built upon the powerful sense of cultural identification generated by *Roots*, the wildly successful 1977 miniseries that tells the multi-generational story of a slave family, from the abduction of Kunta Kinte in Gambia through the Civil War. Like *Roots*, *Holocaust* was designed to be watched by families, so it focused on families. Finally, *Holocaust* coincided with a growing number of programs about Holocaust survivors that singled out the stories of exceptional survivors, rather than focusing on the fates of masses of victims.[4] In short, *Holocaust* emerged from complex cultural conditions that set the stage for an American Holocaust representation about individual Jewish experiences, even if that focus was tempered by the inclusion the experiences of Christian Germans.

If the miniseries represented a turning point for how the Holocaust was represented, it also, with shows like *Roots*, marked a shift in the role of television in American society.[5] Given that many people considered television to be frivolous and superficial, many critics found its use to portray one of the gravest tragedies of modern history distasteful to the point of insulting. The medium became a part of the message, and television itself became obsessed with the topic of its own impact. On September 13, 1980, NBC aired *Holocaust: A Postscript*, a one-hour news special that presented a range of opinions on the quality of the drama and its effectiveness. This self-assessment also claimed that the miniseries set into motion Pope John Paul II's visit to Auschwitz, the President's Commission on the Holocaust (which gave rise to the U.S. Holocaust Memorial Museum), and Germany's extension of the statute of limitations on pursuing Nazi war criminals. In other words, television not only defended *Holocaust* against accusations of trivialization, but also defended itself as a valuable, important medium that could do more than broadcast trashy entertainment.

Repercussions in Germany and beyond

Holocaust also made waves outside the United States. By 1981, its rights had been sold to at least 35 countries, including Australia, Japan, Turkey, and Nicaragua, but the series had the greatest impact in Western Europe.[6] *Holocaust* was first aired in the Federal Republic of Germany in January 1979. As in the United States, the television show was preceded by an intensive information campaign in schools, churches, and public media. But German audiences had a very different relationship to their country's past, individually and collectively. As Wulf Kansteiner points out, they also had their own ways of using television to transmit messages about the past, which also greatly affected the reception of *Holocaust*. While American audiences could see themselves in the story, as Jews or as Americans on the right side of history, Germans for the first time were confronted directly and visually with the "disturbing legacies of the Third Reich," in which they were directly implicated.[7]

Unlike in the United States, the history of the Nazi era did not become an important political issue in West Germany until the 1960s, at which point television programming on the topic began to develop. Kansteiner argues that this philosemitic, or pro-Jewish, programming included not only television but also feature films imported from Eastern Europe and stories about the rescue of Jewish Holocaust victims. These were all usually scheduled around a designated week of "brotherhood" sponsored by Jewish–Christian cooperation societies to further Jewish–Christian dialogue.[8] In the mid-1970s, German television started to produce survivor narratives, both documentaries and features, which tended to portray Jews as either victims or survivors.[9] These shows fit firmly within the strict parameters of philosemitic programming, which permits only positive statements about Jews, who are variously portrayed in stereotypical terms as pious, brilliant, financially adept, or victims. With its own stock Jewish characters, *Holocaust* fits this established pro-Jewish discourse, but whereas few people actually viewed these programs during the 1960s and 1970s, *Holocaust* reached millions of Germans, in no small part because it was able to provide characters with whom audiences could readily identify.[10]

Like American viewers, many Germans criticized *Holocaust* for trivializing the past, but some also questioned whether it was appropriate for an American series to portray German history. Other voices, however, were self-critical, noting that regardless of the show's flaws, it took an American television series to inform mass audiences in Germany about the crimes committed against Jews in their name, when hundreds of previously published German books, plays, and films had failed to do so. According to Anton Kaes, this failure was precisely because those representations tended to "withhold visual and narrative pleasure," of which *Holocaust* offered plenty.[11] Some German critics also pointed out that it was easy for those who wanted to forget the past to embrace Elie Wiesel's dictum that the Holocaust should not be represented on television; but as Germans recognized the pedagogical effectiveness of *Holocaust*, their criticism softened. Still, it did spur director Edgar Reitz to conceive of his own television miniseries, *Heimat*, in order to, as he put it, take German history away from "commercial" American productions and hand it back to the Germans in the form of *Alltagsgeschichte* ("history of everyday life"), a popular contemporary form of writing history that focused not on top political leaders, but on the lives of average people.[12] The irony of *Heimat*, however, was that although it represented an attempt to replace the Jewish point of view with a German perspective, it did so by framing the Germans as victims, thus reversing, but hardly calling into question, the terms of German discourses about Jews.

Even its most vehement critics could not deny that *Holocaust* had a significant impact in Germany. Under public pressure fueled by the show's audience, the government extended the statute of limitations for criminals who had participated in genocide that had been set to expire; this issue had already been under discussion, but *Holocaust* and the furor that surrounded it catalyzed its resolution. Still, in terms of Holocaust representation, German television's focus on stories of Jewish "suffering and survival" continued to suggest that "the Holocaust was a crime without perpetrators or bystanders."[13] Only in the 1990s did German television shows begin to include perpetrators along with survivors, but this occurred at the same time as the role of commercial television became more prominent, and Holocaust productions were shifted out of prime time to make way for more lucrative programming. But because fewer people saw these more complex shows, it is doubtful that any were ever as influential as *Holocaust*.

Holocaust's repercussions

When *Holocaust* initially aired in 1978, Menachem Z. Rosensaft, an advocate for Holocaust survivors, summed up his critical position on the miniseries:

> The problem is that nowadays, anyone with even the slightest intellectual or artistic pretensions feels entitled to deal creatively with the Holocaust. A thorough comprehension of the subject matter has ceased to be a prerequisite. What should be sacred ground characterized by agonized silence and muted elegies which may only be entered with the greatest trepidations has become open territory.[14]

Rosensaft's dismay at the approach taken by *Holocaust*'s producers would be echoed upon the release of Steven Spielberg's film *Schindler's List* in 1993, when critics raised the same kinds of questions that had dogged *Holocaust*. But this time, the voices willing to support the film on the basis of its pedagogical impact, above and beyond its story or production values, were heard more quickly and loudly. As well, nobody asked whether Steven Spielberg had the right to make a movie about the Holocaust; they simply questioned whether he had done so appropriately. Decades after the airing of *Holocaust*, how the Holocaust should be portrayed is still debatable. But the topic of who should be allowed to portray it, and for what audiences, has become much less controversial.

As a melodrama made for mass audiences, *Holocaust* does indeed downplay important historical aspects of the Holocaust and barely addresses some of its most salient moral issues. Yet the television show was undoubtedly a catalyst for American Holocaust memory. In surveys conducted by the American Jewish Committee, more than half of the respondents approved of the program, and 60 percent said that watching it helped them better understand Hitler's treatment of the Jews.[15] Other research showed that *Holocaust* had a significant effect on motivating teachers to teach the Holocaust, even those who thought it was clichéd.

To reach its audience, *Holocaust* juxtaposed the horror of the camps with the triumph of survival. It clearly succeeded in its goal, revealing the powerful role television can play in shaping public memory. As in any medium, however, with that power comes the burden of effectively balancing historical accuracy and narrative pleasure. Holocaust representations that cling so tightly to the truth as to disallow taking pleasure in the storytelling risk losing their audiences; but there is ethical danger when storytelling takes precedence over historical accuracy. One way to address this dilemma is to stop asking whether representations for mass audiences trivialize the Holocaust, for inevitably those representations will frame the Holocaust for that audience and its expectations. Instead, we can ask whether the representation stimulates, rather than forecloses, efforts to learn as much as we can about the mass destruction of the Jews of modern Europe.

PART THREE

The 1980s and 1990s

Did Jews own this house?

Director Claude Lanzmann (left) interviews farmers from the town of Grabów (Poland) in this scene from his epic nine-and-a-half-hour film Shoah *(1985). The villagers live in houses once occupied by the town's Jews, who were deported to the extermination camp in Chełmno 20km away. The scene typifies Lanzmann's approach, relying on oral interviews with witnesses, survivors, bystanders, and even perpetrators rather than on archival documents.*

Screen shot from Shoah, Criterion Collection

10

Shoah (film, 1985):

What is the Role of Witness Testimony in Representations of the Holocaust?

In a 2013 interview on the occasion of the restoration of his groundbreaking nine-hour-and-23-minute film *Shoah*, first shown in Paris in 1985, director Claude Lanzmann was questioned about one of the film's lasting legacies: his decision not to include the film clips, still photographs, and other visual evidence usually found in Holocaust documentaries. Lanzmann provided several reasons for this decision: this visual evidence offers itself up too easily for interpretation, it would have limited his creativity as a filmmaker, and, most importantly, images of what he was trying to represent do not exist. As he put it, "There are no archives of the extermination per se. There isn't a single photo of what goes on inside a gas chamber. Not only no film, but not a picture, nothing."[1] The absence of visual documentation of the gas chambers, he claimed, lay at the heart of his decision to make the film with no visual evidence whatsoever.

Instead, *Shoah* is made up of clips from 350 hours of eyewitness testimony that Lanzmann gathered over twelve years in Europe, the United States, and Israel. From the film's opening scene, which features Simon Srebnik, one of only two survivors of the extermination camp in Chełmno, Poland, to its closing interview with Simcha Rotem, who figured prominently in the Warsaw Ghetto uprising, the film recounts the history of the Holocaust in a chorus of voices sharing their firsthand experiences. Lanzmann occasionally consults textual sources, as when he asks eminent Holocaust historian Raul Hilberg to interpret a document about the transport of Jews. But overall, the eyewitness testimony of people who were physically close to the murders, in some cases even left for dead, drives the film. Filip Müller, for example, was a member of the *Sonderkommando*, the unit of Jewish prisoners forced to work at the crematoria at Auschwitz. At one point he entered the gas chamber himself, but although he planned to die, the other victims pleaded with him to get out, so he could survive to bear witness to their deaths. Müller's powerful testimony, Lanzmann notes, "says more than a thousand images from archives."[2]

Although the testimony of Jewish survivors makes up the heart of *Shoah*, the documentary also features accounts from Polish bystanders including discussions with peasants who lived near the death camps and an interview with Jan Karski, a Catholic resistance fighter who visited the Warsaw Ghetto as a courier for the Polish government-in-exile. The film also includes testimony from former Nazis, including, most dramatically, Franz Suchomel, a former guard at Treblinka, whom Lanzmann surreptitiously filmed while he talked about his involvement in the deaths of Jewish prisoners and even sang the Treblinka camp song.

Shoah's extreme length, absence of voiceover narration, multiple languages (including French, German, English, Polish, Yiddish, and Hebrew), translations, subtitles, and meandering pace enact its core message: the Holocaust is a story that is impossible to tell in its entirety yet whose telling remains imperative. Lanzmann believed that the film's unusual nature would limit its audience, but it received overwhelming international critical acclaim.[3] Though it has been the subject of some criticism, it appears frequently on lists of best documentaries,[4] and even best films,[5] and remains the ultimate yardstick against which all other films on the Holocaust, documentary and fictional, are measured. Nevertheless, because the mainstream film industry now regularly produces movies about the Holocaust, broad audiences are much more likely to learn about the event through feature films. Examining why *Shoah* broke new ground, setting what many consider to be a definitive—and unreachable—standard of truth-telling, helps us understand the limits of Holocaust representation on film. At the same time, comparing *Shoah* to commercial Holocaust films reveals the powerful role of mainstream media in shaping Holocaust memory.

"It was not a world"

Shoah was first shown in 1985, almost twenty-five years after survivors testified at the Eichmann trial in Jerusalem, which was broadcast on television across the world (see Chapter 6). That event made it clear, first, that it is insufficient to speak about the Holocaust only in abstract terms, and, second, that there was no singular Holocaust experience. To uncover the truth of what happened, each and every person involved needed to be able to tell their story. Memoirs, like Elie Wiesel's *Night* (1958, see Chapter 5), and the televised drama *Holocaust: the Story of the Family Weiss* (1978, see Chapter 9) also exposed broad audiences to the experiences of Jewish Holocaust victims. But by 1985, although many films about the Holocaust had been made, none had focused on witness testimony.[6]

Shoah takes the principle of the eyewitness account to its extreme, revealing how testimony depends not only on the witness who provides it, but on the audiences who receive it. Lanzmann relentlessly questions his subjects about the details of their experiences, in interviews that often seem deliberately tedious, overly specific, and even nagging. This style is on full display when he questions Walter Stier, a German railway official who insists he was so busy managing train traffic that he did not notice his trains were transporting Jews to their deaths. Lanzmann asks at length about his duties, even inquiring about the details of the machinery: "What's the difference between a special and a regular train? Are there still special trains now?" In another scene, Lanzmann confronts the convicted Nazi war criminal Josef Oberhauser, now working at a beer hall in Munich. He refuses to answer Lanzmann's persistent and increasingly confrontational questions about his wartime activities. And in one of the film's most haunting scenes, Lanzmann brings Jewish survivor Abraham Bomba out of retirement to cut the hair of what seems to be a barber shop patron, but is actually one of his friends.[7] As Bomba cuts, Lanzmann asks him to remember his job at Treblinka: cutting the hair of Jewish women in the gas chamber before their deaths. Questioning Bomba in a site that simulates his original traumatic experience, Lanzmann pushes his deeply emotional return to that time and place by asking him about the most minute details: "How long did it happen after your arrival in Treblinka?" "How long did the barbers cut the hair inside the gas chamber?" "How did it look, the gas chamber?"[8] Though Bomba breaks down emotionally and obviously wants to stop, Lanzmann urges him to continue, a move which caused some controversy, to which Lanzmann responded: "Some people have suggested some sort of sadism on my part in this perilous scene, while on the contrary I consider it to be the epitome of reverence and supportiveness, which is not to tiptoe away in the face of suffering, but to obey the categorical imperative of the search for and the transmission of truth."[9]

Lanzmann's relentless barrage of specific questions and his determination to press witnesses to their emotional limits in recounting experiences that are often difficult to articulate make *Shoah* a masterpiece of what literary critic and psychoanalytic theorist Shoshana Felman calls the "art of witnessing." According to Felman, *Shoah* is groundbreaking for asking what it really means to bear witness to a catastrophe like the Holocaust. She claims that the truth of the Holocaust can only be transmitted in a work of art, like *Shoah*, precisely because to witness the Holocaust was not merely to observe, record, and remember, but to articulate the experience of a certain position that nobody else could occupy. As Felman asks, "What does testimony mean, if it is the uniqueness of the performance of a story which is constituted by the fact that, like the oath, it cannot be carried out by anybody else?"[10] *Shoah* uses witness testimony to remove the Holocaust from the dangers of abstraction, reminding us of the need for individuals to tell their unique stories, while recognizing that even millions of hours of testimony would not give us a total account.

This emphasis on the uniqueness of testimony also highlights that there is much we cannot know about the Holocaust, not only because its victims have been murdered on such a vast scale, but also because the Nazis took pains to camouflage their actions in an effort to preclude the possibility of witnessing the atrocities. For example, the arrival platforms at extermination camps were built to look like real train stations, with fake schedules of departure times and ticket windows. And in October 1943, Reichsführer-SS Heinrich Himmler, in secret speeches delivered in Poznań (Posen), Poland, explicitly admitted that Germany was perpetrating these crimes but that they should forever be kept secret. Finally, witness testimony is not only about what witnesses say, but about what they do not say. *Shoah* shows how all witnesses have some degree of blindness to the events they experience, whether by design or denial. Thus, the brilliance of the film, Felman reminds us, is that the combined testimony of perpetrators, victims, and bystanders proves what the visual evidence rejected by Lanzmann cannot: that the Holocaust was designed to erase witnessing itself, which highlights the imperative of art to bring witnessing to the fore.

In one compelling segment of testimony that reveals the impossibly ironic role of witnessing without seeing, courier Jan Karski, who worked for the Polish underground, recounts what happened when he tried to tell Allied governments what was happening to the Jews. In mid-1942, Karski met with Jewish leaders from Warsaw who wanted him to bolster his report to Allied government leaders with his own eyewitness testimony. Acceding reluctantly to their request, Karski accompanied them to the Jewish ghetto, a place few outsiders had entered. There he saw mothers with flat breasts feeding babies with crazed eyes and naked bodies lying in the streets, because, he was told, Jews were too poor to hold burials and other ghetto residents needed their clothing. When Lanzmann asks whether it looked like a strange world, Karski explains how difficult it was to articulate: "But I reported what I saw. It was not a world. It was not a part of humanity. I was not part of it. I did not belong there. I never saw such things. I never . . . nobody wrote about this kind of reality. I never saw any theater, I never saw any movie . . . this was not the world. I was told these were human beings—they didn't look like human beings."[11]

Karski's testimony, which includes not only what he saw, but what he did not see (a recognizable world), reveals his limited ability to describe the circumstances of humanity as altered by the Holocaust. His sympathy for the Jews and his pity for those incarcerated in the ghetto bleed from his testimony as strongly as does his distance from them. *Shoah* depends both on the testimonies of Jewish victims, which bring us right up to the edge of their horrific experiences, and descriptions by outsiders, who remain limited by their blindness to or their inability to comprehend, much less articulate, the terms of a horror beyond the bounds of their knowledge.

The critics and Hollywood respond to *Shoah*

Although *Shoah* received critical acclaim and, eventually, widespread international acceptance as an authoritative commentary on the Holocaust, it also garnered its share of criticism. As cultural critics Marianne Hirsch and Leo Spitzer point out, *Shoah* participates, both ironically and unintentionally, in an erasure of gender differences that echoes the ways in which the Nazis dehumanized their victims by erasing gender boundaries. The film privileges testimony by men, incorporating only a few women's voices, mostly bystanders who are interviewed or translators who accompany Lanzmann to interviews. Recognizing how the film mirrors the Nazi gender dynamic is critical for understanding the continued link between past and present mechanisms of dehumanization. Although Jewish men and women were equally targeted for death, they faced different degrees of harassment in the camps, different regulations, and even different selection processes for immediate killing.[12] While gender may have seemed irrelevant to Lanzmann in his quest to uncover the Nazi killing machine, Hirsch and Spitzer show how ignoring the role of gender in the functioning of that machine participates in erasing the status of victims as individuals.[13]

Other critics claimed that Lanzmann unfairly emphasized the anti-Semitism of the poorly educated, impoverished Polish peasants who lived near the camps. In the film, local Poles recount seeing trains laden with wealthy Jews on the way to the camps. They mimic the language spoken by Jews as "ra ra ra," and express little sorrow that Jews no longer live among them. When *Shoah* came out, the Polish press expressed indignation at what they considered its anti-Polish stance, and the government submitted an official letter of protest to the French Ministry of Foreign Affairs, in the erroneous belief that the French government had funded the film.[14] Even Jan Karski said that *Shoah* had erred in not mentioning the gentiles, including thousands of

Poles, who put themselves and their families in danger to save hundreds of thousands of Jews. Karski believed the churches, foreign governments, and other institutions with real power that could have helped the Jews but chose to look away, even after he told them what he had seen, were most deserving of blame.[15]

Other critiques focus on Lanzmann's interviewing technique and what some consider his questionable moral practice of pushing interviewees to discuss traumatic experiences against their will, or even lying to them outright, as in the case of former Treblinka guard Franz Suchomel and German railway worker Walter Stier.[16] Lanzmann had no concerns about his lies, however, explaining that since his efforts to deal honestly with former Nazis had failed, deception was the only way to include them in the film. As he put it, "Frankness and honesty had been repaid with resounding failure; I had to learn to deceive the deceivers, it was my bounden duty."[17]

Despite this criticism, *Shoah* continued to be the film against which subsequent Holocaust films were measured. Its revered status was particularly apparent after the release of *Schindler's List*, Steven Spielberg's 1993 feature film based on the true story of Oskar Schindler, a German businessman who saved 1,100 Polish Jews by hiring them to work in his factory. Praised for its artistry and sensitivity, *Schindler's List* succeeded far beyond expectations for a drama about the Holocaust based on a little-known historical figure. It made a global splash, won numerous Academy Awards, received high marks from prominent critics, and quickly established itself as a master narrative about the Holocaust.[18]

Nevertheless, *Schindler's List* also garnered substantial backlash. Critics pointed out that it highlighted an anomaly, a Christian who endangered himself to save Jewish lives, and trivialized and sensationalized the Holocaust with its redemptive message. One scene in particular violated an unspoken taboo of Holocaust representation, depicting a group of women prisoners being herded into what they—and the audience—think is a gas chamber but turns out to be a shower. As Sara R. Horowitz points out, the scene titillates the audience with the implication that they are about to view something they are not supposed to see: "The anticipated enactment of genocide is thrilling because it is forbidden and at the same time permitted because it is artifice."[19] Such evocations of familiar cinematic responses led critics to complain that *Schindler's List* fails to recognize the singularity of the Holocaust, an event whose unprecedented evil stands outside both history and conventional modes of representation. If *Shoah* aesthetically acknowledges the problematic nature of representation and takes pains to highlight the impossibility of representing events that lack surviving witnesses, *Schindler's List* "does not seek to negate the representational, iconic power of filmic images, but rather banks on this power. Nor does it develop a unique filmic idiom to capture the unprecedented and unassimilable fact of mass extermination; rather, it relies on familiar tropes and common techniques to narrate the extraordinary rescue of a large group of individuals."[20] In short, *Schindler's List* fails where *Shoah* succeeds, because Spielberg's film fails to acknowledge the fundamental limitations of film and, especially, of its own status as a Hollywood movie.

Miriam Hansen reminds us, however, that pitting the two films against each other as mutually exclusive paradigms reduces the challenges of Holocaust representation to a simple binary of showing or not showing, rather than framing the problem as an issue of competing representations and modes of representation. Although she is not a fan of *Schindler's List*, with its flavor of Hollywood glamour, spectacle and entertainment, Hansen concedes that the film serves a purpose in helping us think through how the representation of the Holocaust is shaped by public memory, which, for better or worse, is now predominantly carried by popular culture and mass media. In leaving relatively few survivors—and no survivors of the gas chambers—and destroying longstanding Jewish communities in Europe, the Holocaust dramatically disrupted community and family based traditions of oral and collective memory, leaving the media as a particularly significant form of memory, which we need to accept and understand, not condemn. Though *Shoah* may have been popular, it did not engage ordinary viewers as *Schindler's List* did.[21]

Scholar Barbie Zelizer points out that *Schindler's List* has been lauded as a film that managed to "transcend" Hollywood because of Spielberg's ability to distance his work from the trivializing effects of popular culture.[22] One way he did this was by making the movie look like a documentary, eschewing zoom lenses, using mainly little-known or even unknown actors, and, most famously, shooting mostly in black and white, thus evoking films shot immediately after liberation like *Nazi Concentration Camps* (see Chapter 2). These effects were a conscious choice: Spielberg later said, "I simply tried to pull the events closer to the audience by reducing the artifice" and claimed to have made "a document, not an entertainment."[23] Zelizer argues that the critical acceptance of *Schindler's List* signaled a willingness to recognize the representation of the Holocaust as a legitimate part of Holocaust history and in so doing blurred the boundaries between history and popular culture, one constructed as serious, factual and objective, the other as trivial, specious, and entertaining.[24] In making *Shoah*, Lanzmann did not want the conventions of documentary film to limit his creativity; in making *Schindler's List*, Spielberg sought to legitimize his fictional film by downplaying artifice and mimicking Holocaust documentaries. Together, then, the two films reveal the actual porousness of the perceived dichotomy between history and popular culture.

The value of witness

Shoah takes up issues of filmic representation initially raised by the films of the liberated camps that disseminated some of the first—and ultimately iconic—images of the Holocaust. Prosecutors at the Nuremberg Trials commissioned these films in part because they were convinced that images would provide more effective evidence of the atrocities than eyewitness testimony. *Nazi Concentration Camps* framed its images with sworn affidavits of authenticity from the filmmakers that, ironically, implicitly deny the fact that the films were deliberately constructed to shock and horrify viewers. Miriam Hansen notes that it remains to be seen whether there can be an aesthetic practice "capable of engaging the problematic of representation without disfiguring the memory of the dead."[25] But the film that goes furthest in engaging this problematic is *Shoah*, which, in focusing on witness testimony at length and with great breadth, both rejects the now-conventional visual imagery of the Holocaust and recognizes the limits of Holocaust representation, namely the kinds of facts, meanings, and emotions that Holocaust representations can evoke and those which they cannot. As Lanzmann claimed, "It took time to find the core of this film, and the core is the gas chamber."[26] Though no witnesses survived that gas chamber, only witness testimony can let us approach it.

A page from the Hungarian translation of Art Spiegelman's Pulitzer Prize-winning Maus (1992) is displayed on a subway train in Budapest on March 4, 2005 to advertise the opening of an exhibition of Spiegelman's work. Due to its comic book-like form, Maus marked a turning point in Holocaust representation by drawing attention to the traumas passed on to survivors' children and by blurring the boundaries between fiction and non-fiction.

Attila Kisbendek/AFP/Getty Images

11

Maus: A Survivor's Tale (graphic novel, 1986–1991):

How is the Memory of the Holocaust Transmitted Across Generations?

In 1992, the members of the Pulitzer Prize Board faced a dilemma: they agreed that Art Spiegelman's *Maus: A Survivor's Tale* deserved a prize, but they didn't know which one. The Pulitzer Board was not alone in finding it difficult to categorize the enormously popular graphic novel. Booksellers, readers, and newspaper editors had trouble deciding whether the work was fiction or non-fiction. Their confusion was reasonable: at quick glance, *Maus* looks like fiction, especially because its human characters have animal heads, including mice, cats, frogs, pigs, and dogs. The book's visual and textual devices make it clear that the author was not trying to provide an objective account of his parents' experiences during World War II and the Holocaust. But *Maus* also fulfills several key criteria of non-fiction, including a fact-based narrative and the inclusion of documentary evidence.

When the editors of *The New York Times* placed *Maus* on the fiction best-seller list, Spiegelman formally protested with a letter to the editor:

If your list were divided into literature and nonliterature, I could gracefully accept the compliment as intended, but to the extent that "fiction" indicates that a work isn't factual, I feel a bit queasy. As an author I believe I might have lopped several years off the 13 I devoted to my two-volume project if I could only have taken a novelist's license while searching for a novelistic structure . . . It's just that I shudder to think how David Duke [former Grand

Wizard of the Ku Klux Klan and 1991 Louisiana gubernatorial candidate]—if he could read—would respond to seeing a carefully researched work based closely on my father's memories of life in Hitler's Europe and in the death camps classified as fiction. I know that by delineating people with animal heads I've raised problems of taxonomy for you. Could you consider adding a special "nonfiction/mice" category to your list?[1]

In response to his request, the editors recategorized the book as non-fiction. The Pulitzer Board eventually resolved their conundrum by awarding Spiegelman a Pulitzer Prize Special Citation, in effect, creating its own category.

Though *Maus* was both popular and praised, not everyone was enthralled with Spiegelman's approach to the Holocaust. Some felt that comics, a lowbrow cultural form associated with children's entertainment, were not appropriate for recounting the experience of Holocaust survivors. Others worried that *Maus* might encourage Holocaust deniers and authors of falsified Holocaust accounts (see Chapter 13). In light of these risks, why would an author for whom the dissemination of his parents' true story clearly mattered choose to blur the boundaries between fact and fiction? Spiegelman's answer to this question may seem counterintuitive. He believed that his mode of representation actually enhanced the truth-value of his narrative. Indeed, as Sara R. Horowitz aptly points out, *Maus* shows how blurring the boundaries between fact and fiction can help break down the cognitive and emotional barriers that prohibit a fuller understanding of the past.[2]

Maus instigated a global and lasting shift in how we understand Holocaust representation. It is the most prominent example of a text about the Holocaust written by children of survivors, often referred to as the second generation, who were deeply affected by their parents' traumatic experiences, even if they did not share them. In this context, *Maus* presents the second generation experience of sharing an unlived past in the present, by foregrounding the events Spiegelman's parents experienced alongside the matrix of painful relationships through which knowledge of those events was transmitted to him, their child.

The tale of *Maus*

Maus tells two stories: one about Vladek and Anja Spiegelman, Polish Jews who survived Auschwitz, the other about their son Art, who, like many children of survivors, grew up knowing only parts of what his parents experienced in the Holocaust. Art narrates the text, which begins in 1978, based on conversations he taped with his father about his past in Poland. Vladek recounts his and Anja's experiences in hiding from the Nazis and at Auschwitz. But the book itself frames this narrative of the past with the life of the family after the Holocaust. The first volume begins and ends with scenes of Vladek and Art in the present that depict their emotionally fraught relationship and mutual lack of understanding; a section in the middle, with a very different aesthetic from the rest of the book, recounts Anja's suicide in 1968 and its effect on Art. The second volume also ends with a scene between father and son in which Vladek, about to fall asleep, mistakenly refers to Art as Richieu, the name of his and Anja's first child who did not survive the war. Art dedicates the second volume to Richieu, the brother he never met, whose death as a child in the Holocaust loomed large over Art's own upbringing.

To transmit the complexities of these narratives and relationships, Spiegelman deploys the graphic design skills he pursued even though his parents wanted him to be a dentist. Spiegelman's parents emigrated to the United States from Sweden in 1951, three years after Art was born. When he was six, they moved to Rego Park, Queens. Spiegelman attended the High School for Art and Design in Manhattan, began drawing professionally at age 16, and studied art and philosophy at SUNY-Binghamton's Harpur College. As an adult, he published underground comics and designed Wacky Packages, Garbage Pail Kids and other novelty items for Topps Bubble Gum Company from 1965 until 1987.

What would become the two-volume *Maus* originated as "Maus," a three-page comic published in *Funny Animals* #1 in 1972, four years after Spiegelman's one-month stay in a mental hospital and his mother's suicide a few months later. That same year, Spiegelman began taping interviews with his father about his experiences in the Holocaust, although he did not start work on the book *Maus* until 1978. In 1980, Spiegelman and his wife, Françoise Mouly, founded the avant-garde comics magazine *RAW*. The second issue featured a small, comic book-like supplement that would become the first chapter of the book version of *Maus*. Chapters of the book continued to appear in the magazine as pull-out supplements. Several publishers rejected the full manuscript before Pantheon published *Maus I: A Survivor's Tale: My Father Bleeds History* in 1986. The book won numerous awards and garnered even more attention after Pantheon published the second volume, *Maus II: A Survivor's Tale: And Here My Troubles Began*, in 1991. The two volumes have since been reissued together and in 2011, Pantheon published *MetaMaus*, a book and DVD of interviews, sketches, photographs, and documents that reveal the background and process of the book's creation. Since its initial publication, *Maus* has been translated into dozens of languages, a further testament to its global significance.

What makes *Maus* such an original and striking Holocaust representation is its use—and expansion—of the visual, textual, and aural devices of the comic book for its serious subject matter. Incorporating drawings, diagrams, photographs, narration, accented speech, and textual and visual puns into both panels and narrative allows Spiegelman to convey a breadth and depth of information not easily communicated in more traditional forms of publication. With its talking animals addressing issues of moral complexity, *Maus* also resembles a fable. Depicting Jews as mice, Germans as cats, Poles as pigs, and Americans as dogs invites readers to visually associate individual characters with groups, often via stereotypical traits assigned to that group. German cats and Jewish mice embody the predatory relationship between Nazis and Jews, while also referencing both the Nazi association of Jews with vermin most infamously in the 1940 propaganda film *The Eternal Jew* as well as the violence of cartoon cats and mice (as in the series *Tom and Jerry*).

However, embedded within the visual artifice of talking animals are the actual historical details of Art's parents' lives. Vladek's narration begins in Poland in 1936, the year he met Art's mother Anja. Although Vladek had been involved with another girl, Lucia Greenberg, Vladek implies that he may have left her because of Anja's family's wealth. After they married, Vladek opened a textile factory with the financial support of Anja's parents and in 1938, their first son Richieu was born. A few months later, in an event foreshadowing her depressed state and eventual suicide after the war, Art's mother suffered so severely from postpartum depression that she had to spend time recovering in a sanatorium in Czechoslovakia.

In 1939, after Vladek was called to serve in the Polish army, the Germans subsequently captured and imprisoned him for a number of months in both POW and labor camps. He returned to find Anja and her parents living under both deteriorated political conditions and increased anti-Semitism. Soon, the extended family was forced to move to a ghetto, after which Vladek's father, sister, and nieces and nephews were deported to camps. Vladek recounts that, in 1943, fearing for their son's safety, he and Anja decided to send Richieu to live with relatives in another city. But when the Jews there were about to be deported, Richieu's aunt decided to poison him rather than allow him to be murdered in a camp. The text frequently interrupts Vladek's chronological narrative with scenes from the present that showcase Art's fraught relationship with his father, who in one instance rebukes Art for not helping with household chores, and, in another, disposes of Art's coat in favor of one he finds more agreeable. Such interruptions not only make it difficult to embrace Vladek uncritically as an idealized survivor (see Chapter 5), but also underscore the mediated nature of how Holocaust memory is transmitted across generations.

Vladek continues his narration of the story by describing how he and Anja first went into hiding, then decided to try to make their way to Hungary in order to evade capture by the Nazis, only to be betrayed by their paid smugglers. Here, Spiegelman takes the symbolic dimensions of his unique visual references a step further when Vladek recalls his and Anja's risky attempt to disguise themselves as Poles. The panel shows them wearing pig masks as they set out on a path in the shape of a swastika; the caption reads, in Vladek's broken English, "Anja and I didn't have where to go."[3] Turning the path into a symbol effectively conveys the way Nazi danger surrounded the couple wherever they turned, and the symbol itself literally shows the dead ends they faced, as they were both captured and deported to Auschwitz and then separated, finding each other again only after the end of the war.

As Alan Rosen has pointed out, Spiegelman's textual representation of Vladek's narration adds a powerful aural dimension to the book. The text of Vladek's speech painstakingly recreates his heavy accent and awkward English phrasing, allowing the reader to imagine the sound of his real voice. Audio from Spiegelman's interviews with his father attest to the importance he placed on aural accuracy. Vladek's English also communicates how impossible it is for survivors to tell their full stories. For Vladek, this impossibility is compounded by speaking in a non-native tongue to an audience who was not there, but as Claude Lanzmann's film *Shoah* points out (see Chapter 10), it is a fundamental condition of the survivor's tale. Rosen notes that these textual aural devices work together with Art's foregrounded presence as a listener to underscore this central problem.[4]

The disjunction created by the rigorous accuracy of *Maus*'s representation of sound and the symbolic liberties of its visual representations has been one of the key confusions for those trying to categorize the book as fact or fiction, although, as Marianne Hirsch claims, Spiegelman's insertion of a small number of family photographs at decisive moments in the text disturbs the division between aural verisimilitude and visual imagination. Hirsch also notes that the scattered photographs of Vladek, Anja, Art, and Richieu echo the fragmented nature of the family. She argues that the postwar souvenir photo of Vladek forms the foundation of the entire story and its retelling.[5] As Vladek explains to Art, after the war, he stopped by a photo shop (presumably in Poland) that had a clean survivor uniform in which customers could pose for photographs. He included this picture in a letter he sent to Anja as he tried to reunite with her, and, according to Vladek, she always kept it with her. The photograph contains elements of artifice (the camp uniform, which anyone could wear), yet it also serves as documentary evidence that Vladek was a prisoner in Auschwitz. Hirsch equates the photograph, a simulation of what was real, to *Maus* itself: each contains elements of artifice, yet points to the real.[6]

Spiegelman plays with language and images in other ways. The book's title is in German, the language of its perpetrators. The word *Maus* aurally and visually evokes Auschwitz, but it also sounds the same as the word mouse in English, the language in which Art, like many children of survivors, learned about the Holocaust. Spiegelman makes the Auschwitz pun explicit in the title of the first chapter of the second volume, "Mauschwitz," which situates Vladek and Anja's experience in the camps as part of the larger persecution of millions of Jews (mice). The book's subtitle, "A Survivor's Tale," plays on a mouse's tail and a tail as an ending or what one drags behind, evoking the long-term consequences of the story Vladek tells. These puns defamiliarize the familiar for the English-speaking reader and epitomize the centrality of text and speech to the book. As Marianne Hirsh puts it, "Spiegelman's audacious visual/verbal punning not only lays bare the self-consciousness of his textual production—self-reflexivity that disarmingly pervades his text—it also defines from the beginning the two primary elements of his representational choices, the visual and the aural."[7]

If *Maus* uses language to convey meaning, it also highlights the invisible yet glaring role of silence in Holocaust testimony, sometimes in a comical way. In one scene, Spiegelman and his therapist discuss whether it is meaningful to tell stories about the Holocaust when those who died can't. While Spiegelman agrees with the playwright Samuel Beckett that "Every word is like an unnecessary stain on silence and nothingness," he points out that Beckett "SAID" these words to communicate their meaning.[8] But this brief, humorous interlude points to the deeper, more painful fact that Art will never hear his mother's story, not only because she committed suicide, but also because his father burned her diaries after her death. As a result, Art—and readers—can only learn about Anja's experiences from Vladek. Her absence is most present in the middle of the first volume, in the four-page "Prisoner on the Hell Planet," which stands out from the rest of the book with its heavy black border, fully human characters, photograph of Art and his mother, and angular, expressionist style.[9] By disrupting the book's overall aesthetic and narrative, Art embeds the story of his own suffering into that of his parents' suffering.[10] By depicting himself in a prison cell wearing the striped uniform of an inmate, Spiegelman communicates the painful effects their war memories had on him, as well as his own victimization by his mother's suicide.[11]

As *MetaMaus* shows, Spiegelman is aware that his portrayal of his father is often unflattering. He reveals Vladek's pettiness, lack of sympathy, and casual racism. The point of displaying these character flaws, he explains, is to help readers understand that suffering did not make survivors better people; it just made them suffer.[12] By contrast, Spiegelman's portrait of his mother seems somewhat idealized. Only spare and fragmentary traces of her life emerge in the conversations between her husband and son, whose memories clearly shape and perhaps distort her representation. Yet one of the powerful effects of relating Vladek's story is facing the fact that Anja's story—like so many others—will remain untold. When Vladek insists, again in his broken English, that her story is the same as his own—"I can tell you—she went through the same what me—terrible"—he further implicates himself in her disappearance.[13] One might argue, indeed, that the sum of *Maus*'s textual, visual, and aural devices serves as a representation of the absences the Holocaust left, and what they have meant to those left behind.

Fact or fiction?

We typically view fact and fiction as diametrically opposed categories. Fact reveals something that is considered to be true or actually existing. Fiction is defined as imaginary or invented. But facts alone can obscure reality, while fiction can reveal truths that facts obscure. Art Spiegelman may not have been looking to cross the fact/fiction boundary, but in highlighting the very real divide between the truth of what happened and the truth of how it is remembered, *Maus* addresses the crucial question of how the Holocaust is remembered and represented across generations, beginning with eyewitness testimony. Spiegelman does not always quote verbatim from his taped conversations with his father; rather, he selected key words around which he built the dialogue between father and son that appears in *Maus*. To the best of their abilities, father and son remain committed to recounting their understanding of what actually occurred. Yet *Maus*'s comic book frames and talking animals always reminds us of the story's constructedness.

Whatever its format, Holocaust testimony occupies a special place in the history of Holocaust representation. Yet that testimony is inevitably mediated by the lenses of time, memory, and experience (see Chapter 10). In this context, *Maus* can be seen as a deeper form of truth about the Holocaust, for it both offers testimony and foregrounds how that testimony is mediated—and thus inevitably limited. *Maus* also highlights the double nature of mediation that occurs when children who experienced the effects of their parents' trauma tell their families' Holocaust stories—and their own. Spiegelman was certainly not the first child of a survivor to write about his experiences. But the international attention *Maus* garnered helped create the category of second-generation Holocaust representation. Whether Holocaust survivors saturated their children with stories of their survival or, as was often the case, remained silent about the past, it is clear that how a family tells (or doesn't tell) its story plays an important role in how the Holocaust is remembered. As *Maus* shows, Art may not have been an eyewitness to the Holocaust, but it affects him each and every day. Erin McGlothlin calls this dissonance a "crisis of signification," because the trauma the second generation experiences in their family life is "essentially divorced from the Holocaust experience that engendered it. The signifier remains, but it is unable to locate its referent, resulting in a truncated relationship between experience and effect."[14] When the children of Holocaust survivors write about the Holocaust, they must attempt to bridge this gap between experience and effect.[15]

Although the term second generation initially designated children of Holocaust survivors, scholars and researchers have broadened it to include the children of perpetrators. Despite their obvious differences, there are some significant similarities in how these two groups have been deeply affected by the secondhand trauma of the Holocaust, leading historian Dan Diner to label them "a community of opposites" with regard to Holocaust memory.[16] Their writing engages what Marianne Hirsch calls the work of "postmemory," defined as "the response of the second generation to the trauma of the first." According to Hirsch, "Postmemory is a powerful form of memory precisely because its connection to its object or source is mediated not through recollection but through representation, projection, and creation—often based on silence rather than speech, on the invisible rather than the visible."[17] *Maus* embodies this constantly self-reflexive form of Holocaust memory by intertwining the events of the Holocaust and the present, making every effort to break the illusion of a smooth narrative and stressing the difficulty of separating the facts of the past from their representations in the present.

By his own admission, Spiegelman was determined to distance his work from existing representations of the Holocaust. Although he had already begun work on *Maus* before the popular TV miniseries *Holocaust* aired (see Chapter 9), he was distressed and alienated by its glibness, although he admired its ability to reach so many people: "I was appalled by the ersatz acting, the stupidity of the narrative choices being made, but was still fascinated that somebody had woven something together intended for a mass audience."[18] He also recognized the paradoxical power of iconic Holocaust images to shape (or distort) individual truth, as apparent in the first panel of the 1972 version of "Maus," which references Margaret Bourke-White's iconic photograph of liberated prisoners in Buchenwald. Spiegelman outlined his drawing of the photo as if it were part of a family album and drew an arrow with the word "poppa" pointing to one of the mouse prisoners. Rather than suggesting that his father was one of the still-unidentified men in the actual Bourke-White photograph, the drawing points to the impossibility of separating his father's personal story from the iconic images which have come to signify the Holocaust.

The generational challenge

Maus made waves by telling the story of Holocaust survivors from the perspective of the next generation and thus highlighting the degree to which memory influences what we can know about the past. The book shows how the process of recovering the past and the family dynamics of Holocaust survivors have become just as much a part of Holocaust history as the testimony of eyewitnesses. By walking the line between fact and fiction, *Maus* reveals that the truth of what happened cannot be separated from how it is remembered, and exemplifies how a Holocaust representation can address both the facts of history and the way we recover those facts. *Maus* is a turning point in Holocaust representation because it is not only aware of the challenges inherent in Holocaust representation, but also willing to expose those challenges and take aesthetic and emotional risks to address them.

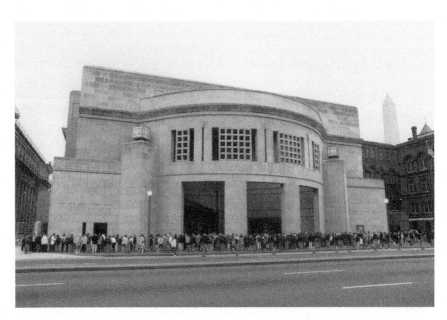

Visitors line up in front of the United States Holocaust Memorial Museum in Washington, DC on April 27, 2000. Located just off the National Mall, the museum is America's "national institution for the documentation, study, and interpretation of Holocaust history, and serves as [its] memorial to the millions of people murdered during the Holocaust."

United States Holocaust Memorial Museum

12

United States Holocaust Memorial Museum (museum, 1993):

How Do Countries Outside Germany Commemorate the Holocaust?

When leaders of American Jewish organizations convene for lunch, it usually doesn't make the front page of *The New York Times*. But on October 25, 1985, when representatives from the World Jewish Congress, the Union of American Hebrew Congregations, and the United States Holocaust Memorial Council had lunch with German Chancellor Helmut Kohl, it was front page news. As the *Times* reported, the luncheon included a "soul-baring" and frank discussion of Germany's efforts to redress its Nazi past.[1] Kohl had requested the meeting to address lingering ill will toward his country among American Jews, which had been exacerbated by recent events.

Tensions had been high since American President Ronald Reagan's controversial visit to the Kolmeshöhe military cemetery in Bitburg, Germany, five months earlier, as part of ceremonies commemorating the 40th anniversary of the end of World War II. Before the visit, it was discovered that several members of Hitler's Waffen-SS were buried alongside the Allied soldiers Reagan planned to honor. Although Reagan was informed about the SS graves before leaving the United States, he went ahead with his visit. Adding insult to injury, Reagan justified his decision in terms that equated the SS soldiers with their Jewish victims, stating, "They were victims just as surely as the victims in the concentration camps."[2] His position elicited widespread dismay and official protests from Jewish leaders, veterans' groups, and politicians. Famous Holocaust survivor and future Nobel Prize-winner Elie Wiesel (see Chapter 5) implored Reagan not to visit the cemetery, saying "That place, Mr. President, is not your place. Your place is with the victims of the SS."[3] To quell the furor, Reagan and Kohl went to the concentration camp at Bergen–Belsen immediately after Bitburg, but many saw this as a further conflation of perpetrators and victims. The outrage was so widespread that The Ramones, a well-known punk band, wrote a protest song, "Bonzo Goes to Bitburg," which The Village Voice included among its top singles for 1985.[4]

The Bitburg controversy made many American Jews question the longstanding American commitment to Holocaust survivors, many of them liberated by American forces and then welcomed as refugees to the United States. But Reagan's actions called this commitment into question, and the lunch with Chancellor Kohl didn't exactly help. Kohl defended the Bitburg visit by explaining that the graves belonged to SS soldiers who had been drafted and played no role in the concentration camps. But Jewish leaders felt he had missed the point, failing to grasp the heavy symbolic weight of a visit to an SS cemetery, regardless of the stories of particular SS members. As Rabbi Alexander Schindler of the Union of American Hebrew Congregations bluntly told Kohl, "You really do not understand what bothered us so much."[5]

The timing of this controversy was significant. On October 16, 1985, just nine days before the luncheon, the groundbreaking ceremony for the United States Holocaust Memorial Museum (USHMM) took place in Washington, DC. The Bitburg incident, in other words, occurred at the precise moment when the United States was formalizing its own official relationship to the genocide, highlighting on one hand its triumphal role in liberating the camps and, on the other, admitting that the United States failed to adequately aid European Jewish refugees. Rather than serving to unite Germany and the United States, the establishment of the USHMM at the literal and symbolic centers of American democracy underscored the two countries' very different relationships to and attitudes toward the Holocaust.

Holocaust memorials in Germany play many roles: they honor the dead, express contrition for crimes, and educate younger generations (see Chapter 16). But whatever their purpose, all of these sites are part of a "Topography of Terror," as a Berlin museum built on the site of the Gestapo and SS headquarters is called. German memorials occupied haunted spaces where crimes against humanity were planned and perpetrated, and they are geared to an audience whose very nationality implicates them in—or at least connects them to—those crimes. But it is a different thing to publicly commemorate the Holocaust outside Germany, at a remove from its events, perpetrators, and victims. The nature of those commemorations, whether memorials, museums, or both, is closely linked to a country's proximity to and relationship with Germany, especially during World War II. While Holocaust museums and memorials dot the American map (see Chapter 14), the USHMM, located on the National Mall in Washington, DC, resonates most deeply as an official statement of America's relationship to this past, revealing how Americans have used and continue to use Holocaust history for the purposes of national self-identification. Whether adjacent to Europe's killing fields or thousands of miles away, museums and memorials, no matter how self-critical, filter their countries' official relationships to Holocaust and memory through powerful national myths.

A museum on the mall: The "opposite" of the Holocaust

The earliest Holocaust memorials were established at atrocity sites; prisoners began to create them even as killings were still taking place.[6] In the United States, an inscribed cornerstone dedicated to a museum and memorial was laid in New York City's Riverside Park on October 19, 1947, though the future plans never came to fruition. Across the United States, however, as Hasia Diner points out, there was plenty of local commemoration. Synagogues established memorial spaces for Jewish Holocaust victims, and immigrant support associations (*landsmanshaftn*) published memorial books (yizkor books) to honor the dead (see Chapter 3).[7] But the USHMM has dwarfed them all, drawing more than 36 million visitors since it opened to the public in 1993.[8]

The USHMM emerged out of decades of growing Holocaust consciousness, beginning with the Eichmann trial in 1961 (see Chapter 6) and continuing with the Six-Day War in 1967, when many Israelis felt that Jews were again under attack. In the late 1970s, the Holocaust gained new prominence in American public discourse as a result of the 1978 broadcast of the television miniseries *Holocaust: The Story of the Family Weiss* (see Chapter 9) and a national debate about the limits of free speech sparked when neo-Nazis planned a march in the heavily Jewish town of Skokie, Illinois, where one in six residents was a Holocaust survivor.[9] One tangible result of this heightened interest was the establishment of the President's Commission on the Holocaust, chaired by Elie Wiesel. On September 27, 1979, the Commission submitted a report recommending the "establishment of a living memorial that will speak not only to the victims' deaths but of their lives, a memorial that can transform the living by transmitting the legacy of the Holocaust." This living memorial's three components would be a memorial/museum, an educational foundation, and a

Committee on Conscience.[10] In 1980, an act of Congress established the United States Holocaust Memorial Council, which worked to bring this living memorial into being.

At the USHMM groundbreaking, participants mixed soil from concentration camps and Warsaw's Jewish cemetery into the building's foundation to symbolically link the new American museum with Europe's spaces of death. The building's location also has symbolic significance: it stands adjacent to the National Mall with its many memorials to American heroes and democratic values, as well as the spot where Rev. Martin Luther King, Jr. advocated racial tolerance in his "I Have a Dream" speech. The site thus establishes Holocaust memory as a powerful piece of American memory—and values—as also reflected in the USHMM's mission to provide "a powerful lesson in the fragility of freedom, the myth of progress, and the need for vigilance in preserving democratic values."[11] At the same time, aligning the Holocaust with American war veterans and the architects of American democracy implicitly distances the United States from German fascism and the Holocaust. In other words, beginning with its very location, the USHMM helped the United States define its values as antithetical to the Holocaust. As Michael Berenbaum, Project Director of the USHMM from 1988 to 1993, put it, "the history described [in the USHMM] cuts against the grain of the American ethos," and the events of the Holocaust embody "a violation of every essential American value."[12]

The architecture of memory

Although its placement on the National Mall was a powerful statement of the USHMM's symbolic significance, the site presented a difficult balancing act for architect James Ingo Freed. Freed's challenge was to find a way for the museum to blend in with neighboring neoclassical government buildings yet still evoke a genocide that took place thousands of miles away. With their heavy façades and bureaucratic feel, nearby buildings like the Bureau of Engraving and Printing and the U.S. Department of Agriculture convey the solidity, stability, and permanence of government power. But neoclassicism was also the preferred style of Nazi architects, so Freed could not simply adopt it. Indeed, he had been hired because earlier designs were too grandiose, uncomfortably evoking the dehumanizing aspects of neoclassicism.[13]

In the end, Freed struck a balance by using materials similar to those of neighboring structures but designing a building that embodies the painful themes of the Holocaust. New York Times architecture critic Herbert Muschamp described the museum's shattering physical impact: "Images of confinement, observation, atrocity and denial surface and recede within the building's hard industrial forms: expanses of brick wall bolted with steel, floating glass bridges engraved with the names of devastated cities, lead pyramids clustered in sentry-box rooflines."[14] It was praised as "an overwhelming visual experience, even if the objects displayed tell a horrible tale."[15]

The suggestive architecture provides a deeply emotional experience for visitors. The building is intentionally disorienting, confusing, and claustrophobic. As Freed explained, "Brick walls, exposed beams, boarded windows . . . will let visitors know that they are in a different place—that the Holocaust is an event that should disturb and be felt as well as perceived."[16] To this end, the exposed metal and bolts of the elevators resemble prison cells or cattle cars, and the frames around the elevators and doors resemble gates to concentration camps or the semicircular doors of crematoria ovens. Walkways above the lobby in effect place museum-goers under surveillance. One walkway, between the library and photo archives on the Museum's top floor, resembles the bridges that linked the residential areas of Jewish ghettos to the factories where they toiled. Overall, the Museum's architecture pushes visitors to experience the Holocaust in diametrical opposition to the neighboring Mall's temples of democracy.

The permanent exhibition

If the lobby of the USHMM removes visitors from the open spaces of the National Mall, the permanent exhibition removes them a step further.[17] Somber, darkly lit, and intentionally claustrophobic, this exhibition covers three floors of the museum. Its wide array of artifacts, film clips, explanatory texts, maps, and interpretive displays lead visitors through a linear, chronological narrative of the Holocaust. Generally downplaying any controversial aspects of Holocaust history, "the permanent exhibition appears as a seamless tale, presenting its story through an anonymous voice that conceals those who shaped the exhibition."[18] The focus remains squarely on victims throughout; swastikas, Nazi paraphernalia, and images of Hitler are few and far between, by design. Indeed, the permanent exhibition is designed to actively encourage identification with victims. When the USHMM first opened, visitors were assigned identity cards of actual victims, with biographical details and brief notes about the person's experiences before and during the war. They could check in on the status of their victims at computer stations located in different parts of the exhibition. However, lines of visitors waiting for computers created bottlenecks that ultimately made this experience unworkable.

Besides promoting identification, the USHMM tries to personalize the genocide by showing visitors the faces behind abstract statistics and body counts. Perhaps the most conspicuous example of this approach is "A Shtetl: The Ejszyszki Shtetl Collection," which is displayed in a three-storey tower that serves as a transitional space between floors. This collection consists of approximately 1,500 photographs of residents of Ejszyszki (also known as Eishyshok), a *shtetl* (market town) in Lithuania. On September 21, 1941, the SS murdered over 4,000 Ejszyszki Jews, ending 900 years of Jewish history in the area. The display is the work of Yaffa Eliach, who survived the massacre as a child and later researched her hometown and gathered photographs from survivors and their families. The tall, narrow tower evokes the chimneys of concentration camp crematoria, and the tower and collection together make a powerful link between the machinery of killing and the people who were killed.

One place where museum-goers do not identify with or focus on victims is the start of the permanent exhibition, where they experience the perspective of the American GIs who liberated the concentration camps in 1945. Video monitors in the elevator display historical film footage and the voice of an American soldier recounts the first time he entered a concentration camp. Exiting the elevator, visitors are confronted with large atrocity photographs from the Ohrdruf concentration camp, liberated by the Americans on April 4, 1945 (see Chapter 2). The disturbing images of bodies take visitors directly to the end of the Holocaust. The rest of the permanent exhibition narrates the history that led to this end in three parts—"The Nazi Assault, 1933–1939," "The Final Solution, 1940–1945," and the "Last Chapter"—spread out over three floors.

Unlike German memorials and museums (see Chapter 16), the USHMM operates on the premise that its visitors are typically Americans unfamiliar with German history. Hence the first section includes displays about prewar Jewish life in Europe and traces German political and social history leading up to the Holocaust. Galleries show visitors how the Nazi regime incrementally ratcheted up pressure on the Jews, through displays about race science, book burnings, Germany's discriminatory laws and expansionist foreign policy, and the anti-Jewish violence on *Kristallnacht* (November 9–10, 1938), as well as a 14-minute video about anti-Semitism in Germany. But the USHMM does not whitewash the less than stellar U.S. record of support for European Jews, nor does it free American visitors of historical responsibility. This section also tells the story of the "Voyage of the Damned," when the United States forced the S.S. *St. Louis*, a ship carrying Jewish refugees, to return to Europe in June 1939. Many of the passengers later died in concentration camps. Another display recounts the failure of the July 1938 Evian conference in France, where 32 nations met to discuss Europe's Jewish refugee crisis. Due to prevailing anti-immigrant sentiments, the United States (and many other nations) refused to ease immigration restrictions to help the refugees.

The permanent exhibition's second section shifts from the Holocaust's historical and ideological origins to the war years. By design more intense and graphic, these displays cover topics such as the euthanasia of the disabled, the incarceration of Jews in ghettos, and the actions of *Einsatzgruppen* (Nazi mobile killing units) after Germany invaded the Soviet Union in June 1941. Visitors walk through a gate cast from the entrance to Auschwitz emblazoned with the iconic slogan *Arbeit macht frei* (Work makes you free) to enter "The Concentration Camp Universe," where audio recordings by survivors recount malnourishment, torture, and murder, and photographs and a detailed scale model of an Auschwitz crematorium illustrate the horror. Piles of shoes taken from the murdered at Majdanek add to the exhibition's emotional impact.

But the permanent exhibition does not end with these brutal depictions of the death camps. Rather, its third and final section turns to rescue, resistance, and liberation, followed by the aftermath of the Holocaust and stories of displaced persons, refugees from Europe, and the establishment of the State of Israel. This section concludes with a short film, *Testimony*, in which survivors "recount their experiences of loss, suffering, and anguish, as well as rescue, resistance, compassion, and hope."[19] When visitors leave the permanent exhibition, they find themselves near the Hall of Remembrance, a six-sided structure with an eternal flame that reframes the preceding exhibition through the perspective of American nationalism. This "simple, solemn space designed for public ceremonies and individual reflection" marks a dramatic shift in tone. Rich in symbolism—the hexagonal shape suggests both the six million murdered Jews and a Star of David—the Hall of Remembrance offers the possibility of hope and even redemption. The narrow windows provide the natural light the permanent exhibition lacks and offer views of the Washington Monument and the Jefferson Memorial. Leaving the Holocaust, visitors find themselves back in the United States, its opposite.

Memorials beyond the killing fields

Holocaust memorials and museums far from the killing fields of Europe do more than keep the memory of the Holocaust alive; they help clarify and shape a national relationship to the Holocaust. Israel offers a useful point of comparison to the United States. In 1948, when nearly half the population of Jewish Palestine consisted of Holocaust survivors, the Holocaust provided unmatched evidence for the Zionist argument justifying the need for the State of Israel. Israel's Holocaust authority, Yad Vashem, was founded in 1953, specifically to formalize this narrative of a nation that arose from the ruins of the Holocaust. Yad Vashem's official subtitle, the Martyrs' and Heroes' Remembrance Authority, foreground the importance of Holocaust fighters and martyrs to Israeli national self-understanding. But Yad Vashem is not a static institution and has changed in response to changing perceptions of the Holocaust and Israel. In the early part of this century, Israel spent $100 million to remodel the memorial site, including a new Holocaust museum, designed by star Israeli architect Moshe Safdie, which opened in 2005. At the end of the exhibition at the renovated Yad Vashem, visitors find themselves looking out over Jerusalem, which suggests that Israel is the rightful endpoint of the history of the Holocaust. Tom Segev suggests that the remodeling was an effort to maintain Israel's "monopoly" on Holocaust memory and not let newer museums and memorials, such as the USHMM and Germany's Memorial to the Murdered Jews of Europe overshadow Yad Vashem. Segev may overstate the case for this "Holocaust memory arms race," but the urge to keep up with the times underscores the continued importance of official Holocaust memory for Israel.[20]

In contrast to Israel and the United States, with their many Holocaust representations and memorials, Europe has, until recently, paid less attention to memorializing Jews. In Western Europe, in the years immediately following World War II, Jewish groups sometimes created memorials to victims of Nazi persecution, but in Eastern Europe, if they were memorialized at all, Jewish victims tended to be subsumed under Polish, Soviet, and other national war fatalities.[21] As John-Paul Himka and Joanna Beata Michlic point out, although most Jewish victims of Nazi persecution died in those countries, few of their World War II representations, including literature, art, and film, featured Jews. Rather, those countries' communist regimes downplayed Jewish suffering and conflated it with narratives of suffering of all of its citizens as victims of Nazi aggression. Moreover, continued anti-Semitic prejudices in those countries and strict censorship laws constricted the few Jews who lived there from openly commemorating the destruction of their communities.[22] Yet, despite the lack of national Holocaust commemoration activities, poets, photographers, writers, and artists did their best to create and circulate small-scale representations that kept memory alive, particularly in the Soviet Union, though these depictions did not circulate widely, in good part because of the Cold War.[23]

With the end of the Cold War, the countries of Eastern Europe began to come to terms with their pasts.[24] Poland, where many camps and ghettos were located and roughly half the six million murdered Jews lived, has seen a proliferation of Holocaust events and memorials since the late 1990s.[25] Despite Poland's still-tiny Jewish population (2009 estimates suggest there are 5,000–20,000 Jews out of 40 million Poles), the country now has more Jewish-themed events than many countries with much larger Jewish populations.[26]

Clearly, Holocaust memorials are never just about the Holocaust. Rather, they reflect ever-evolving relationships to the traumatic past and illustrate how posterity—in this case national posterity—mobilizes the past to serve the present. As James E. Young notes, "public memory of the Holocaust . . . is never shaped in a vacuum, its motives never pure."[27] These museums and memorials use architecture, exhibit contents, and even emerging digital technologies to articulate missions that go well beyond objectively commemorating the Holocaust. As technology evolves, for instance, and actual physical sites play a smaller role in the Holocaust memorial experience, American Holocaust memorials are, like Yad Vashem, racing to keep up with the times: the USHMM has a presence in the virtual world Second Life, where participants can visit an exhibit on *Kristallnacht*, and the University of Southern California is turning interviews with survivors into interactive holograms for use in museums. Even as Holocaust memory continues to evolve in the United States, some argue that the Holocaust has taken over Jewish life, which could be better served by a focus on other issues, such as declining religious observance.[28] But the persistent popularity of the USHMM suggests that the Holocaust remains an important part of American self-identification, for Jews and for other Americans.

Binjamin Wilkomirski, author of Fragments: Memories of a Wartime Childhood *is pictured in Zürich on September 15, 1999 holding an artistic depiction of World War II. Wilkomirski proclaimed himself to be a Latvian Jew who survived the Holocaust but his assertions fell apart under closer scrutiny.*

Getty Images

13

Fragments: Memories of a Wartime Childhood (fiction, 1996):

What Does it Mean to Lie About the Holocaust?

In 1995, one of Germany's most prestigious publishers published Binjamin Wilkomirski's *Bruchstücke. Aus einer Kindheit 1939–1948*, a book that raised important questions about the cultural status of Holocaust survivors and the historical value of their memoirs. Translated as *Fragments: Memories of a Wartime Childhood*, Wilkomirski's book was lauded for its delicate prose, gripping testimony, and what appeared to be its profound insights into the experience of a childhood Holocaust survivor. *Fragments* became an international literary sensation. In a slew of overwhelmingly positive reviews in both the popular press and academic journals, it drew comparisons to Elie Wiesel's *Night* (see Chapter 5), Anne Frank's *The Diary of a Young Girl* (see Chapter 4), and Primo Levi's *Survival in Auschwitz*.[1] A reviewer for *The New York Times* praised it for being written "with a poet's vision; a child's state of grace,"[2] while Jonathan Kozol gushed in *The Nation* that "This stunning and austerely written work is so profoundly moving, so morally important and so free from literary artifice of any kind at all that I wondered if I even had the right to try to offer praise."[3] *Fragments* won a National Jewish Book Award and the Prix Mémoire de la Shoah of the Fondation du Judaïsme Français. Soon, however, doubts emerged about many of the book's claims, and eventually *Fragments* was debunked as a fake.

Though many have dismissed the scandal as an ordinary literary fraud, it nevertheless serves as a teachable moment for the study of Holocaust representation. "The Wilkomirski Affair," as it is known, highlights the interpretive challenge that survivor memoirs pose with regard to historical truths. While readers generally approach first-hand accounts of the Holocaust as authentic records of individual experience, the Wilkomirski Affair cautions us against such a naïve understanding of memory, reminding us that all memories involve interpretations. Wilkomirski's rise and fall exposed what we might call the scripts according to which survivor memoirs are constructed. Audiences have developed specific expectations about the content of Holocaust memoirs, appropriate public responses to them, and the cultural status and moral authority of their authors. The Wilkomirski Affair revealed that the explosion in the number of Holocaust memoirs was not simply a proliferation of memories of a set of historic events, but a symptom of an age that valorizes victimhood and embraces public confessions of victimization in autobiographies, talk shows, and reality television.

Fragments details an adult's memories of an early childhood shattered by the Holocaust. Wilkomirski tells of losing his family, a sojourn in the Riga Ghetto in Latvia, escaping from the Nazis on a boat, hiding on a Polish farm, incarceration in Auschwitz and Majdanek, a postwar stint in a Kraków orphanage, his flight to Switzerland, and adoption by a childless Swiss couple who switched his identity with that of a Christian orphan. The short, episodic chapters are written in a simple, vivid style that reproduces the perspective of a traumatized child. As one critic puts it, the book is structured "according to the logics of trauma, made up of fragmentary half-digested images barely sewn together, bound only by an undergirding sense that hostile, impersonal forces . . . had swept the narrator along during his most vulnerable years."[4] *Fragments* also shows how trauma persists when the author revisits his past. "My earliest memories," he writes in the opening chapter, "are a rubble field of isolated images and events. Shards of memory with hard knife-sharp edges, which still cut flesh if touched today. Mostly a chaotic jumble, with very little chronological fit; shards that keep surfacing against the orderly grain of grown-up life and escaping the flaws of logic."[5] Despite its narrative gaps, or perhaps because of them, *Fragments* is powerfully gripping. By including the scenes and characters that readers have come to expect from survivor testimonies—episodes of Nazi cruelty, deportation in rail cars, loss of family, horrendous conditions in concentration camps, characters who commit unthinkable crimes or generous acts of kindness—it allows readers to fill in the holes with their own imaginations.

Fragments concludes with Wilkomirski noting that he "wrote these fragments of memory with the hope that perhaps other people in the same situation would find the necessary support and strength to cry out their own traumatic childhood memories, so that they too could learn that there really are people today who will take them seriously, and who want to listen and to understand."[6] Indeed, as a survivor, Wilkomirski became an inspirational figure for other people who survived the Holocaust as children. Survivors have acquired significant moral authority since they first took the stand at the trial of Adolf Eichmann, sharing the details of their Holocaust ordeals (see Chapter 6). In critic Anne Rothe's account, the Holocaust survivor became a contemporary alternative to classic notions of heroism. "While the heroes of old altruistically risked their own lives to save another's," Rothe writes, the modern-day antihero seeks simply to survive.[7] As an apparent Holocaust survivor, Binjamin Wilkomirski was accorded significant moral authority. He lectured widely, participated in academic conferences, and even went on a fundraising tour for the United States Holocaust Memorial Museum. His book inspired other Holocaust survivors to go public with their own stories and empowered victims of other childhood traumas to come forward and confront their pain. Then, almost as dramatically as his star had risen, Wilkomirski found himself embroiled in serious controversy.

The Wilkomirski Affair

On August 27, 1998, Swiss journalist and novelist Daniel Ganzfried leveled serious charges against Wilkomirski in the magazine *Die Weltwoche*. Ganzfried claimed that *Fragments* was a work of fiction and "Binjamin Wilkomirski" was the pseudonym of Bruno Grosjean, an illegitimate child born in 1941 in Switzerland to a factory worker named Yvonne Grosjean, whose mental and physical illnesses left her unable to care for him. After an early childhood filled with neglect and abuse by parents and foster parents, the boy was adopted in 1945 by a well-off Zürich couple, Kurt and Martha Dössekker. According to Ganzfried, "Binjamin Wilkomirski, alias Bruno Dössekker . . . knows Auschwitz and Majdanek only as a tourist."[8]

Ganzfried's stunning allegations ignited a firestorm of controversy that soon spread beyond Switzerland. Because Holocaust survivors command such moral authority, Wilkomirski's publishers had dismissed early concerns about *Fragments*, some expressed even before the book's publication. But it became impossible to ignore important Holocaust scholars such as Raul Hilberg and Yehuda Bauer, as they shared their longstanding doubts about Wilkomirski's veracity. According to Hilberg, the story told in *Fragments*, "hovers between the highly unlikely and the utterly impossible" because many of its historical details contradict verified chronologies.[9] In one passage, Wilkomirski claimed to have seen a tank at a time when there were no German tanks in Latvia.[10] In another, he remembered someone shouting "Watch it: Latvian militia!" but Latvian collaborators were called "auxiliary police," not militia.[11]

In the face of such charges, Wilkomirski retreated to a position of victimhood, pointing out that he was a traumatized Holocaust survivor who could not be expected to know every detail perfectly. Moreover, he indignantly protested, he should not be subjected to such attacks, given all he had endured, and he continued to adamantly insist that his story was true. The afterword of *Fragments*, added to address early doubts, supported his case, by emphasizing that he was one of many "children without identity" who lacked information about his past given its chaos. When critics argued that his birth date of February 12, 1941 made many details in *Fragments* impossible, Wilkomirski pointed to his adoption, saying that "As a child, I also received new identity, another name, another date and place of birth" and adding "this date has nothing to do with either the history of this century or my personal history."[12]

As the controversy broadened, a number of Holocaust survivors came to Wilkomirski's defense, recognizing similarities in their life stories and sympathizing with his traumatic tale. One man even recognized Wilkomirski as his own son, although DNA testing soon disproved this claim. Some survivors sought to mobilize scholars in Wilkomirski's support. Holocaust testimony expert Lawrence Langer recalls receiving a letter from a child survivor requesting that he intervene in the situation on the behalf of all children who, like her, had survived the Holocaust but later learned their Jewish parents had been murdered. According to Langer, such survivors worried that, "suspicions about Wilkomirski's honesty might threaten their own fragile identities."[13]

To settle the matter definitively, the publishers of *Fragments* asked Swiss historian Stefan Maechler to verify Wilkomirski's authenticity.[14] Maechler received unrestricted access to documents and correspondence and conducted numerous interviews, including with Wilkomirski himself. In his final report, released in 2000 in Switzerland and published in English in 2001 as *The Wilkomirski Affair: A Study in Biographical Truth*, Maechler stated that, "the elements of Wilkomirski's story are full of contradictions both in their particulars and in regard to historical reality" and "incompatible with his own biographical reality." The report presented evidence that in 1981 Wilkomirski had contested the will of Yvonne Grosjean and even referred to her in writing as "my birth mother."[15] Maechler concluded that "the story he wrote in *Fragments* and has told elsewhere took place solely within the world of his thoughts and emotions."[16]

By early 1999, knowledge of the accusations had spread. Journalists around the world publicly questioned Wilkomirski's story. In February 1999, the American television news magazine *60 Minutes* reported critically on the case, and in June that same year, *The New Yorker* published an unflattering article about Wilkomirski, tellingly headlined "The Memory Thief." In October

1999, Suhrkamp, the German publisher of *Fragments*, decided to withdraw the book from bookstores based on a draft of Maechler's report. In November 1999, Schocken, the American publisher, followed suit.[17]

Even as publishers, historians, and the popular media lost faith in *Fragments*, the American Orthopsychiatric Association (ORTHO) decided in April 1999 to cast its lot with Wilkomirski, awarding him its Max Hayman Award for "distinguished scholarship in the mental health disciplines that contributes to the elimination of genocide and the remembrance of the Holocaust." Orthopsychiatry is the study, prevention, and treatment of emotional and behavioral problems, especially among children. Apparently untroubled by either the factual inconsistencies surrounding Wilkomirski's personal history or Wilkomirski's refusal to submit to DNA testing, ORTHO saw his insistence on the truth of his story in the face of harsh public criticism as an example of courage. They believed he was standing up for all child survivors whose traumas had no witnesses and who suffer from not being believed.[18] Wilkomirski had been a victim, the award implied, and now he was being victimized again in the court of public opinion.

Holocaust memory and the era of the witness

The Wilkomirski Affair left many questions unanswered, foremost among them whether Grosjean-Dössekker-Wilkomirski was a con man, who knowingly and systematically lied, or if he genuinely believed his own story. While the former is possible, the latter seems more likely. Because *Fragments* straddles the boundary between fiction and authentic memoir, one critic has classified it separately, as an example of a "deluded or false memoir."[19] Maechler never explicitly labeled Wilkomirski a fraud, but his report concluded that "the evolution of Wilkomirski's story displays many features typical of invented or false memory."[20] False memory—in which, usually with the help of a therapist, a person retrieves and comes to believe in traumatic memories that never actually happened—received significant media attention in the United States in the 1990s, due to lurid cases in which children reported ritual sacrifices by devil worshippers, as well as an epidemic-level number of cases of reported childhood sexual abuse, many of which turned out not to have happened.

False memory often follows distinct cultural trends, and for Wilkomirski, the trend was the Holocaust. Throughout his adulthood and well before he published *Fragments*, he surrounded himself with therapists, Holocaust survivors, and other enablers who helped him make sense of his own traumatic early childhood of neglect and foster homes. Over the years, Wilkomirski's story continually evolved. He renamed himself, for instance, after the famous Polish violinist Wanda Wilkomirska, whom he saw in concert in 1972 and believed he resembled. As the people, places, and events of the Holocaust became well-known during the Holocaust memory boom of the 1980s and 1990s, it became the conceptual scaffold upon which he fastened his own newly rediscovered memories.

Two figures who especially encouraged Wilkomirski to identify with Eastern Europeans and Holocaust victims were Elitsur Bernstein, an Israeli psychotherapist living in Switzerland, and Laura Grabowski, another supposed child survivor. Wilkomirski and Bernstein met when Bernstein approached Wilkomirski for music lessons in the late 1970s. Over the course of their friendship, Bernstein encouraged Wilkomirski to write down his nightmares and was the first reader of what eventually became *Fragments*.[21] Bernstein rejected accusations that he implanted false memories, but he nevertheless played a significant role in encouraging Wilkomirski to expand his story. Laura Grabowski claimed to know Wilkomirski from Auschwitz, and he turned to her to corroborate his claims. She lost all credibility, however, when investigators discovered that, before switching traumas to the Holocaust, she had published, as Lauren Stratford, *Satan's Underground: The Extraordinary Story of One Woman's Escape*, a memoir of her victimization by devil worshipers. The roles of Elitsur Bernstein and "Laura Grabowski" dramatically demonstrate how memory is not just a private recovery of experience, but has a profoundly social dimension. External influences in the present can significantly condition how we remember and interpret the past.

An audience hungry for stories of the Holocaust and opportunities to identify with its victims no doubt contributed to Wilkomirski's fabrication. The publication of *Fragments* coincided with a period of intense and systematic efforts to establish archives of Holocaust testimonies. Beginning in the late 1970s, Yale University's Fortunoff Video Archive for Holocaust Testimonies began to assemble and catalogue survivor testimonies; in 1995, it received a major grant from Steven Spielberg to expand its efforts to record the stories of elderly survivors before they died (Spielberg and his Shoah Foundation have actively supported diverse efforts to create testimony archives). Today various universities and institutes in the United States and Israel, including Yad Vashem, the Hebrew University, the USHMM, Yale, and the University of Southern California feature extensive collections of survivor testimonies. During this "era of the witness," to use French historian Annette Wieviorka's term, "feelings and psychological problems began to be exhibited publicly."[22] Radio, television, video, and, soon, the Internet, contributed to the development of a culture in which ordinary people could share their experiences of trauma to voyeuristic audiences hungry for authentic stories of catastrophe.

The initial hesitancy to confront Wilkomirski showed how the Holocaust survivor had acquired significant moral authority in a public culture that validates and celebrates confessions of the victimized, often in an emotionally charged atmosphere. Wilkomirski cultivated both this sense of moral authority and its emotional resonance, sometimes even accompanying actors who read passages from his book with sentimental Eastern European clarinet melodies. The scandal around *Fragments* revealed the dangers in approaching Holocaust history primarily through survivor memoirs. Expressing his frustration with the valorizing of Holocaust survivors and the adopting of uncritical positions of reverence towards them, Raul Hilberg criticized the notion that "any survivor, no matter how inarticulate, is superior to the greatest Holocaust historian who did not share in the experience."[23] The Wilkomirski Affair underscores the need to corroborate personal testimonies with theoretically informed, dispassionate research.

The Wilkomirski Affair and the abuse of memory

For all of the controversy it generated, *Fragments* was neither the first example of a Holocaust fraud nor the last. Around the same time as the Wilkomirski Affair, scholars discredited Belgian author Misha Defonseca's *Misha: A Mémoire of the Holocaust Years* as invented. Decades earlier, Polish author Jerzy Kosiński published *The Painted Bird* (1965), which the American newspaper *The Village Voice* revealed in 1982 was possibly plagiarized or written by Kosiński's editors. More recently, in his 2008 Holocaust romance *Angel at the Fence: The True Story of a Love that Survived*, Holocaust survivor Herman Rosenblat initially claimed to have first met his future wife when she passed him food through the fence during his incarceration at Buchenwald, only to say later that it wasn't true. Still, it is important to recognize that these and other Holocaust frauds are exceptions.

To those who believe the memory of the Holocaust has been over-commercialized in books, movies, museums, and monuments, Wilkomirski was an accident waiting to happen. Phillip Gourevitch, one of the journalists who discredited Wilkomirski, lamented, "I am more fearful for and depressed by the culture that received him as an apostle of memory than I am for the man himself, whoever he thinks he is."[24] Clearly, the ubiquity of Holocaust memory left audiences gullible to deceptions like Wilkomirski's. Yet it may still be possible to draw a positive conclusion from the scandal. With many genocides, the will to remember has never been strong enough to generate sufficient testimonies to enable a full-scale deception like Wilkomirski's. There are no heavily publicized false memoirs of the 1915 Armenian genocide or the 1994 genocide in Rwanda. It was only possible for Wilkomirski to write *Fragments* because of the thousands of real survivor accounts and testimonies that exist. The people, places, objects, and events in those memoirs have become so familiar that they can be imitated and still seem true to the uncritical eye. But such frauds are not proof of the failure to remember. If anything they are about remembering too much.

PART FOUR

The 2000s and Beyond

This October 2012 image shows a World War II-era rail car of the type used to transport prisoners to concentration camps. It is the centerpiece of the Children's Holocaust Memorial in Whitwell, Tennessee. It houses 11 million paper clips, one for each victim of the Holocaust, which Whitwell students collected for a project to learn about tolerance and diversity.

Daniel H. Magilow

14

The Children's Holocaust Memorial (memorial, 2001):

How is the Holocaust Used to Teach About Diversity?

A rural community, Whitwell, Tennessee is one of the last places one might expect to find a Holocaust memorial. Like many small towns in the American South, its roughly 1,700 inhabitants are overwhelmingly white, evangelical Protestants. No Jews live there and the town has no historical connection to the Holocaust. But since 2001, Whitwell Middle School has hosted the Children's Holocaust Memorial, a representation of the Holocaust that first attracted attention for its unorthodox form. The memorial consists of 11 million paper clips, one for each victim of Nazi Germany, which Whitwell students collected for a project aiming to teach about tolerance and diversity. The paper clips are displayed in a rail car once used to transport victims to death camps.

Although it has faded into relative obscurity in recent years, the Whitwell paper clip project received international media coverage in the late 1990s and early 2000s. People sent paper clips and letters of encouragement from around the world; donors included presidents, actors, athletes, and celebrities. The undertaking drew praise from Jewish community leaders and political figures, including First Lady Laura Bush, and it inspired two children's books, the 2004 documentary *Paper Clips*, and similar collecting memorials. Organizations like the Anti-Defamation League frequently recommend the Children's Holocaust Memorial and the *Paper Clips* documentary for middle- and high school curriculum units about tolerance and diversity. On June 28, 2001, New York Congressman Benjamin A. Gilman even commended the Whitwell project in the House of Representatives and invited his colleagues, "to help the Whitwell Middle School realize their noble goal, and in the process, spread their vital message of tolerance and compassion and to remember this devastating, inhumane chapter of world history."[1] Yet the Children's Holocaust Memorial still draws praise today for its novel approach. On January 25, 2014, *The New York Times* indirectly praised it when describing *And Every Single One Was Someone*, a new book consisting only of the word "Jew" repeated six million times. The *Times* emphasized that this book—really an art project—by the Orthodox Jewish educator Phil Chernofsky was not entirely original because "more than a decade ago eighth graders in a small Tennessee town set out to collect six million paper clips, as chronicled in a 2004 documentary."[2] Like the Whitwell project, Chernofsky's book attempted to make comprehensive the overwhelming statistic that 6,000,000 Jews died in the Holocaust.

But the Children's Holocaust Memorial has also had its fair share of critics. Some questioned why Whitwell students didn't focus instead on local histories of intolerance. Others pointed to the problematic myths that underlie the choice of paper clips, the trivializing effects of that choice, and what they consider the offensive use of powerful Nazi and Jewish symbols without proper context. Still, now-retired Whitwell Middle School Principal Linda Hooper repeatedly emphasized the project's tremendous value for students, teachers, and staff, noting that "the Paper Clip project has allowed our students, staff, and community to forcefully confront our own prejudices."[3]

When the project first developed, many also dismissed the Children's Holocaust Memorial as Holocaust kitsch. Yet we cannot deny that this amateur, local memorial resonated with wider audiences. For better or worse, the debates it incited about contemporary Holocaust representations oriented toward children extend far beyond Whitwell and continue to influence Holocaust memorials. With its use of ubiquitous Holocaust symbols, such as Anne Frank, cattle cars, and swastikas, the Whitwell memorial exemplifies the popular tendency, especially prevalent in Holocaust education, to interpret the genocide through a series of well-known icons that create a redemptive moral narrative about the dangers of bigotry and intolerance. Its establishment in 2001 also reveals how popular Holocaust memory in the United States developed during the spike in interest that followed the 1993 opening of the United States Holocaust Memorial Museum and the success of Steven Spielberg's *Schindler's List* that same year. Yet ultimately, the debates around the Children's Holocaust Memorial and other projects like it invite questions that remain open: who owns the history of the Holocaust and who can decide how best to represent it? To what extent is it acceptable for projects by and/or for children to simplify history if their goal is to educate tomorrow's citizens to be tolerant of difference? How much simplification is acceptable, especially when, as some scholars have argued, the moral obligation for historical accuracy is greater than usual for Holocaust representations that target juvenile audiences?[4] To address such questions, it is useful to examine the origins and development of the Children's Holocaust Memorial and then to examine the objections to it in greater detail.

The project's origins

The defining characteristic of the Children's Holocaust Memorial is that it was created out of a collection of paper clips. To understand this curious choice of material, we must return to its origins in a class project. In 1998, Whitwell Middle School teacher David Smith attended a regional conference on youth enrichment programs. Inspired by a presentation about the Holocaust, Smith and colleague Sandy Roberts set out "to develop a program that teaches tolerance for students who grow up in a homogeneous society and then leave for college," noting that "Many of these students return to the area after graduating from high school because they can't deal with the diversity in the bigger world."[5] They chose the Holocaust as their focus so that, as the children's book *Six Million Paper Clips: The Making of a Children's Holocaust Memorial* puts it, the project would "demonstrate what intolerance is and what it can lead to."[6] The project developed over several years, with the support of parents and the school principal. Each year, new classes learned about the history of the Holocaust, but rather than just looking at the specific politics, ethnic conflicts, and regional history of mid-twentieth century Europe, they learned about the genocide as a worst case scenario for the evils of prejudice, an educational strategy that dates back to the popularity of Anne Frank in the 1950s (see Chapter 4).

The paper clip memorial emerged out of student efforts to comprehend the overwhelming statistic that 6,000,000 Jews died in the Holocaust. In the documentary *Paper Clips*, one student explains how the idea to collect 6,000,000 paper clips came from a website, where they learned that Norwegians wore paper clips on their lapels and shirt pockets during World War II, as a sign of resistance to German occupation and anti-Semitism (this account was in fact inaccurate, as discussed below). Duly inspired, the Whitwell students began to collect paper clips, which they originally intended to have melted down into the raw material for a memorial, possibly a stop sign in which a paper clip would diagonally block out a swastika, in the manner of a No Smoking sign. This idea proved infeasible, given that different kinds of paper clips are made of different materials. Ultimately, the students decided just to collect 6,000,000 paper clips, with no clear plan for what to do with them, at least at first.

As news about the Whitwell project spread, two Washington, DC-based German journalists, Peter Schroeder and Dagmar Schroeder-Hildebrand, became its advocates. They met with the teachers in Whitwell and publicized the undertaking through their media contacts. As a result of this publicity, thousands of letters and, ultimately, millions of paper clips came to Whitwell from around the world, although mainly from the United States and Germany. Heartfelt letters of support accompanied paper clips offered to commemorate specific victims. In the end, Whitwell far surpassed its goal, receiving approximately 30 million paper clips, leaving teachers and students to decide what to do with them. Inspired by their experience in an authentic World War II-era cattle car at the United States Holocaust Memorial Museum, Dagmar Schroeder-Hildebrand and Linda Hooper decided to recreate that experience in Whitwell. The Schroeders began searching for a cattle car and eventually found one near Chełmno, Poland, the former site of a death camp. They had it shipped to Whitwell in the autumn of 2001. On November 9, 2001, the 63rd anniversary of *Kristallnacht*, the Children's Holocaust Memorial was officially dedicated. Local dignitaries spoke and a Hebrew school class from Atlanta recited *kaddish*, the Jewish mourner's prayer.

In its final form, the Children's Holocaust Memorial—like many youth-oriented Holocaust projects—brings together a diverse set of references and objects related to the Holocaust, Judaism, and American popular culture. The memorial's centerpiece, the rail car, has two display areas behind protective glass, with a small viewing area in between them. The display areas house 11 million paper clips along with letters and other memorial objects sent to Whitwell. Many of the memorial objects are clearly created by and/or meant for children, including a suitcase with letters of apology to Anne Frank and a Scrabble board with words about the project like Jews, Holocaust, tolerance, and compassion. Others include a *kippah* (skullcap), a dollar bill folded into a Star of David, and a baseball cap with the phrase "You had me at Shalom" in mock-Hebrew script. The threshold of the train car features a *mezuzah*, the ceremonial parchment placed on the doorframe of Jewish homes.

Reinforced to support the weight of millions of small pieces of metal and plastic, the rail car sits on a small set of train tracks in a gravel field next to the school. The field is decorated with another key motif of the memorial: mosaic tiles of butterflies. Numbering eighteen because eighteen in Hebrew numerology signifies *chai* (life), these butterflies refer a poem by Pavel Friedman, a young Czechoslovak Jew who was sent to the Theresienstadt concentration camp in April 1942. There he composed "The Butterfly," a short poem about his longing for natural beauty while "Penned up inside this ghetto," that ends with the lines:

Only I never saw another butterfly.
That butterfly was the last one.
Butterflies don't live in here,
in the ghetto.

The poem's brevity and clear symbolism have made it a staple of American Holocaust education, but the Children's Holocaust Memorial takes the butterfly symbolism a step further, interpreting it as an act of interfaith dialogue between Christians and Jews. In the words of the memorial's website, butterflies are "the Christian symbol of renewal and the Children of [the concentration camp] Terezine [sic]."[7] A plaque on the gravel field adapts the famous quotation by cultural anthropologist Margaret Mead, "Never doubt that a small group of thoughtful, committed citizens can change the world. Indeed, it is the only thing that ever has." The Whitwell plaque states, "Never Doubt that a group of thoughtful, committed students can: 'CHANGE THE WORLD—ONE CLASS AT A TIME.' " A few feet away, inside Whitwell Middle School, a resource room houses a library of Holocaust books and dozens of binders containing the letters that accompanied the paper clips donated to the project. It also houses a few binders of hate mail from white supremacists and Holocaust deniers with, among other things, paper clips bent into the shape of swastikas.

Criticisms of the project

The creators of the Children's Holocaust Memorial developed it with laudable intentions: as an educational opportunity for children, a memorial to the Holocaust victims, a gesture of interfaith reconciliation, and, more broadly, as proof that people far removed from centers of power and commerce can contribute to public discourse in meaningful ways. The director of the Anti-Defamation League, Abraham Foxman, had a copy of *Paper Clips* sent to President George W. Bush and praised the film for showing "how the Holocaust can be relevant today, even in middle-America" and for becoming "a catalyst to teach others about the lessons of the Holocaust."[8] To such supporters, the Children's Holocaust Memorial was a resounding success.

To its critics, however, the project failed to fulfill these noble intentions, and their lines of criticism reveal powerful unspoken protocols for how the memory of the Holocaust should be represented in public. One argument is that the Holocaust is inappropriate subject matter for teaching tolerance in the American South, which has its own histories of racial intolerance. Another is that the memorial's defining motif, the paper clip, in fact lacks the very historical connections to the Holocaust used to justify its use and instead carries much more ominous overtones. Finally, some critics argue that the memorial's use of Nazi and Jewish symbols is insensitive and that rather than honoring Holocaust victims, it instead reflects the project's fascination and over-identification with them. These concerns imply that there are proper rules of engagement for Holocaust memory—the who, what, where, and how—that can easily be violated when individuals fail to properly contextualize the event. Given that the Children's Holocaust Memorial originated as an educational project, one understandable response to these criticisms is to point out that it was a project for children. But this response also raises the question of what kind of leeway we provide for the sake of educating the young.

The after-school program at Whitwell Middle School that culminated in the Children's Holocaust Memorial was in many ways typical of Holocaust education programs for children in the United States. For the sake of tolerance education, these programs often focus on a handful of iconic figures, images, and places, such as Anne Frank, cattle cars, and Auschwitz. Rather than seeking to understand what motivated the perpetrators, they center on the experiences of Jewish victims, using identification with innocent victims as an educational strategy.[9] Although the Holocaust is a powerful example, critics allege that American history offers many instances of intolerance that the students at Whitwell could have studied, including some in which their families and neighbors might have been implicated as perpetrators. They could, for instance, have created memorials to honor local victims of intolerance: the Ku Klux Klan was founded in 1865 in nearby Pulaski, Tennessee, and in the 1830s, the U.S. Government expelled indigenous Cherokee. Studying more recent episodes of local racial intolerance might have led the students to the stories of Rosa Parks refusing to give her up bus seat to a white passenger in Montgomery, Alabama, lunch counter boycotts in North Carolina, or even to Byron De La Beckwith, the white supremacist who assassinated civil rights leader Medgar Evers in 1963 and who until his 2001 death lived in Signal Mountain, Tennessee, just 20 miles from Whitwell. One uncomfortable explanation for the Whitwell students' Holocaust focus choice may have been that studying the history of American intolerance in the Jim Crow South would have been too close to home for a politically conservative small town. Studying the Holocaust gave Whitwell and its students a comfortable, low risk way to talk about intolerance without having to consider their own possible commonalities with Germans and their collaborators in the 1930s and 1940s. But this approach was not unique to Whitwell's program. To the contrary, it exemplifies how Holocaust education programs can allow many Americans to avoid potentially painful self-reflection.

The memorial's lack of historical rigor, particularly in the matter of paper clips, has been another concern. During World War II, some nationalistic Norwegians did wear paper clips (*binders* in Norwegian) to symbolize standing together during a time of national crisis. They chose the paper clip because Norwegians consider it a Norwegian invention, though in point of fact, Norwegian Johan Vaaler only invented a particular paper clip design.[10] Still, wearing a paper clip for Norway did not necessarily translate into support for persecuted Norwegian Jews. When Germany invaded in April 1940, Norway's Jewish population was tiny, totaling about 1,700 (including 200 refugees from Austria and Germany), essentially the same size as Whitwell; it would not have registered as significant for most Norwegians. Though some paper clip-wearing Norwegians may have opposed anti-Semitism, the vast majority wore the symbol to protest their country's loss of sovereignty and demonstrate loyalty to the exiled King Haakon VII and his government-in-exile in London.[11] Thus, the Whitwell students falsely equated symbolic Norwegian resistance to German occupation as support for persecuted Jews, reducing historical complexity to a simple binary of bad Germans and Nazis and their good—and united—enemies.

A related historical problem concerns the failure of the Whitwell students and teachers to grasp—or acknowledge—the ominous echoes of their Paper Clip Project. "Operation Paperclip" was a top secret U.S. government program that whitewashed the political histories of Nazi scientists after World War II. This cover-up allowed the United States, rather than its archrival the Soviet Union, to benefit from these scientists' technological know-how at the height of the Cold War. Established by the Office of Strategic Services, the forerunner to the Central Intelligence Agency, the program violated official U.S. government policy against recruiting German scientists who had belonged to the Nazi party or actively supported the German war effort. The name "Operation Paperclip" derived from the paper clips used to attach sanitized biographies to the scientists' official American personnel files. In this case, paper clips symbolized ignoring crimes in the name of political expediency. Thus, albeit unintentionally, the Whitwell "Paper Clip Project" referenced an unseemly chapter in the aftermath of World War II and the Holocaust when, far from condemning Nazism, the American government engaged in a cover-up and welcomed Nazis into the United States. At no place in the Children's Holocaust Memorial is this historical affinity even acknowledged.

The third line of criticism about the memorial concerns its casual, even offensive, use of powerful symbols. As we have seen, the project assembles well-known Holocaust tropes, including butterflies, a cattle car, Anne Frank, and Stars of David, alongside the millions of paper clips. Critics such as rabbi and columnist Marc Gellman denounced the use of paper clips for essentially equating human lives with disposable office supplies, thereby trivializing the Holocaust and dehumanizing its victims, an act that historians argue served as the first step on the path to genocide.[12] Rather than represent victims' lives as rich, complex, and indispensable, the memorial turns each life into an identical, disposable piece of metal. Furthermore, the association of paper clips with office work alludes to, but hardly repudiates, the Holocaust's profoundly bureaucratic character. As Hannah Arendt argued (see Chapter 6), the genocide happened at such a large scale in good part because of the efforts of bureaucrats like Adolf Eichmann who managed its logistics.

Perhaps the most serious criticism of the Whitwell project was that, as it gained attention and paper clips began pouring in, it lost sight of its goal and became more about Whitwell than the Holocaust. In his review of the documentary *Paper Clips*, film critic A.O. Scott recorded his uneasiness with the sense of accomplishment displayed in the documentary:

> I found myself bothered by the sense of self-congratulation that radiated through the film, and that seemed to tug against the gravity of the historical cataclysm that the students were meant to be studying. The dedication ceremony at the Whitwell memorial, which includes a German railway car once used to transport people to the death camps, is touching, but also a little strange. It testifies not only to the hard work and high-mindedness of the people of Whitwell, but also to the stubbornly affirmative character of American educational culture, which can turn even the most unfathomable horrors of history into a reason for people to feel good about themselves.[13]

Scott's critique gets to the heart of the concerns about the Whitwell project and teaching the Holocaust to schoolchildren. To what extent has the Children's Holocaust Memorial been celebrated as a project that effectively commemorates the victims of the Holocaust, and to what extent has it garnered so much attention because it was made in rural Tennessee by schoolchildren? Some scholars, such as Lawrence Langer, have argued persuasively about the dangers of searching for meaning in and putting redemptive endings on Holocaust testimonies and representations.[14] Is it ever permissible for the Holocaust to become a feel-good redemption story?

The criteria for success

In spite of the criticism that has been leveled at it, the Children's Holocaust Memorial still commands attention and the praise of respected adult voices, including the Anti-Defamation League, Elie Wiesel, and even the United States House of Representatives. Recognizing that the teachers and students at Whitwell undertook their project with the sincerest of intentions and that it raised awareness in ways other Holocaust education efforts could not, they have been willing to overlook its historical errors and inadvertent insensitivities. Certainly the project's goals—to raise awareness and promote diversity—fundamentally resembled those of Holocaust education programs in schools, colleges, and local communities across the United States. What made the Whitwell project a worldwide—and controversial—phenomenon was a unique confluence of factors: the fact this small town would produce a Holocaust memorial at all, the memorial's use of millions of paper clips as its material, and the vocal advocacy of two professional journalists who could direct attention to the project.

The project's most immediate legacy—and an argument in its favor that it has helped raise awareness—is the number of other collecting projects it has inspired, including the Peoria Holocaust Memorial Project's collection of six million buttons, the Holocaust Museum Houston's 1.5 million paper butterflies, and Project6Million, which seeks to collect six million statements about tolerance, memory, and diversity. Several projects aim to collect six million pennies for charity, a curious choice given the notorious anti-Semitic stereotype of Jews as miserly penny pinchers.[15] While the criticisms of the Children's Holocaust Memorial and other such projects are significant, many people still recognize them as positive gestures toward teaching children to appreciate diversity. The impetus to somehow make tangible the horrific enormity of the murder of six million Jews continues to preoccupy Americans and others interested in teaching children about the Holocaust. Ultimately, however, one must ask if well-intended but historically flawed efforts to represent and commemorate the Holocaust actually do what they intend, and even if they do not, whether they are nevertheless more valuable than no attempts at all. We may not know the answer until the children who collect paper clips, butterflies, and pennies become adult citizens facing the everyday demands for tolerance in a multicultural society.

LEGO Concentration Camp, *by artist Zbigniew Libera, is displayed as part of the* Mirroring Evil: Nazi Imagery/Recent Art *exhibit at the Jewish Museum in New York City. The exhibit attracted controversy from critics who saw it as insensitive to Holocaust victims, while supporters argued that the artworks drew needed attention to the commercialization of the Holocaust.*

Mario Tama/Getty Images

15

Mirroring Evil: Nazi Imagery/ Recent Art (museum exhibition, 2002):

Has the Memory of the Holocaust Become Too Commercial?

On September 9, 2001, *The New York Times* published a preview of the season's upcoming cultural events. Among the descriptions of new museum and gallery shows was a listing for *Mirroring Evil: Nazi Imagery/ Recent Art*, scheduled to run from March 17 to June 30, 2002, at New York's Jewish Museum. Its one-sentence blurb read: "While much art about the Holocaust centers on its victims, the 13 contemporary artists in the exhibition use images associated with its perpetrators to explore the nature of evil."[1] *Mirroring Evil* was a group show of 13 artists from eight different countries. Some of them were Jewish, and all were born after the Holocaust ended. Their 19 images, sculptures, and video installations criticized popular Holocaust representations for their widespread commercialization and tendency to fall back on clichés and iconic photographs rather than engage the genocide in all its historical and moral complexity. They also challenged the ways those representations invite people to create simplistic dichotomies of good and evil, easily identify with victims, and thereby imagine that they have nothing in common with perpetrators. By contrast, as described by curator Norman L. Kleeblatt, the artists in the show "created works in which viewers would encounter the perpetrators face to face in scenarios in which ethical and moral issues cannot be easily resolved."[2]

Shows at New York's Jewish Museum do not usually receive national attention. But scarcely 48 hours after the listing for *Mirroring Evil* appeared in *The New York Times*, hijackers flew airplanes into the World Trade Center, and evil suddenly moved to the forefront of public attention. Responding that evening to the day's traumatic events, President George W. Bush announced that "Today, our nation saw evil." A few months later, in early 2002, he used his State of the Union Address to denounce Iran, Iraq, and North Korea as an "Axis of Evil." In this radically changed cultural context, *Mirroring Evil* erupted into a full-blown scandal, as the national media got wind of the intentionally provocative, ironic, and offensive nature of its artworks, which relied heavily on Nazi imagery and references. Among the more eyebrow-raising pieces were a set of poison gas canisters emblazoned with Tiffany, Chanel, and Prada logos, boxes for an imaginary *LEGO Concentration Camp*, and a digitally manipulated photograph that placed its artist in an iconic Holocaust photograph holding a can of Diet Coke. Defending these confrontational artworks, the Jewish Museum's Director Joan Rosenbaum underscored the show's radically different approach to Holocaust representation, explaining that instead of offering up pathos-laden images of victims for viewers to identify with, its artists all "dare to invite the viewer into the world of the perpetrator."[3]

Mirroring Evil was hardly the first multi-artist show of Holocaust art. The decades after 1980 saw an outpouring of artistic representations of the Holocaust, in parallel with the proliferation of Holocaust books and films. Yet artworks remained less visible than these other media because they could only be seen in exhibition spaces, museums, and galleries, often for a limited amount of time.[4] While some of this art challenged the written and unwritten rules surrounding Holocaust representation, the intensely self-reflexive and provocative nature of the work showcased in *Mirroring Evil* took this challenge to another level, forcing viewers to confront their own biases and avoidance mechanisms about the Holocaust.

Although *Mirroring Evil* had been in development long before 9/11, the terrorist attacks provoked new questions about the exhibition and its underlying principles, and revived old questions with new urgency: Was it appropriate to exhibit art focused on perpetrators when Holocaust survivors were still alive? Could it ever be appropriate to exhibit that art? Was the Jewish Museum a suitable venue for the exhibition? Was the exhibition's timing inappropriate, given that New York was a newly victimized city? Or did the trauma of 9/11 make the exhibition even more relevant?[5] Many critics of *Mirroring Evil* framed their questions by drawing explicit 9/11 analogies: "Imagine if a performance artist walked over to Ground Zero and mocked those who had been burned alive and crushed to death," one wrote. "Everyone would repudiate such artistic license as being morally repulsive. How is what the Jewish Museum has done any different?"[6]

These questions clearly extended far beyond the exhibition's original mandate to challenge the commercialized nature of Holocaust representations. In the decade since the exhibition, they have continued to be raised and examined, not only through art exhibitions, but in the construction of new memorials and museums dedicated specifically to the memory of the Holocaust (see Chapters 12, 14, and 16). By revisiting the works displayed in *Mirroring Evil* and the controversy that surrounded them, this chapter delves into the important issues related to Holocaust representation that the exhibition first brought to a broad public audience. The show intentionally represented the Holocaust with obscene and offensive images in order to argue that the ways in which popular culture commercializes and trivializes the memory of the Holocaust are themselves obscene. But the negative response it received showed that it also unintentionally foregrounded questions about the implicit rules that govern the exhibition of Holocaust art, including when, if ever, it will no longer be too soon to represent the Holocaust ironically or playfully. Ultimately, *Mirroring Evil* made a plausible case for the value of Holocaust representations that go beyond factually recounting events and reverentially mourning the dead.

(Pre)Judging *Mirroring Evil*

Controversy began to envelop *Mirroring Evil: Nazi Imagery/Recent Art* months before it opened. By its opening, on March 17, 2002, as art critic Eleanor Heartney notes, "Many people had already formed an opinion about the show."[7] The exhibition catalogue had appeared already in December 2001, offering a clear overview of the show, but also fueling the controversy in advance of its opening. Published by a reputable academic press, it featured essays by art critics, curators, and scholars who provided rigorous intellectual and historical contexts for the artworks. On January 10, 2002, however, *The Wall Street Journal* took the conversation in another direction when it suggested that *Mirroring Evil* could become the next *Sensation*. *Sensation* was a 1999 exhibition at the Brooklyn Museum of Art that then-Mayor Rudolph Giuliani denounced for its inclusion of sacrilegious artworks such as Andres Serrano's *Piss Christ* (an eerily beautiful close-up photograph of a crucifix in a glass of Serrano's urine) and Chris Ofili's *The Holy Virgin Mary* (pejoratively described as the *Elephant Dung Madonna*). Giuliani threatened to revoke the museum's public funding and even evict it from its building. The episode raised many issues about controversial art, including censorship and public funding, which were widely debated. Soon after *The Wall Street Journal* article, other newspapers began reporting on the upcoming show, often offering preemptive criticism.[8] Two months before it opened, a commentator who obviously had not yet seen the artworks wrote in *The New York Daily News* that "These images will generate thousands of words and deep visceral responses. To count as art, these responses—verbal or otherwise—would have to go beyond the predictable. I doubt they will."[9]

Recognizing the sensitive nature of *Mirroring Evil*, the Jewish Museum planned the exhibition's catalogue and physical layout to make it clear that the show was designed not to trivialize the Holocaust, but rather to confront visitors with difficult but important questions about its representation. Even so, the advance protests put the museum on the defensive. In response to the media storm, curators placed an explicit disclaimer at the beginning of the exhibit, noting that some Holocaust survivors had found the show disturbing, and visitors might find some or all of the artworks offensive. An additional exit was added so visitors could leave in the middle, before they encountered the most incendiary pieces.[10]

In its final form, the exhibition's design juxtaposed two very different museum experiences. On the one hand, Reesa Greenberg points out, white walls, bright lighting, and an uncluttered installation focused on *Mirroring Evil* as art. On the other, protective devices such as the dark, empty transitional room between the Museum lobby and the exhibition, the introductory disclaimer, the carefully plotted route, and a "decompression space" at its end highlighted the show's solemn and reflective dimensions.[11] Through this hybrid exhibition design, *Mirroring Evil* thus evoked both the exploratory, playful, experimental tone of contemporary art spaces and the darker, more somber tone of commemorative historical exhibitions, such as the United States Holocaust Memorial Museum (see Chapter 12). The intent was clearly not to insult, and the Jewish Museum took pains to accommodate those who alleged the contrary.

In early 2002, as the media continued to publicize the exhibition, the storm around *Mirroring Evil* intensified. Much of the resentment arose less from objections to individual artworks, which the public had not yet seen, and more from the belief that a respected, mainstream Jewish cultural institution had no business legitimizing representations that might be perceived as devaluing the Holocaust. Brooklyn Assemblyman Dov Hikind, whose district included the heavily Orthodox Jewish neighborhood of Borough Park, even called for a boycott of the exhibition. One the loudest voices of dissent was Menachem Z. Rosensaft, a prominent New York attorney, advocate for children of Holocaust survivors, and long-time member of the United States Holocaust Memorial Council. Rosensaft objected to how the venue "gives the imprimatur of the Jewish Museum to this exhibition and . . . thereby legitimizes all future trivializations of the Holocaust by others."[12] In an op-ed in the Jewish newspaper, *The Forward*, Rosensaft supported his point with an explicit 9/11 analogy. Referring to Zbigniew Libera's *LEGO Concentration Camp* (1996) and Alain

Séchas's *Enfants Gâtés* (*Spoiled Children,* 1997), which depicted five Disney-like animals with Hitler moustaches, Rosensaft asserted that the Jewish Museum would not have been likely "to feature a LEGO model of the ravaged World Trade Center, surrounded by severed plastic heads with tiny NYPD and FDNY caps, alongside a benign 'Disney-like' depiction of Osama bin Laden."[13]

While they say there is no such thing as bad publicity, the uproar around *Mirroring Evil* did not translate into huge crowds of museum-goers. Approximately 100 yeshiva students, Holocaust survivors, and concerned community members briefly protested on opening day, chanting "Shame on you!" and "Don't go in!" to museum visitors. While these individuals denounced the show without seeing it, even critics generally receptive to experimental art responded negatively to the exhibition. Writing in *The New York Times*, art critic Michael Kimmelman described the issue as "not whether the museum can do the show, but whether it has taken minor art, elevated it to the status of significance by exhibiting it, thereby provoking an inevitable reaction, then defended its action as part of its responsibility to show significant art, even if it is offensive to some Jews."[14] One had only to read the headline of the review in *The New York Observer* to know how the reviewer felt: "Jewish Museum Show Full of Vile Crap, Not to Be Forgiven."[15]

Amid this barrage of negativity and indignation, a few critics dared to speak out in support of *Mirroring Evil*. Art historian Linda Nochlin praised the show for uniting a disparate array of artworks that, through their very diversity, rejected the notion that there was only one way to narrate the history of the Holocaust.[16] Nochlin also recognized that *Mirroring Evil* marked a generational shift in the representation of the Holocaust. Its artists grew up in the 1960s and 1970s, and, she noted, they "make clear their complete separation—temporal, spatial, ideological—from that *univers concentrationaire* [the world of the concentration camp] that is their ostensible subject."[17] Unlike older generations, these artists never experienced a world that didn't speak about the Holocaust. Rather, they came of age in a media landscape saturated with memorials, films, documentaries, plays, novels, memoirs, and other Holocaust representations. From these myriad representations, they "vicariously" experienced the traumas of the past.[18] Whereas earlier artists protested the obscenity of staying silent about the genocide, the artists in *Mirroring Evil* argued that a culture oversaturated with mass-produced, hackneyed Holocaust imagery was itself obscene. Such an environment lets posterity delude itself with the self-satisfied belief that it has mastered the past and will not repeat its errors, despite significant evidence to the contrary. The only way to draw attention to this perceived obscenity, these artists believed, was to co-opt, exaggerate, and satirize these formulaic commercialized representations. In Nochlin's words, "The horror of the Holocaust . . . has been so often iterated that it has sunk to the level of cliché. What can bring back the original shock? Reviving the corpse of feeling with a salutary slap in the face."[19]

"Duchamp is our Misfortune": *Mirroring Evil* and the avant-garde

One important response to *Mirroring Evil* was not an essay, but an editorial cartoon. Drawn by Art Spiegelman, best known for his graphic novel *Maus* (see Chapter 11), it appeared in the March 25, 2002 issue of *The New Yorker*. Spiegelman's sharply critical take on the exhibition consisted of six panels. In the first five, a skinhead with a paintbrush and paint bucket stealthily looks to see if the coast is clear and defaces a brick wall with a large red swastika. The final panel zooms out to reveal the wall as one of the artworks at the Jewish Museum. Still dressed like a thug, but now with one hand in his pocket and the other cradling a glass of wine, the skinhead has become an artist who chats about his transgressive project at an art opening. Spiegelman's cartoon echoed the argument that *Mirroring Evil* legitimized tasteless, low quality, shock artwork by granting it the prestige of a show in a New York museum.

Spiegelman's cartoon also helps clarify the intent and art historical lineage of *Mirroring Evil*. Its caption, "Duchamp is our Misfortune," refers to a popular Nazi propaganda slogan, *Die Juden sind unser Unglück* (The Jews are our misfortune), and French Dadaist Marcel Duchamp (1887–1968). Duchamp scandalized the early twentieth-century art world with his "readymades": mundane, everyday objects—in one notable case a urinal, in another a cheap postcard reproduction of Leonardo da Vinci's *Mona Lisa*—which he slightly altered, signing the urinal "R. Mutt" and drawing a moustache on the *Mona Lisa*, and submitted to exhibitions. Duchamp's readymade artworks asked to what extent art depends on galleries, museums, collectors, critics and other institutions to acquire its monetary and social value. Art historians consider them examples of modernist avant-garde art, which as Peter Bürger defines it, is art that critiques the institutions that control how artworks are produced, exchanged, and consumed.[20] Spiegelman's caption acknowledges that that the avant-garde Holocaust artworks in *Mirroring Evil* sought to draw attention to the ways in which contemporary culture has reduced the Holocaust to a set of stock images and clichés. But in insisting that "Duchamp is our misfortune," he points out that Duchamp's anti-institutional gestures have themselves been so frequently imitated that they are no longer shocking. The implication is that claiming the status of avant-garde art is simply a way for *Mirroring Evil* to inoculate itself against legitimate criticisms about its propriety.

Several artworks in *Mirroring Evil* explicitly cited Duchamp. In *Zugzwang* (*Forced movement*, 1995), the German artist Rudolf Gerz arranged copies of portrait photographs of Marcel Duchamp and Adolf Hitler in an alternating checkerboard pattern. Both photographs were taken by Heinrich Hoffmann, who photographed Duchamp in 1912 and became Hitler's personal photographer two decades later (Hoffman's studio assistant Eva Braun became Hitler's wife). In German, a *Zugzwang* is a situation in chess when a player is forced into an undesirable move. According to Gerz, the thesis of *Zugzwang* is that "one can not speak or even think about modern art, one can not make art without having Hitler and Duchamp in one's head, however conveyed."[21] Like Gerz, Israeli artist Boaz Arad also referenced Duchamp, but more playfully. Arad's video project *Marcel Marcel* manipulates a well-known scene of Hitler making a speech in Leni Riefenstahl's Nazi propaganda film *Triumph of the Will* (1935). Arad mimics Duchamp's defacement of the *Mona Lisa* with a moustache. As his speech becomes jumbled, Hitler's own moustache comes to life, dancing around his head, lengthening and shortening, morphing into a beard, entering his nostrils, and otherwise drawing attention away from his speech to mock how he has become an icon in his own right, much like the *Mona Lisa*.

Other artworks in *Mirroring Evil* evoke Duchamp less explicitly. The American artist Tom Sachs contributed the found object projects *Giftgas Giftset* (1998) and *Prada Deathcamp* (1998). Curator Norman Kleeblatt noted that "Sachs turns the strategies of Marcel Duchamp around by 180 degrees."[22] Where Duchamp took everyday objects and made them art, *Giftgas Giftset* takes luxury objects and makes them banal instruments of murder. *Giftgas Giftset* puns on the German *Giftgas* (poison gas). It consists of three empty canisters that resemble the containers for Zyklon-B, the pellets that produced the toxic gas used to murder Jews at Auschwitz. Sachs took discarded Chanel, Hèrmes, and Tiffany wrapping materials and wrapped them around the canisters, creating a poison gas giftset, which he placed in a white display cube to make the luxury gas canisters appear even more exclusive and valuable. Sachs's other project, "Prada Deathcamp" is a small model of a concentration camp built on a discarded cardboard Prada hatbox. Describing how his artwork relates to fascism and the Holocaust, Sachs said, "I'm using the iconography of the Holocaust to bring attention to fashion. Fashion, like fascism, is about loss of identity."[23] Sachs seemed to be comparing Holocaust victims to fashion victims in the kind of self-absorbed statements that surely contributed to reviews of *Mirroring Evil*, such as Peter Schjeldahl's in *The New Yorker*, which argued that the artworks said less about the Holocaust and more about how controversial the artists believed themselves to be. "Overall," Schjeldahl wrote, "the show suggests an emergency ward for narcissism."[24]

Like Sachs, Polish artist Maciej Toporowicz juxtaposes Nazi imagery and luxury consumer goods in *Obsession* (1993). Toporowicz's five-and-a-half minute video montage jumps between clips of 1930s Nazi propaganda films, scenes from 1970s Italian *sadiconazista* films, such as Liliana Cavani's *The Night Porter* (1974) and Luchino Visconti's *The Damned* (1969) (see Chapter 8), and television commercials for the Calvin Klein perfume "Obsession," exposing profound stylistic similarities between these ostensibly different kinds of representations. The idealized and sexualized bodies of Nazi propaganda films and *sadiconazista* movies closely resemble the attractive fashion models in the perfume advertisement, as Toporowicz underscores the extent to which Nazified imagery has uncritically entered contemporary advertising culture. In Kleeblatt's description, *Obsession* forces viewers "to a self-examination about the continuing seduction of Nazi imagery."[25] At the same time, its title refers to the ongoing, commercialized obsession with the Holocaust in popular culture.

Another Polish artist, Piotr Uklański, examines this commercialization in perhaps its most visible venue: cinema. Uklański's *The Nazis* (1998) is a frieze constructed from 166 identically sized photographs. Each photograph shows a famous leading man playing a Nazi. The actors include Clint Eastwood, Tom Selleck, Michael Douglas, Ralph Fiennes, Frank Sinatra, Harrison Ford, and even Ronald Reagan. The project began when Uklański noticed a magazine article about best dressed-actors that ignored the fact that many were clad as Nazis; he assembled the photographs and movie stills into a long line of images that reveal how cinema and celebrity culture make Nazis desirable. In its sheer length, the series of portraits resembles a long roll of film. As it exposes the mass media's complicity in perpetuating images of handsome Nazis, it also implicates the moviegoers who flock to each new Nazi movie, perpetuating the cycle of commercialization. Another artist in the exhibition, Austrian Elke Krystufek, appropriated the images that Uklański had already appropriated and placed them alongside naked paintings of herself, often holding a camera. These images ask whether deriving pleasure from looking at Nazis (in films) has become fundamentally pornographic.

Playing with the Holocaust?

Of all the inflammatory artworks in *Mirroring Evil*, Zbigniew Libera's *LEGO Concentration Camp* (1996) was among the most controversial, though it is also one of the most useful for understanding the exhibition's legacy. Because Libera's project literally represented the Holocaust as a toy, it gave critics an easy example to cite when dismissing *Mirroring Evil* as juvenile, trivializing, and offensive. In point of fact, however, *LEGO Concentration Camp* was not a toy at all; it was a set of empty boxes that demanded that museum visitors imagine what such a toy might look like. By taking as its theme the idea of "playing the Holocaust" and using "play and toys to represent the Holocaust or Nazi Germany," or "playing the Holocaust," as Ernst van Alphen calls it, it hints at what might prove to be the show's most significant legacy.[26] *Mirroring Evil* fundamentally challenged the traditional role of Holocaust representations, namely to memorialize the dead in a reverential and historically accurate manner. In an exhibition catalogue essay about Libera's project and other "Holocaust toys," van Alphen explained that linking toys and the Holocaust would spark controversy almost by definition, because, "in the context of Holocaust education and remembrance, it is an unassailable axiom that historical genres and discourses, such as the documentary, memoir, testimony, or monument, are much more effective and morally responsible in teaching the historical events than imaginative discourses."[27]

By providing a reputable forum for imaginative approaches to the Holocaust, *Mirroring Evil* challenged this "unassailable axiom." It showed how transforming, challenging, and even playing the Holocaust does not necessarily entail trivializing it. Indeed, it can accomplish the opposite. Properly contextualized, art that plays the Holocaust can potentially help one approach the genocide in ways traditional genres and discourses cannot by highlighting not only the sadness, but also the trauma triggered by Holocaust remembrance. *Mirroring Evil* suggested that confronting the trauma of the Holocaust demands more than simply learning the historical events, or even facing, understanding, and accepting what happened. It also requires that one confront the range of emotions that the Holocaust provokes. In a culture where Holocaust representations had become and arguably remain profoundly unimaginative, this exhibition showed how imagination can force us to engage the past in new ways that make it meaningful once again.

Peter Eisenman's Memorial to the Murdered Jews of Europe, just south of the Brandenburg Gate in the center of Berlin in May 2011. With its 2,700 concrete slabs, known as stelae, the memorial has drawn praise for suggesting the open-ended character of memory but also criticism for not being clear enough about its purpose.

Eric D. Gedenk

16

Memorial to the Murdered Jews of Europe (memorial, 2005):

Is There an End to Holocaust Memory?

In January 2013, BuzzFeed.com, a website that promotes viral content on the Internet, picked up a story that was rapidly gaining traction. Titled "14 Grindr Profile Pics Taken At The Holocaust Memorial," the post highlighted what it called a "disturbing new trend" on Grindr, a popular dating smartphone app for gay men.[1] In their dating profiles, men were posting photographs of themselves standing among, leaning on, and climbing on top of the concrete slabs, known as stelae, that make up the Memorial to the Murdered Jews of Europe in Berlin. Undoubtedly, these romance-seekers were drawn to the eye-catching aesthetic and profile-enhancing possibilities of the field of 2,700 evenly spaced coffin-like stelae of varying heights (some as tall as 13 feet), stretching in rows over nearly 19,000 square meters. Commentators were appalled by this tawdry use of the memorial, but Grindr members were not deterred. By the end of 2013, *Totem and Taboo*, a blog launched in November 2011 specifically to document the trend, had registered more than 100 such photos.[2]

The Grindr furor was only one of many incidents that have incited public outcry over supposedly inappropriate uses of the memorial. In 2009, the budget airline easyJet withdrew almost 300,000 copies of its in-flight magazine after numerous passengers and Jewish organizations complained about an eight-page fashion shoot, titled "A Quick Guide to the Chic Side of Berlin," that posed stylishly dressed models next to the stelae, as well as in front of Berlin's Jewish Museum. Unlike easyJet, the magazine's publisher defended the photo shoot, arguing that the article would encourage more tourists to visit the Jewish sites. Indeed, the article identifies them as must-see attractions for savvy tourists: "Ravaged by war and torn in two by conflicting ideologies, Berlin may not be a picture-perfect jewel . . . but it's a treasure trove for the culture vulture . . . no visit would be complete without exploring testaments to the city's turbulent past, such as . . . the Jewish Museum and the Holocaust Memorial."[3]

These incidents are only some of the most recent instances of the controversies Berlin's Holocaust memorial began inciting long before it opened to the public in 2005. Complaints started pouring in as soon as Germany's parliament, the Bundestag, approved architect Peter Eisenman's design in June 1999, the chief concern being that it was too abstract to serve as a memorial at all, let alone a Holocaust memorial.[4] German author Martin Walser dismissed the design as a "nightmare the size of a football-field."[5] But Eisenman staunchly defended the memorial as a counterbalance to traditional monuments, which evoke nostalgia, allowing people to remember the past they desire, rather than the past as it really was.[6]

Unlike most monuments, Berlin's Memorial to the Murdered Jews of Europe has no focal point for visitors. It has no beginning or end, and visitors can enter and exit from any direction. There are no plaques or inscriptions that would transform it into a more concrete representation. In a BBC interview on the occasion of its opening, Eisenman noted, "I fought to keep names off the stones, because having names on them would turn it into a graveyard," adding "I like to think that people will use it for short cuts, as an everyday experience, not as a holy place."[7] While Eisenman may not have anticipated dating websites or fashion shoots when he defended the memorial's anonymity and envisioned its use, his design purposefully did nothing to discourage such engagements.

Given the centrality of the Nazis, Berlin, and Germany in instigating and carrying out the murder of Europe's Jews, it might seem obvious that Berlin should have a Holocaust memorial. But the long, fraught story behind the monument's development reveals that its construction, sixty years after the end of World War II, represents both a turning point in Germany's postwar *Vergangenheitsbewältigung* (coming to terms with the past) and a change in how we perceive Holocaust memorials more generally. Since the opening of the memorial, the discussions over its meaning and use have continued, as thousands of people visit the site every day, some crying as they reflect upon the Holocaust, others playing hide and seek, skateboarding, and sunbathing. The Memorial to the Murdered Jews of Europe thus brings crucial questions about Holocaust memorials into sharp relief: What exactly is the function of a Holocaust memorial, especially in Germany? What is the relationship between the sites where the Holocaust actually took place—the prisons, death camps, and mass graves—and a newly fabricated site like this monument? And are there unwritten rules for how one should behave at a Holocaust memorial?

Germany's countermonuments

The idea of constructing a national Holocaust memorial in Berlin was initiated in 1988 by German television talk show host Lea Rosh and historian Eberhard Jäckel. But the history of Holocaust memorials in Germany precedes their effort, and that history includes a number of memorials by artists who questioned whether traditional monuments, ironically, impede public memory rather than encourage it.[8] If a Holocaust memorial too closely references or symbolizes a real event, that is, if it is too easy to interpret, they argued, it could also be too easy to forget. James E. Young sums up this critique:

> Under the illusion that our memorial edifices will always be there to remind us, we take leave of them and return only at our convenience. To the extent that we encourage monuments to do our memory-work for us, we become that much more forgetful. In effect, the initial impulse to memorialize events like the Holocaust may actually spring from an opposite and equal desire to forget them.[9]

Perhaps in part because of what we might call this forgetting effect, when it comes to the Holocaust, many Germans have expressed a desire to draw a *Schlussstrich* (concluding line) to bring this dark chapter of their history to an end and allow them to move on.

Even before a competition was announced for the memorial in Berlin, a number of German artists had designed memorials that they felt would emphasize the difficulty of memorializing the Holocaust, precisely for the purpose of perpetuating its memory. James E. Young helpfully terms these efforts "countermonuments," since they, ironically, purport to do the opposite of what they are supposed to do. Rather than constructing edifices to commemorate the destruction of a people, they attempt to highlight empty space as a way of drawing attention to people who are no longer there. Where traditional memorials are made out of materials designed to last, the countermonument deliberately challenges the idea that memorials should stand the test of time and aims to disappear or change over the years. Rather than standing untouched, a countermonument invites violation and desanctification. In terms of the Holocaust, a countermonument commemorates a vanished people with a "vanished" monument, aiming to provoke its visitors rather than console them.[10]

One of the first countermonuments in Germany was the Anti-Fascist Memorial constructed by artists Jochen Gerz and Esther Shalev-Gerz to memorialize the victims of fascism in Hamburg's Harburg neighborhood. The memorial consisted of a 12-meter pillar that, between 1986 and 1993, was lowered further into the ground every year until all that remained was its top, a lead plaque, now level with the ground, which marks the project. In Kassel, in 1987, German artist Horst Hoheisel recreated the *Aschrott-Brunnen* (Aschrott Fountain), a 12-meter neo-Gothic pyramid surrounded by a pool, as an inverted countermonument buried in the ground. The Nazis had destroyed the fountain because it was built with funds provided by a Jewish businessman from Kassel named Sigmund Aschrott. By creating a mirror image of the fountain, rather than recreating the fountain as it had existed, Hoheisel turned its destruction into a symbol of the subsequent deportation and murder of Kassel's 463 Jewish residents. As James E. Young notes, "the negative space of the absent monument will now constitute its phantom shape in the ground," thus preserving the absence of the monument and, along with it, the knowledge of how and why it was destroyed.[11] The monument is still a functioning fountain, and the sound of water rushing underground offers a ghostly reminder of a lost past.

A unique memorial in Berlin formalizes the absence of the Jewish population by incorporating the memory of the Holocaust's effect on the everyday lives of Nazi Germany's Jews into contemporary everyday life. In 1993, Renata Stih and Frieder Schnock, two artists based in Berlin, created Places of Remembrance: Memorial to the Deported Jewish Citizens of the Bayerische Viertel in a Berlin neighborhood where many Jews murdered in the Holocaust once lived. The memorial consists of eighty signs with images on one side and texts of Nazi laws and decrees on the other, such as an empty ashtray and the inscription "Jews are allowed no more cigarettes or cigars. 11.6.1942," or a pair of swimming trunks and "Berlin public pools may no longer be entered by Jews. 3.12.1938." Word and image function together to emphasize the seemingly banal beginnings of the exclusion of Jews from German society that culminated in their deportation and extermination. This decentralized memorial allows residents and passersby to experience history as they go about their daily business in the neighborhood, where the signs blend in with the local cityscape, and symbolize how deeply anti-Semitism was enmeshed in the everyday life of local Germans.[12]

The history of the Holocaust Memorial in Berlin, 1988–2013

Unlike the localized countermonuments of the 1980s and 1990s, the Berlin Memorial to the Murdered Jews of Europe was intended, from the start, as a grand national gesture. It was conceived in an atmosphere of dramatic transition, as the fall of the Berlin Wall (1989) and German reunification (1990) raised questions about what it meant to return to a single German state that had not existed since the Nazi era, causing Germans to reflect once more on the role of the past in German self-identification. Germans sought not to forget the past, journalist Jane Kramer writes, but to make it usable, as a source of positive identification. This entailed identifying with its victims, rather than focusing on its perpetrators, or, as Kramer put it, describing Chancellor Helmut Kohl's vision, using the politics of commemoration to "put Germany on the winning side."[13] In other words, deeply political agendas shaped all stages of the debate surrounding the memorial.

This was the context in which plans for the memorial took root and developed. With the support of historian Eberhard Jäckel, television talk show host Lea Rosh—a Protestant whose maternal grandfather was Jewish, and who had changed her name from Edith to the more Jewish-sounding Lea— used her celebrity connections to raise twelve million dollars and extracted a promise from Chancellor Kohl that the memorial would be located on prime real estate in central Berlin, near the ruins of Hitler's bunker. From the start, Rosh's enthusiastic and unsophisticated approach to Holocaust memory rankled Berlin intellectuals and others, some of whom claimed that Germans had no place memorializing victims when they should be focusing on their own role in the destruction. But by the mid-1990s, argues Kramer, most Germans were "absorbed in an elaborate exercise in 'solidarity,' if not identification, with Hitler's victims," which combined with Rosh's relentless promotion of the idea, described aptly by Kramer as "ghoulish public entertainment," to provide the conditions for the project's success. After Kohl announced his support for the project, an open competition was launched and 523 designs were submitted.[14]

One key topic of debate was whom the memorial should commemorate. Although Rosh had, from the beginning, insisted that the memorial would be a German initiative to memorialize Jews, this proposed limitation sparked controversy, for many other memorials commemorated Jewish victims of Nazi persecution together with Sinti and Roma (gypsies), homosexuals, and other victims of fascism. The memorial's location also proved controversial. Originally, Kohl had promised that it would be built on the site of the former Gestapo headquarters in central Berlin, but that idea fell through as many people thought this was an inappropriate location if the memorial was going to commemorate only Jews, not all of Hitler's victims. Others felt that the memorial project would detract from the actual sites where killings took place, like the Ravensbrück and Sachsenhausen concentration camps, which, as many pointed out at the time, were falling into disrepair and badly in need of funds, making the "most expensive memorial project in Berlin's history" (the memorial ultimately cost $35.7 million) a lamentable irony.[15]

But the deepest and most lasting controversy surrounded the memorial's design. Lea Rosh was among those who envisioned a traditional-style memorial heavy on symbolism. By the mid-1990s, German attitudes toward memorializing the Holocaust had swung away from countermonuments, and the winning design in the initial 1994 competition was a huge concrete slab on which the names of the millions of victims would be engraved, much like a symbolic tombstone. Under heavy criticism, however, Chancellor Helmut Kohl rejected the design, and a second competition was launched in 1997, which resulted in the design that was eventually built just south of the Brandenburg Gate in Berlin. But media debates continued, both about the still-controversial focus on Jewish victims, and about the failure of the design to adequately educate visitors about the Holocaust. Eisenman added an underground library and study center to the design, the Bundestag approved the revised plan in 1999, and funds were raised over the next several years. Ultimately, the idea that Jewish victims were deserving of their own memorial, as the only group singled out for complete destruction, prevailed. And, indeed, in many ways the memorial has fulfilled its intent: to allow non-Jewish Germans to tell the story of the Holocaust from the "victims' perspective" at a different kind of memorial designed to complement "authentic" sites of Holocaust memory.[16]

Experiencing the Memorial

Controversy over the memorial did not end with its opening in 2005; it simply shifted, as visitors engaged with the vast countermonument. It soon became apparent that many visitors did not even know what the stelae were, so the planned library and study center was transformed into a formal Information Center that plays an important role, through its presentation of texts, images, and audiovisual material, in mediating how individuals experience the memorial. The Information Center offers group guided tours, an audio tour, workshops, a searchable video archive, and informational materials about the memorial, the Nazi campaign against the Jews, and preparing for and processing a visit. Hosts are stationed near the entrances to the Information Center to offer guidance and keep order at the site, which is also monitored by cameras and live security.[17]

As sociologist Irit Dekel notes, visitors experience the memorial in a wide variety of ways. While the media is quick to pounce on blatantly exploitative uses, like the dating profile pictures and fashion shoots described above, Dekel's research shows that many visitors to the memorial do learn about the Holocaust and reflect upon the memory of its victims, whether they use the Information Center or not. She explains how the memorial's open-ended layout sets the stage for a variety of unregulated memorial encounters: visitors can enter and exit from different points, and the rules for entering and exiting are purposefully left open, which encourages reflection. Those who work at the memorial are aware of the range of emotions that the abstract and open nature of the memorial encourages, and they urge visitors to experience it however they like, often using the phrase "Everything goes. There are no wrong answers."[18] When visitors have no knowledge about the Holocaust and anti-Semitism, guides invite them to visit the Information Center. Marita Sturken observes that merely walking among the stelae provokes emotional responses in many visitors, as the memorial foregrounds distance and reflection, rather than easy identification or pathos:

> visitors can feel the shifting terrain, as the pillars change in height and one goes from light to cavernous spaces to undulating stones. If we see others walk into the field of pillars, their heads disappear within it—we know they are there, but they are lost to us . . . As one gets deeper into the chasms and loses the city behind, one catches glimpses of others moving through, fleeting and then gone, never to be seen again. Thus, in walking through the memorial, visitors can experience the arbitrariness of life, its tenuousness.[19]

In 2010, the number of visitors reached 461,000. According to a public survey from 2009, about half of the Information Center's visitors are German, while the other half come from other countries. As per its original intent, those who work at the memorial consider the memorial to be primarily for the benefit of non-Jewish Germans, suggesting that one of the most significant political implications of the site is the way it maintains German memory of the Holocaust.[20]

The end of Holocaust memory?

As Karen E. Till notes, "The Holocaust Memorial, of course, is not just a replica of memorials elsewhere. It was an outcome of negotiated German and international cultures of memory, each defined by distinct hauntings, political perspectives, social relations, and histories."[21] Today, the Memorial to the Murdered Jews of Europe is part of a surge in new sites of memory in Berlin, including the Memorial to the Homosexuals Persecuted under the National Socialist Regime, and the Memorial to the Sinti and Roma of Europe Murdered under the National Socialist Regime. It also serves as a counterpart to architect Daniel Libeskind's Jewish Museum Berlin, dedicated in 2001. Libeskind's design also incorporates countermonument elements, notably absence, emptiness, and the invisible, which express the disappearance of Jewish culture in the city. The museum is constructed in the form of a straight line repeatedly intersected by a zigzag. The straight line represents the continuities of German–Jewish history, while the zigzag speaks to unexpected twists, turns, and periods of exclusion and persecution. Unlike the permanent exhibition at the United States Holocaust Memorial Museum (see Chapter 12), the building itself disrupts any attempt to understand the history it presents as a smooth progression or seamless narrative. Although it, too, has over time received its share of criticism, Libeskind's design has also drawn much praise because rather than smoothing over the tensions in German–Jewish history, it masterfully gives physical form to Germany's fraught relationship with its Jewish minority. In many ways, the Memorial to the Murdered Jews of Europe and the Jewish Museum Berlin function in tandem: the memorial can be seen as an open museum, while, in its very structure, the museum functions as a kind of monument.

The 17-year period between Lea Rosh's initial idea and the final construction of the Memorial to the Murdered Jews of Europe incited renewed pessimism about memorials, as well as doubts about the efficacy of countermonuments. Some commentators suggested that the uproar that inevitably accompanies the construction of monuments is their only beneficial outcome: scholar Gert Mattenklott noted, "the only valuable thing about monuments is the discussion they provoke." For others, the very act of commemoration, ironically, serves to diminish its effect: as scientist and political activist Jens Reich remarked, "It seems the more we commemorate, the more we dilute the seriousness of commemoration; the better we describe, the less we mean."[22]

Some feel that the Memorial to the Murdered Jews of Europe veers too far in the direction of the countermonument in its efforts to prevent forgetting and nostalgia. To those critics, Peter Eisenman's defense of the memorial as the cutting edge of memory work falls short of its goals precisely because of its insistence on providing only a figurative experience. In Eisenman's words, "Our memorial attempts to develop a new idea of memory . . . In our memorial there is no aim, no end, no way in or out . . . In this context, there is no nostalgia, no remembrance of the past, only a living memory of individual experience."[23] But even today many remain concerned that in attempting to address all the concerns of memorialization at once, the memorial ends up serving none of them.

Ultimately, the controversy surrounding the memorial shows that there is no single way of commemorating the Holocaust that will satisfy every need. Other complementary memorials will always be necessary. One such continuing effort throughout Europe is artist Gunter Demnig's *Stolpersteine* (stumbling blocks) project that commemorates the victims of Nazi persecution through plaques embedded in the ground near their homes. Any individual can sponsor a small, commemorative brass plaque at a cost of 120 Euros; as of the end of December 2013, over 43,500 *Stolpersteine* had been placed in over 610 locations throughout Germany, Austria, and other countries.[24] Demnig sees the plaques as an antidote to the Berlin memorial: "The monument in Berlin is abstract and centrally located. But if the stone is in front of your house, you're confronted. People start talking. To think about six million victims is abstract, but to think about a murdered family is concrete."[25] But even this small-scale memorial has its detractors, who think the possibility of people stepping on or ignoring the small, unobtrusive plaques fails to keep the memory of the victims intact. In a similar but more ephemeral direction, a Munich-based technology firm recently released a smartphone app that displays the names and pictures of Holocaust victims on the phones of those who pass by their former residences, thereby creating "a virtual, floating museum over Munich."[26]

Photo shoots, picnicking, skateboarding, and tanning at the memorial only confirm the judgments of its staunchest critics. Yet it may be more fruitful not to condemn the memorial as a failed site of remembrance, but to consider how visitor engagements with the site, whether casual or profound, can be understood as acts of remembrance more broadly construed. In other words, as Irit Dekel notes, what happens at the memorial can help us understand how Holocaust memory is always mediated—through filters of time, place, and social codes—and how unwritten codes of remembering still shape the experience of every visitor. The process of memory work and self-understanding is "performed in the act of remembrance and the reflection on that act."[27] As such, whether people like it or not, the Memorial to the Murdered Jews of Europe opens up new possibilities for engagement with Holocaust memory, some perhaps more meaningful than others, but each relevant in its own way.

Memorials are signs of their times, as well as the past they represent. Given the conditions in which it was envisioned, designed, and built, Berlin's Memorial to the Murdered Jews of Europe may very well have been the best possible answer to the question of how a Germany newly reunited, sixty years after World War II, might best commemorate the Jews of Europe murdered by the Nazis. Over the years, a more traditional monument with easy symbolism and clear directives for behavior could easily fall into obscurity. Perhaps a controversial structure that constantly points to its own limits, even as it forces visitors to determine their own paths through both its current space and the past it represents, best signals the continuation of Holocaust memory rather than its end.

Notes

Introduction

1   Jeffrey Shandler, *While America Watches: Televising the Holocaust* (New York: Oxford University Press, 1999), xii.

2   Two recent works intended for students that overview some of these debates are: Donald Niewyk, *The Holocaust: Problems and Perspectives of Interpretation*, 4th edition (Stamford: Cenage Learning, 2011) and Tom Lawson, *Debates on the Holocaust* (Manchester: Manchester University Press, 2010).

3   Alvin H. Rosenfeld, *The End of the Holocaust* (Bloomington: Indiana University Press, 2011), 8.

4   In the introduction to the *Oxford Handbook of Holocaust Studies*, Peter Hayes and John K. Roth describe some of the problems associated with these terms for the Holocaust's "protagonists." See Peter Hayes and John K. Roth, eds., *Oxford Handbook of Holocaust Studies* (New York: Oxford University Press, 2010), 6.

5   Berel Lang, *Holocaust Representation: Art within the Limits of History and Ethics* (Baltimore, MD: Johns Hopkins University Press, 2000), ix–x.

6   For more on the history of the term "Holocaust" and its usage, see Jon Petrie, "The Secular Word HOLOCAUST: Scholarly Myths, History, and 20th century Meanings," *Journal of Genocide Research* 2, no. 1 (2000): 31–63.

7   James E. Young, *Writing and Rewriting the Holocaust: Narrative and the Consequences of Interpretation* (Bloomington: Indiana University Press, 1990), 85.

8   The Roma, the group pejoratively known as "gypsies," use the term *porajmos* (literally "devouring" or "destruction"). However, this term only came into use in the 1990s, when Romani activists sought to draw attention to their unique experiences and not let their history simply be subsumed as the collateral damage of violence to Jews. Ian Hancock, "On the interpretation of a word: Porrajmos as Holocaust," http://www.radoc.net/radoc.php?doc=art_e_holocaust_interpretation&lang

9   "Holocaust," Shoah Resource Center, http://www.yadvashem.org/odot_pdf/Microsoft%20Word%20-%206419.pdf

10 David G. Roskies, *Against the Apocalypse: Responses to Catastrophe in Modern Jewish Culture* (Syracuse, NY: Syracuse University Press, 1999), 262.

11 Edward T. Linenthal, *Preserving Memory: The Struggle to Create America's Holocaust Museum* (New York: Penguin, 1995), 52–56. See also Donald L.

Niewyk and Francis R. Nicosia, *The Columbia Guide to the Holocaust* (New York: Columbia University Press, 2000), 45–52.

12 "Introduction to the Holocaust," United States Holocaust Memorial Museum, http://www.ushmm.org/wlc/en/article.php?ModuleId=10005143

13 For an overview of the term, see W.J.T. Mitchell, "Representation," in *Critical Terms for Literary Study*, ed. Frank Lentricchia and Thomas McLaughlin (Chicago: University of Chicago Press, 1995), 11–22.

14 Theodor W. Adorno, *Prisms* (Cambridge: The MIT Press, 1982), 34.

15 Gene Ray, *Terror and the Sublime in Art and Critical Theory: From Auschwitz to Hiroshima to September 11* (Basingstoke: Palgrave Macmillan, 2005), 64.

16 Terrence Des Pres, "Holocaust Laughter," in *Writing and the Holocaust*, ed. Berel Lang (New York: Holmes and Meier, 1988), 217.

17 Rosenfeld, 11.

18 For more on the "memory boom" in general see Jay Winter, "The Generation of Memory: Reflections on the 'Memory Boom' in Contemporary Historical Studies," *Bulletin of the German Historical Institute* 27, no. 3 (2000): 69–92; see also Frank Rich, "Journal; The Holocaust Boom," *The New York Times*, April 7, 1994. Regarding the "museum boom" and specifically the "Jewish museum boom," see Barbie Zelizer, *Remembering to Forget: Holocaust Memory Through the Camera's Eye* (Chicago: University of Chicago Press, 1998), 194–95 and Diana Muir Applebaum, "Other Outlooks; Is the Jewish Museum Boom a Good Thing?" *Jewish Outlook*, November 1, 2011.

19 "Holocaust Survivor Stories Live on in Holograms," *Here and Now* with Robin Young and Jeremy Hobson, 90.9 WBUR Boston, April 8, 2013. http://hereandnow.wbur.org/2013/04/08/holocaust-survivor-holograms

Chapter 1

1 Marianne Hirsch, "Nazi Photographs in Post-Holocaust Art: Gender as an Idiom of Memorialization," in *Phototextualities: Intersections of Photography and Narrative*, ed. Alex Hughes and Andrea Noble (Albuquerque: University of New Mexico Press), 19.

2 Cornelia Brink, "Secular Icons: Looking at Photographs from Nazi Concentration Camps," *History & Memory* 12, no. 1 (2000): 135–50.

3 Martin Kemp, *Christ to Coke: How Image Becomes Icon* (New York: Oxford University Press, 2012), 3.

4 Barbara Engelking and Jacek Leociak, *The Warsaw Ghetto: A Guide to the Perished City* (New Haven, CT: Yale University Press, 2009), 481–93.

5 Samuel Kassow, *Who Will Write Our History?: Emanuel Ringelblum, the Warsaw Ghetto, and the Oyneg Shabes Archive* (Bloomington: Indiana University Press, 2007), 90–143.

6 Debórah Dwork, *Children With a Star: Jewish Youth in Nazi Europe* (New Haven, CT: Yale University Press, 1991), xi.

7 Kassow, 260.

8 Richard Raskin, *A Child at Gunpoint: A Case Study in the Life of a Photo* (Aarhus: Aarhus University Press, 2004), 35–36.

9 Jürgen Stroop, *The Stroop Report: The Jewish Quarter of Warsaw is No More!* (New York: Pantheon Books, 1979).

10 "Nazi Terrorism in Poland is Brought to Light," *The New York Times*, December 26, 1947.

11 "Photographer at War," *The New York Times*, December 27, 1945.

12 Raskin, 31–32.

13 Joachim Jahns, *Der Warschauer Ghettokönig* (Leipzig: Dingsda Verlag, 2009).

14 Raskin, 82–94. Raskin examines three named "candidates": Artur Dąb Siemiątek, Tsvi Nussbaum, and Levi Zeilinwarger, plus a fourth anonymous individual. Barbie Zelizer adds Israel Rondel to the list of claimants. See Barbie Zelizer, *About to Die: How News Images Move the Public* (New York: Oxford University Press, 2010), 141.

15 The subsequent details of Joseph Blösche come from Dan Porat's *The Boy: A Holocaust Story* (New York: Hill and Wang, 2010), which interweaves the story of the photograph with a narrative of the perpetrators and their postwar trials.

16 Porat, 181–85.

Chapter 2

1 "War-Crimes Court Sees Horror Films," *The New York Times*, November 30, 1945, 6.

2 David Bathrick, "The Afterlife of Triumph of the Will: The First Twenty-five Years," in *Riefenstahl Screened: An Anthology of New Criticism*, ed. Neil Christian Pages, Mary Rhiel, and Ingeborg Majer-O'Sickey (New York: Continuum, 2008), 89.

3 For example, Billy Wilder, who was born in Austria-Hungary and emigrated to the U.S. after Hitler came to power in Germany, was already a successful writer, producer, and director in Hollywood when he worked on these documentary films. He later directed Marilyn Monroe in popular movies such as *The Seven-Year Itch* (1955) and *Some Like it Hot* (1959).

4 Anton Kaes, *From Hitler to Heimat: The Return of History as Film* (Cambridge, MA: Harvard University Press, 1989), 196.

5 Lawrence Douglas, *The Memory of Judgment: Making Law and History in the Trials of the Holocaust* (New Haven, CT: Yale University Press, 2001), 14, 21.

6 Douglas, 12–16.

7 Douglas, 30.

8 Douglas, 17–18.

9 Letter from General Dwight D. Eisenhower to General George C. Marshall, April 15, 1945, http://www.ushmm.org/research/research-in-collections/search-the-collections/bibliography/liberators

10 Douglas, 29.

11 Kay Gladstone, "Separate Intentions: The Allied Screening of Concentration Camp Documentaries in Defeated Germany in 1945–46: *Death Mills* and *Memory of the Camps*," in *Holocaust and the Moving Image: Representations in Film and Television since 1933*, ed. Toby Haggith and Joanna Newman (London: Wallflower Press, 2005), 54. There is evidence that, from the start, the filmmakers knew that their productions would be used not only in court at Nuremberg, but also to thwart future Holocaust deniers. Gladstone, 54.

12 One atrocity film, *The Nazi Plan*, does include images of Nazi signs instructing Germans to "liberate themselves" from Jews and advocating the boycott of Jewish shops.

13 Gladstone, 54.

14 Gladstone, 53.

15 Caroline Joan S. Picart and David A. Frank, *Frames of Evil: the Holocaust as Horror in American Film* (Carbondale: Southern Illinois University Press, 2006), 23–24.

16 Director Stanley Kramer's popular Oscar-winning film *Judgment at Nuremberg* (1961), features actual clips from the film, as does its less well-known remake, *Nuremberg* (2000).

17 Grisela Pollock and Max Silverman, eds., *Concentrationary Cinema: Aesthetics as Political Resistance in Alain Resnais's* Night and Fog (New York: Berghahn, 2011), 3.

Chapter 3

1 David Cesarani and Eric J. Sundquist, eds., *After the Holocaust: Challenging the Myth of Silence* (London: Routledge, 2012), 1.

2 Peter Novick, *The Holocaust in American Life* (New York: Houghton Mifflin, 1999), 103–104.

3 Cesarani and Sundquist, 1.

4 Hasia R. Diner has recently explored this argument at length. See Diner, *We Remember with Reverence and Love: American Jews and the Myth of Silence after the Holocaust, 1945–1962* (New York: New York University Press, 2009).

5 Jeffrey Herf, *Divided Memory: The Nazi Past in the Two Germanys* (Cambridge, MA: Harvard University Press, 1997), 1–12.

6 Sharon Kangisser Cohen, *Child Survivors of the Holocaust in Israel: Finding Their Voices. Social Dynamics and Post-War Experiences* (Brighton: Sussex Academic Press, 2005), 230.

7 Tom Segev, *The Seventh Million: Israelis and the Holocaust*, trans. Haim Watzman (New York: Hill & Wang, 1993), 180.

8 Mark L. Smith, "No Silence in Yiddish: Popular and Scholarly Writing about the Holocaust in the Early Postwar Years," in Cesarani and Sundquist, 55–66; 55.

9 See Laura Jokusch, *Collect and Record!: Jewish Holocaust Documentation in Early Postwar Europe* (New York: Oxford University Press, 2012), 4.

10 Margarete Myers Feinstein, "Re-imagining the Unimaginable: Theater, Memory, and Rehabilitation in the Displaced Persons Camps," in Cesarani and Sundquist, 39–54; 39–44.

11 David G. Roskies, and Naomi Diamont, *Holocaust Literature: A History and Guide* (Waltham, MA: Brandeis University Press, 2012), 105–108.

12 Diner, 1–17.

13 Yizkor (Holocaust Memorial) Books, New York Public Library, accessed July 31, 2013, legacy.www.nypl.org/research/chss/jws/yizkorbooks_intro.cfm

14 Jonathan Boyarin, "Yizker-bikher", The YIVO Encyclopedia of Jews in Eastern Europe, accessed July 31, 2013, www.yivoencyclopedia.org/article.aspx/Yizker-bikher.

15 Michlean Amir, "Israel as the Cradle of Yizker-Books," in *Memorial Books of Eastern European Jewry: Essays on the History and Meanings of Yizker Volumes*, ed. Rosemary Horowitz (Jefferson, NC: McFarland, 2011), 29.

16 Jack Kugelmass and Jonathan Boyarin, eds. and trans., *From a Ruined Garden: The Memorial Books of Polish Jewry*, 2nd edition (Bloomington: Indiana University Press), 25–27. See also James E. Young, *The Texture of Memory: Holocaust Memorials and Meaning* (New Haven, CT: Yale University Press, 1993), 7.

17 Rosemary Horowitz, ed., *Memorial Books of Eastern European Jewry: Essays on the History and Meanings of Yizker Volumes* (Jefferson, NC: McFarland, 2011), 11.

18 Mellech Bakalczuk-Felin, ed., *Yizker-bukh Khelm* (Johannesburg: Chelmer landsmanshaft in Johannesburg, 1954).

19 *Yizker-bukh Khelm*, "Preface," iii.

20 *Yizker-bukh Khelm*, 327.

21 *Yizker-bukh Khelm*, 331.

22 *Yizker-bukh Khelm*, 334.

23 Jacob Shatzky, "Review of Yizker Books 1955," in Horowitz, ed., 73.

24 *Yizker-bukh Khelm*, 585–86.

25 Kugelmass and Boyarin, 22.

26 *Yizker-bukh Khelm*.

Chapter 4

1 Frances Goodrich and Albert Hackett, *The Diary of Anne Frank* (New York: Random House, 1956), 172–73.

2 Barbara Kirshenblatt-Gimblett and Jeffrey Shandler, "Introduction: Anne Frank, The Phenomenon," in *Anne Frank Unbound: Media Imagination Memory*, ed. Barbara Kirshenblatt-Gimblett and Jeffrey Shandler (Bloomington: Indiana University Press, 2012), 1.

3 As this chapter concerns Anne Frank's posthumous image rather than her biography, readers in search of more details about her life can consult, among other works, Melissa Müller's *Anne Frank: The Biography* (New York: Metropolitan Books, 2013). David Barnouw and Gerrold van der Stroom's *The Diary of Anne Frank: The Revised Critical Edition* (New York: Doubleday, 2003) also includes extensive biographical material. The United States Holocaust Memorial Museum's website offers an extensive bibliography of Anne Frank related scholarship at: http://www.ushmm.org/research/research-in-collections/search-the-collections/bibliography/anne-frank

4 For more on the history of Jewish life in the Netherlands during World War II and the Holocaust, see Peter Tammes, "Jewish immigrants in the Netherlands during the Nazi occupation," *Journal of Interdisciplinary History* 37, no. 4 (2007): 543–62 and Marnix Croes, "The Holocaust in the Netherlands and the Rate of Jewish Survival," *Holocaust and Genocide Studies* 20, no. 3 (2006): 474–99.

5 See, for instance Diane L. Wolf, *Beyond Anne Frank: Hidden Children and Postwar Families in Holland* (Berkeley: University of California Press, 2007) and Alexander Zapruder, ed., *Salvaged Pages: Young Writers' Diaries of the Holocaust* (New Haven, CT: Yale University Press, 2002).

6 Willy Lindwer, *The Last Seven Months of Anne Frank* (New York: Random House, 1991), 104. Quoted in Alvin Rosenfeld, "Anne Frank and the Future of Holocaust Memory," Joseph and Rebecca Meyerhoff Annual Lecture, October 14, 2004 (Washington, DC: United States Holocaust Memorial Museum) 9.

7 See the essays in Helene Flanzbaum, ed., *The Americanization of the Holocaust* (Baltimore, MD: Johns Hopkins University Press, 1999).

8 Rosenfeld, 2–3.

9 Barnouw and van der Stroom, 669.

10 Jeffrey Shandler, "From Diary to Book" in Kirshenblatt-Gimblett and Shandler, eds., 28.

11 Shandler, 29.

12 Gerrold van der Stroom, "The Diaries, *Het Achterhuis* and the Translations," in Barnouw and van der Stroom, 63.

13 Molly Driscoll, "Michigan school: 'Anne Frank' will stay," *Christian Science Monitor*, May 13, 2013.

14 Barnouw and van der Stroom, 253–57.

15 Barnouw and van der Stroom, 251.

16 See Meyer Levin, *The Obsession* (New York: Simon and Schuster, 1973).

17 Meyer Levin, "Life in the Secret Annex," *The New York Times*, June 15, 1952.

18 Lawrence Graver, *An Obsession with Anne Frank: Meyer Levin and the Diary* (Berkeley: University of California Press, 1995), 25–27.

19 Francine Prose, *Anne Frank: The Book, The Life, The Afterlife* (New York: HarperCollins, 2009), 183–84.

20 Edna Nashon, "Anne Frank From Page to Stage," in Kirshenblatt-Gimblett and Shandler, 66–67.

21 Nashon, 67.

22 Barnouw and van der Stroom, 622.

23 Barnouw and van der Stroom, 716.

24 Vincent Canby, "A New 'Anne Frank' Still Stuck in the 50s," *The New York Times*, December 21, 1997.

Chapter 5

1 "Union of Polish Jews of Argentina Celebrates 25th Anniversary," *Jewish Telegraphic Agency*, October 23, 1950.

2 For more on Holocaust discussions during this time, as well as the myth that the Holocaust was not discussed at all, see Chapter 3.

3 From 1960, when it was first translated into English, to 2008, an estimated 10 million copies of *Night* were sold. See Rachel Donadio, "The Story of *Night*," *The New York Times*, January 20, 2008.

4 Zev Garber, and Bruce Zuckerman, "Why do we call the Holocaust 'The Holocaust'? An Inquiry into the Psychology of Labels," *Modern Judaism* 9, no. 2 (1989): 202.

5 Gary Weissman, "Questioning Key Texts: a Pedagogical Approach to Teaching Elie Wiesel's *Night*," in *Teaching the Representation of the Holocaust*, ed. Marianne Hirsch and Irene Kacandes (New York: Modern Language Association, 2004), 325–26.

6 Cardinal Jean-Marie Lustiger, "The Absence of God? The Presence of God? A Meditation in Three Parts on *Night*," *America* 159, no. 15 (November 19, 1988): 402–406. Reprinted in "Elie Wiesel's *Night*," ed. Harold Bloom (New York: Infobase Publishing, 2010), 29.

7 Ruth R. Wisse, *The Modern Jewish Canon: A Journey Through Language and Culture* (Chicago: University of Chicago Press, 2000), 213.

8 Elie Wiesel, *Night* (New York: Bantam Books, 1982), 35.

9 Wiesel, 64–65.

10 Wiesel, 66.

11 Lustiger, 32.

12 Wiesel, 109.

13 Alvin H. Rosenfeld, "Améry, Levi, Wiesel: The Futility of Holocaust Testimony," in *Elie Wiesel: Jewish, Literary, and Moral Perspectives*, ed. Steven T. Katz and Alan Rosen (Bloomington: Indiana University Press, 2013), Chapter 19.

14 Naomi Seidman, "Elie Wiesel and the Scandal of Jewish Rage," *Jewish Social Studies*, New Series 3, no. 1 (Autumn, 1996), 14–15.

15 Seidman, 8.

16 Elie Wiesel, *Un di velt hot geshvign* (Buenos Aires: Tsentral-Farband fun poylishe yidn in Argentina, 1956), 244, cited in Seidman, 7.

17 Seidman, 8.

18 Wiesel, *Night*, 109.

19 Elie Wiesel, *Un di velt hot geshvign*, as cited in Seidman, 7.

20 Seidman, 15.

21 Many have pointed out that Wiesel's vocal protests of President Reagan's 1985 visit to a cemetery in Bitburg where several members of the Nazi SS had been buried played a role in his being awarded the Nobel Peace Prize.

22 Anne Rothe, *Popular Trauma Culture: Selling the Pain of Others in the Mass Media* (New Brunswick, NJ: Rutgers University Press, 2011), 32.

23 Rothe, 32–35.

24 Rothe, 40–41.

25 Jeffrey Shandler, *Jews, God, and Videotape: Religion and Media in America* (New York: New York University Press, 2009), 128.

26 Shandler, 128.

27 Elie Wiesel, "Art and Culture after the Holocaust," in *Auschwitz: Beginning of a New Era?*, ed. Eva Fleischner (New York: Ktav, 1977), 409.

28 Alain Finkielkraut, *The Imaginary Jew* (Lincoln: University of Nebraska Press, 1994), 36.

Chapter 6

1 At the trial, which lasted ten months, more than 120 prosecution witnesses testified and the court reviewed more than 1,400 exhibits.

2 Lawrence Douglas, *The Memory of Judgment: Making Law and History in the Trials of the Holocaust* (New Haven, CT: Yale University Press, 2001), 6.

3 John McGowan, *Hannah Arendt: An Introduction* (Minneapolis: University of Minnesota Press, 1998), 2–4. The Varnhagen biography was not published until well after World War II.

4 Hannah Arendt, *The Jewish Writings*, ed. Jerome Kohn and Ron H. Feldman (New York: Schocken, 2007), xiv.

5 Elisabeth Young-Bruehl, *Hannah Arendt: For Love of the World* (New Haven, CT: Yale University Press, 2004), 189.

6 Anson Rabinbach, "Eichmann in New York: The New York Intellectuals and the Hannah Arendt Controversy," *October* 108 (Spring, 2004): 97–111: 104.

7 McGowan, 9.

8 Hannah Arendt, *Eichmann in Jerusalem: A Report on the Banality of Evil* [1963], intr. Amos Elon (New York: Penguin, 2006), ix.

9 For a concise summary of the debate, including direct quotes, see Deborah Lipstadt, *The Eichmann Trial* (New York: Schocken, 2011), 148–49.

10 Ravit Reichman, *The Affective Life of Law: Legal Modernism and the Literary Imagination* (Stanford, CA: Stanford University Press, 2009), 140–41.

11 Arendt, 252.

12 Arendt, 287–88.

13 David Cesarani points out, for example, that she only stayed for a few days of Eichmann's testimony. See *Becoming Eichmann: Rethinking the Life, Crimes, and Trial of a "Desk Murderer"* (Cambridge, MA: Da Capo Press, 2006), 15. The fact that Arendt had failed to cite Hilberg as the source of some information in her original reports for *The New Yorker* ired the author himself for many years. Ironically, Arendt was one of the peer reviewers who turned down Hilberg's book. See http://www.thenation.com/article/conscious-pariah

14 Lipstadt, xix.

15 Bettina Stangneth, *Eichmann vor Jerusalem. Das unbehelligte Leben eines Massenmörders* (Zürich: Arche, 2011), 22. Recently published in English as *Eichmann Before Jerusalem: The Unexamined Life of a Mass Murderer* (New York: Knopf, 2014)

16 Roger Berkowitz, "Arendt & Eichmann," *New York Review of Books*, December 19, 2013, in response to Mark Lilla, "Arendt & Eichmann: The New Truth," *New York Review of Books*, November 21, 2013.

17 Arendt, 125.

18 See, for example, Richard J. Bernstein, *Hannah Arendt and the Jewish Question* (Cambridge, MA: The MIT Press, 1996), 161–65.

19 "*Eichmann in Jerusalem*: An Exchange of Letters between Gershom Scholem and Hannah Arendt," *Encounter* 22 (January 1964): 51–56, reprinted in *Hannah Arendt: the Jew as Pariah: Jewish Identity and Politics in the Modern Age*, ed. Ron H. Feldman (New York: Grove Press, 1978), 240–51; 248.

20 Jeffrey Shandler, "The Man in the Glass Box," in *Visual Culture and the Holocaust*, ed. Barbie Zelizer (New Brunswick, NJ: Rutgers University Press, 1998), 105.

21 Susan Sontag, "Reflections on *The Deputy*," in *Against Interpretation and other Essays* (New York: Delta, 1966), 125.

22 Arendt, 233.

23 Darcy C. Buerkle, "Affect in the Archive: Arendt, Eichmann, and The Specialist," in *Visualizing the Holocaust: Documents, Aesthetics, Memory*, ed. David Bathrick, Brad Prager, and Michael David Richardson (Rochester, NY: Camden House, 2008), 217.

24 Buerkle, 211.

25 Buerkle, 215.

26 Arendt, 229.

Chapter 7

1   Eric Bentley, ed., *The Storm Over The Deputy: Essays and Articles About Hochhuth's Explosive Drama* (New York: Grove Press, 1964), 8.

2   Susan Zuccotti, *Under His Very Windows: The Vatican and the Holocaust in Italy* (New Haven, CT: Yale University Press, 2000), 1.

3   "Vietnam in Basel," *Der Spiegel*, October 2, 1963, 84–88.

4   Stephen J. Whitfield, "The Deputy: History, Morality, Art," *Modern Judaism* 30, no. 2 (2010): 154.

5   "Character Assassination" [editorial], *America*, March 7, 1964, in Bentley, 39.

6   Hasia R. Diner, *We Remember with Reverence and Love: American Jews and the Myth of Silence after the Holocaust, 1945–1962* (New York: New York University Press, 2009), 257–59.

7   Rainer Taëni, *Rolf Hochhuth* (Munich: Edition + Kritik, 1977), 14.

8   Historian Michael Marrus first referred to the Allies, neutral powers, the Vatican, and Jews in unoccupied countries as bystanders in *The Holocaust in History* (Hanover, NH: Published for Brandeis University Press by University Press of New England), an influential historiographical study that he published in 1987; five years later, the term would be used by Raul Hilberg in the title of his influential book *Perpetrators, Victims, Bystanders*, thus cementing its use by scholars. David Cesarani and Paul A. Levine, eds., *Bystanders to the Holocaust: a Re-Evaluation* (London: Frank Cass, 2002), 1–4.

9   Several dramas dealing with the Holocaust and its aftermath had been performed in German theaters or broadcast on the radio, but none was as controversial. These include Wolfgang Borchert's *The Man Outside* (1947), Günter Eich's radio play *Dreams* (1953), and Max Frisch's *Andorra* (1958) and *The Fire Raisers* (1958). As Andreas Huyssen points out, a number of plays dealing with these topics were performed in Germany between 1961 and 1965, but they tended to focus on a critique of German society after the war. The only other plays that deal with the events of the Holocaust were Heinar Kipphardt's *Joel Brand* and Peter Weiss's *Die Ermittlung* (*The Investigation*), both performed in 1965. However, unlike these plays, *The Deputy* was performed more often outside Germany than inside. See Andreas Huyssen, *After the Great Divide: Modernism, Mass Culture, Postmodernism* (Bloomington: Indiana University Press, 1986), 106.

10   Gene A. Plunka, *Holocaust Drama: The Theater of Atrocity* (New York: Cambridge University Press, 2009) 173.

11   Rolf Hochhuth, *The Deputy* (Baltimore, MD: The Johns Hopkins University Press, 1997), 287.

12   Susan Sontag, "Reflections on *The Deputy*," *New York Herald*, March 1, 1964, in Bentley, 121.

13   Bertolt Brecht, "Alienation Effects in Chinese Acting," in *Brecht on Theatre: The Development of an Aesthetic*, ed. and trans. John Willett (New York: Hill and Wang, 1964), 91–99.

14 Taëni, 47–48.

15 Hochhuth, 95.

16 Margaret E. Ward, *Rolf Hochhuth* (Boston: Twayne Publishers, 1977), 37.

17 Ward, 34.

18 Whitfield, 156.

19 Hochhuth, 223.

20 Hochhuth, 224.

21 Peter Demetz, *Postwar German Literature: A Critical Introduction* (New York: Pegasus, 1970), 141.

22 Lawrence L. Langer, *Admitting the Holocaust* (New York: Oxford University Press, 1995), 95–96.

23 Hochhuth, 256.

24 Hochhuth, 284–85.

25 Michael R. Marrus, "Pius XII and the Holocaust: Ten Essential Themes," in *Pope Pius XII and the Holocaust*, ed. Carol Rittner and John K. Roth (London: Leicester University Press, 2002), 43.

26 Michael Phayer, *Pius XII, The Holocaust, and The Cold War* (Bloomington: Indiana University Press, 2008), 134.

27 See, for instance, John Cornwell, *Hitler's Pope: The Secret History of Pius XII* (New York: Penguin, 1999).

28 G.B. Cardinal Montini, "Pius XII and the Jews," *The Tablet*, June 1963, in Bentley, 68.

29 Rolf Hochhuth, "The Playwright Answers," *Atlas*, June 1963, in Bentley, 77.

30 "Acts and Documents of the Holy See Relative to the Second World War," http://www.vatican.va/archive/actes/index_en.htm

31 Zuccotti, 6.

32 Kevin P. Spicer, "Catholics", in *The Oxford Handbook of Holocaust Studies*, ed. Peter Hayes and John K. Roth (New York: Oxford University Press, 2010), 245.

33 Hannah Arendt, "*The Deputy:* Guilt by Silence," *New York Herald Tribune Magazine*, February 23, 1964, in Bentley, 90.

34 See for instance, Doris Bergen, *Twisted Cross: The German Christian Movement in the Third Reich* (Chapel Hill: University of North Carolina Press, 1996) and Richard Steigmann-Gall, *The Holy Reich: Nazi Conceptions of Christianity, 1919–1945* (New York: Cambridge University Press, 2004).

35 Carol Rittner and John K. Roth, "Introduction: Calls for Help," in Rittner and Roth, 4.

36 Zuccotti's *Under His Very Windows*, Phayer's *Pius XII, The Holocaust, and The Cold War*, and Cornwell's *Hitler's Pope: The Secret History of Pius XII* all belong to this new generation of scholarship about the Catholic Church and the Holocaust. For representative defenses of the Catholic Church, see *The Pius War: Responses to the Critics of Pius XII*, ed. David G. Dalin and Joseph Bottum (Lanham, MD: Lexington Books, 2010).

37 Sidra DeKoven Ezrahi, *By Words Alone: The Holocaust in Literature* (Chicago: University of Chicago Press, 1980), 44.

Chapter 8

1 Raul Hilberg, *The Destruction of the European Jews*, 3rd edition (New Haven, CT: Yale University Press, 2003).

2 Jeffrey Shandler, *While America Watches: Televising the Holocaust* (New York: Oxford University Press, 1999).

3 Aaron Kerner discusses these two related genres in *Film and the Holocaust: New Perspectives on Dramas, Documentaries, and Experimental Films* (New York: Continuum, 2011), 101–19, 139–54.

4 Alongside *The Night Porter*, other notable examples include Luchino Visconti's *La caduta degli dei* (*The Damned*, 1969), Lina Wertmüller's *Pasqualino Settebellezze* (*Seven Beauties*, 1975), Tinto Brass's *Salon Kitty* (1975), and Pier Paolo Pasolini's *Salò o le 120 giornate di Sodoma* (*Salò, or the 120 Days of Sodom*, 1975).

5 J. Hoberman, "100 Best Films of the 20th Century by the Village Voice Critics Poll", *Village Voice*, January 4, 2000. Reproduced at http://www.filmsite.org/villvoice.html

6 Vincent Canby, "The Night Porter is Romantic Pornography," *The New York Times*, October 31, 1974.

7 Roger Ebert, "*The Night Porter*," *Chicago Sun-Times*, February 10, 1975.

8 Kriss Ravetto, *The Unmaking of Fascist Aesthetics* (Minneapolis: University of Minnesota Press, 2001), 151.

9 Teresa de Lauretis, "Cavani's *The Night Porter*: A Woman's Film?" *Film Quarterly* 30, no. 2 (Winter, 1976): 35–38.

10 Eric Schaefer, *"Bold! Daring! Shocking! True!": A History of Exploitation Films, 1919–1959* (Durham, NC: Duke University Press, 1999), 4.

11 Lynn Rapaport "Holocaust pornography: Profaning the sacred in Ilsa, She-Wolf of the SS," *Shofar: An Interdisciplinary Journal of Jewish Studies* 22, no.1 (2003): 58.

12 Kerner, 103.

13 Monik Korno [pseud.] *Hayiti kalbato ha-peratit shel kolonel Shults* [I was Colonel Schulz's Private Bitch] (Tel Aviv: Eshet, 1962). See Amit Pinchevski and Roy Brand, "Holocaust perversions: The Stalags pulp fiction and the Eichmann trial," *Critical Studies in Media Communication* 24, no. 5 (2007): 387–407.

14 Annette Insdorf, *Indelible Shadows*, 3rd edition (New York: Cambridge University Press, 2003), 131.

15 Susan Sontag, "Fascinating Fascism," in *A Susan Sontag Reader*, ed. Elizabeth Hardwick (New York: Farrar, Straus and Giroux, 1982), 317.

16 Saul Friedländer, *Reflections of Nazism: An Essay on Kitsch and Death* (New York: Harper and Row, 1984), 14.

17 Alicia Kozma, "Ilsa and Elsa: Nazisploitation, Mainstream Film and Cinematic Transference," in *Nazisploitation!: The Nazi Image in Low-Brow Cinema and Culture*, ed. Daniel H. Magilow, Kristin T. Vander Lugt, and Elizabeth Bridges (New York: Continuum, 2012), 55–71; 57.

18 Kozma, 57.

19 Joel Meares, "How Führer Fav Filmmaker Inspired Depictions of Power," *Wired*. http://www.wired.com/magazine/2011/08/pl_prototype_leni/

20 Kozma, 67.

21 Michael D. Richardson, "Sexual Deviance and the Naked Body in Cinematic Representations of Nazis," in *Nazisploitation!: The Nazi Image in Low-Brow Cinema and Culture*, ed. Daniel H. Magilow, Kristin T. Vander Lugt, and Elizabeth Bridges (New York: Continuum, 2012), 38–54; 48. For more on *The Reader* see William Collins Donahue, *Holocaust as Fiction: Bernhard Schlink's Nazi Novels and their Films* (New York: Palgrave Macmillan, 2010).

Chapter 9

1 Elie Wiesel, "Trivializing the Holocaust: Semi-Fact and Semi-Fiction," *The New York Times*, April 16, 1978.

2 *Imaginary Witness: Hollywood and the Holocaust*. Directed by Daniel Anker (USA, 2004).

3 Jeffrey Shandler, *While America Watches: Televising the Holocaust* (New York: Oxford University Press, 1999), 113.

4 Annette Insdorf, *Indelible Shadows: Film and the Holocaust* (New York: Cambridge University Press 2002), 20.

5 Shandler, 113.

6 David L. Paletz, ed., *International Journal of Political Education. Special Double Issue: Reactions to "Holocaust,"* 4, nos.1 and 2 (May 1981), Introduction, 2.

7 Wulf Kansteiner, *In Pursuit of German Memory: History, Television and Politics after Auschwitz* (Athens: Ohio University Press, 2006), 152.

8 Kansteiner, 112–13.

9 Kansteiner, 115 and Wulf Kansteiner, "What is the Opposite of Genocide? Philosemitic Television in Germany, 1963–1995," in *Philosemitism in History*, ed. Jonathan Karp and Adam Sutcliffe (New York: Cambridge University Press, 2011), 292.

10 Kansteiner, *In Pursuit*, 179.

11 Anton, Kaes, "The American television series Holocaust is shown in West Germany," in *Yale Companion to Jewish Writing and Thought in German Culture 1096–1996*, ed. Sander L. Gilman and Jack Zipes (New Haven, CT: Yale University Press, 1997), 784–86.

12 Kaes, 784–86.

13 Kansteiner, *In Pursuit*, 117–22.

14 Menachem Z. Rosensaft, "Distorting the Holocaust," *Midstream*, June/July, 1978, 55.

15 American Jewish Committee, "Americans Confront the Holocaust," 7.

Chapter 10

1 Interview with Claude Lanzmann by Serge Toubiana, http://www.criterion. com/current/posts/2817-claude-lanzmann-on-shoah, posted on June 25, 2013, accessed August 15, 2013.

2 Interview with Claude Lanzmann by Serge Toubiana.

3 The audience nevertheless exceeded the expectations of Lanzmann, who claimed in a February 26, 2005 interview in *Le Monde* that he believed only a few thousand people would see his film. See *Claude Lanzmann's* Shoah*: Key Essays*, ed. Stuart Liebman (New York: Oxford University Press, 2007), 19 note 9.

4 For many years, *Shoah* was the "most profitable documentary film ever released in the United States." Liebman, 5.

5 For instance, *Shoah* appeared at number 29 on the list of Top 50 Greatest Films of All Time in the September, 2012 issue of *Sight & Sound*, the journal of the British Film Institute. http://www.bfi.org.uk/news/50-greatest-films-all-time

6 Up to that point, popular films tended to adapt Holocaust and World War II themes to well-known genres such as spy films, war movies, and science fiction. Independent films with smaller audiences that predated *Shoah*, such as *The Night Porter* and other neo-Nazisploitation films, had their own agendas in using the Holocaust as a historical backdrop (see Chapter 8).

7 Claude Lanzmann, *The Patagonian Hare: A Memoir* (New York: Macmillan, 2012), 432.

8 Claude Lanzmann, *Shoah: An Oral History of the Holocaust. The Complete Text of the Film* (New York: Pantheon, 1985), 133 and 111–12.

9 Lanzmann also notes that he and Bomba remained on good terms, even after Bomba had seen the film. Lanzmann, *Patagonian Hare*, 435.

10 Felman, Shoshana, and Dori Laub, *Testimony: Crises of Witnessing in Literature, Psychoanalysis, and History* (New York: Routledge, 1992), 206.

11 Lanzmann, *Shoah*, 174.

12 For example, see Dalia Ofer and Lenore J. Weitzman, eds., *Women in the Holocaust* (New Haven, CT: Yale University Press, 1998); Carol Rittner and John K. Roth, eds., *Different Voices: Women and the Holocaust* (New York: Paragon House, 1993); and Sonja M. Hedgepeth and Rochelle G. Saidel, eds., *Sexual Violence against Jewish Women during the Holocaust* (Waltham, MA: Brandeis University Press, 2010).

13 Marianne Hirsch and Leo Spitzer, "Gendered Translations: Claude Lanzmann's *Shoah*," in *Gendering War Talk*, ed. Miriam Cook and Angela Woollacott (Princeton, NJ: Princeton University Press, 1993), 16.

14 Jean-Charles Szurek, "*Shoah*: From the Jewish Question to the Polish Question," in Liebman, 149–69; 153.

15 Jan Karski, "*Shoah*," in Liebman, 171–74; 171. Lanzmann seems to have addressed this issue in the release of his 2010 film, *The Karski Report*, which includes the rest of the footage from the interview he conducted with Karski in 1978. In that film, Karski recalls that United States Supreme Court Justice Felix Frankfurter, upon hearing of the horrors to the Jews he witnessed in Poland, stated firmly "I do not believe you."

16 Lanzmann readily admits that he had no intention of respecting Suchomel's condition that he remains anonymous. And when interviewing Stier, he pretended to be a researcher from a fictitious history research center at the University of Paris who was studying how the Reichsbahn managed to carry out its extraordinary mission during the war. Lanzmann, *Patagonian Hare*, 446–50.

17 Lanzmann, *Patagonian Hare*, 449, 454.

18 Yosefa Loshitzky, ed., *Spielberg's Holocaust: Critical Perspectives on Schindler's List* (Bloomington: Indiana University Press, 1997), 2.

19 Sara R. Horowitz, "But is it Good for the Jews?: Spielberg's Schindler and the Aesthetics of Atrocity," in Loshitzky, 119–39; 128.

20 Miriam Hansen, "*Schindler's List* is not *Shoah*: The Second Commandment, Popular Modernism, and Public Memory," *Critical Inquiry* 22 (Winter, 1996): 302.

21 Hansen, 296, 310.

22 Barbie Zelizer, "Every Once in a While: *Schindler's List* and the Shaping of History," in Loshitzky, 18–35; 21.

23 Zelizer, 28.

24 Zelizer, 29.

25 Hansen, 302.

26 "Filmmaker who bore witness to Holocaust," *Harvard Gazette*, March 28, 2012. http://news.harvard.edu/gazette/story/2012/03/filmmaker-who-bore-witness-to-holocaust/, accessed November 2, 2013.

Chapter 11

1 Spiegelman, Letter to the editor, *The New York Times Book Review*, December 29, 1991, 4.

2 Sara R. Horowitz, *Voicing the Void: Muteness and Memory in Holocaust Fiction* (Albany: State University of New York Press, 1997), 7.

3 Art Spiegelman, *Maus: A Survivor's Tale*. Vol. I (New York: Pantheon Books, 1986–1991), 125.

4 Alan Rosen, "The Language of Survival: English as Metaphor in Spiegelman's *Maus*," *Prooftexts* 15, no. 3 (September 1995), 249.

5   Art Spiegelman, *Maus: A Survivor's Tale*. Vol. II (New York: Pantheon Books, 1986–1991), 134.

6   Marianne Hirsch, "Family Pictures: Maus, Mourning, and Post-Memory," *Discourse* 15, no. 2, *Special issue: the Emotions, Gender, and the Politics of Subjectivity* (Winter, 1992–93), 12, 15, 25.

7   Hirsch, 12.

8   Spiegelman, *Maus: A Survivor's Tale*. Vol. II, 134.

9   Spiegelman, *Maus: A Survivor's Tale*. Vol. I, 100–103.

10 Art Spiegelman, *MetaMaus* (New York: Pantheon Books, 2011), 35.

11 Hirsch, 18.

12 Spiegelman, *MetaMaus*, 36.

13 Spiegelman, *Maus: A Survivor's Tale*. Vol. I, 158.

14 Erin McGlothlin, *Second-Generation Holocaust Literature: Legacies of Survival and Perpetration* (Rochester, NY: Camden House, 2006), 10.

15 For a useful selection of texts by children of Holocaust survivors, some translated from German and Hebrew, see *Nothing Makes you Free: Writings by Descendants of Jewish Holocaust Survivors*, ed. Melvin Jules Bukiet (New York: Norton, 2002).

16 Dan Diner, "Negative Symbiosis: Germans and Jews after Auschwitz," in *Reworking the Past: Hitler, the Holocaust and the Historians' Debate*, ed. Peter Baldwin (Boston, MA: Beacon Press, 1990), 251.

17 Hirsch, 8–9.

18 Spiegelman, *MetaMaus*, 48.

Chapter 12

1   "Kohl Meets with Jewish Leaders," *The New York Times*, October 26, 1985, 1.

2   "Remarks of President Reagan to Regional Editors," White House, April 18, 1985, as cited in *Bitburg in Moral and Political Perspective*, ed. Geoffrey Hartman (Bloomington: Indiana University Press, 1986), 239–40; 240.

3   Edward T. Linenthal, *Preserving Memory: The Struggle to Create America's Holocaust Museum* (New York: Columbia University Press, 1995), 130.

4   "The 1985 Pazz & Jop Critics Poll," *Village Voice*, February 18, 1986.

5   "Kohl Meets with Jewish Leaders," *The New York Times*, October 26, 1985.

6   Harold Marcuse, "Holocaust Memorials: the Emergence of a Genre," *American Historical Review* 115 (February 2010): 53–89; 55.

7   Hasia R. Diner, *We Remember with Reverence and Love: American Jews and the Myth of Silence after the Holocaust, 1945–1962* (New York: New York University Press, 2009), 36–37.

8   Its rich archival collections also make it a key destination for Holocaust researchers worldwide, many of whom find it easier to access documents in

Washington, DC than in the very countries whose history they are studying. http://www.ushmm.org/information/about-the-museum/museum-history

9 Linenthal, 11.

10 "President's Commission on the Holocaust," http://www.ushmm.org/m/pdfs/20050707-presidents-commission-holocaust.pdf

11 "About the Museum," United States Holocaust Memorial Museum, http://www.ushmm.org/information/about-the-museum

12 Michael Berenbaum, *The World Must Know: The History of the Holocaust as Told in the United States Holocaust Memorial Museum*, 2nd edition (Washington, DC: United States Holocaust Memorial Museum, 2006), xx.

13 Linenthal describes in detail the controversies about the initial design and subsequent hiring of Freed. Linenthal, 72–108.

14 Herbert Muschamp, "Shaping a Monument to Memory," *The New York Times*, April 11, 1993.

15 Liliane Weissberg, "In Plain Sight," in *Visual Culture and the Holocaust*, ed. Barbie Zelizer (London: Athlone Press, 2001), 13–27; 19.

16 Linenthal, 91.

17 Linenthal, 170.

18 Linenthal, 168.

19 "Permanent Exhibition Narrative," United States Holocaust Memorial Museum, 15. http://www.ushmm.org/m/pdfs/20060925-PEnarrative.pdf

20 http://www.theguardian.com/artanddesign/2005/mar/15/heritage.israelandthepalestinians

21 Omer Bartov discusses the ignoring of Jewish victims and the active erasure of their past in *Erased: Vanishing Traces of Jewish Galicia in Present-day Ukraine* (Princeton, NJ: Princeton University Press, 2007).

22 John-Paul Himka and Joanna Beata Michlic, eds., *Bringing the Dark Past to Light: the Reception of the Holocaust in Postcommunist Europe* (Lincoln: University of Nebraska Press, 2013), 4–6.

23 Olga Gershenson, *The Phantom Holocaust: Soviet Cinema and Jewish Catastrophe* (New Brunswick, NJ: Rutgers University Press, 2013), 1–3.

24 Himka and Michlic, 3.

25 Martin Gilbert, *The Atlas of Jewish History* (New York: William Morrow, 1992), 98.

26 Erica T. Lehrer, *Jewish Poland Revisited: Heritage Tourism in Unquiet Places* (Bloomington: Indiana University Press, 2013), 1.

27 James E. Young, "Memorials and Museums," in *The Oxford Handbook of Holocaust Studies*, ed. Peter Hayes and John K. Roth (New York: Oxford University Press, 2010), 491.

28 Alan L. Mintz, *Popular Culture and the Shaping of Holocaust Memory in America* (Seattle: University of Washington Press, 2001), 161. For a detailed discussion see Peter Novick, *The Holocaust in American Life* (Boston: Houghton Mifflin, 1999).

Chapter 13

1   Stefan Mächler, *The Wilkomirski Affair: A Study in Biographical Truth* (New York: Schocken, 2001), 114.

2   Julie Salomon, "Childhood's End," *The New York Times*, January 12, 1997.

3   Jonathan Kozol, "Children of the Camps," *The Nation*, October 28, 1996.

4   Timothy D. Neale, " '. . . the credentials that would rescue me': Trauma and the Fraudulent Survivor," *Holocaust and Genocide Studies* 24, no. 3 (2010): 432.

5   Binjamin Wilkomirski, *Fragments: Memories of a Wartime Childhood* (New York: Schocken Books, 1996) 4.

6   Wilkomirski, 155.

7   Anne Rothe, *Popular Trauma Culture: Selling the Pain of Others in the Mass Media* (New Brunswick, NJ: Rutgers University Press, 2011), 8.

8   Mächler, 129.

9   Harvey Peskin, "Holocaust Denial: A Sequel. The Case of Binjamin Wilkomirski's *Fragments*," *The Nation*, April 19, 1999.

10 Blake Eskin, *A Life in Pieces: The Making and Unmaking of Binjamin Wilkomirski* (New York: Norton, 2002), 76–77.

11 Mächler, 167.

12 Wilkomirski, 154.

13 Lawrence L. Langer, *Using and Abusing the Holocaust* (Bloomington: Indiana University Press, 2006), 56.

14 Mächler, vii.

15 Mächler, 268.

16 Mächler, 268.

17 "Publisher Drops Holocaust Book," *The New York Times*, November 3, 1999.

18 Peskin.

19 Susan Rubin Suleiman, "Problems of Memory and Factuality in Recent Holocaust Memoirs: Wilkomirski/Wiesel," *Poetics Today* 21, no. 3 (2000): 543–59.

20 Stefan Machler and Moira Moehler-Woods, "Wilkomirski the Victim: Individual Remembering as Social Interaction and Public Event," *History & Memory* 13, no. 2 (2001): 67.

21 Jay Geller, "The Wilkomirski Case: Fragments or Figments?" *American Imago* 59, no. 3 (Fall 2002): 358.

22 Annette Wieviorka, *The Era of the Witness*, trans. Jared Stark (Ithaca, NY: Cornell University Press, 2006), 97.

23 Edward T. Linenthal, *Preserving Memory: the Struggle to Create America's Holocaust Museum* (New York: Penguin, 1995), 216.

24 Philip Gourevitch, "The Memory Thief," *The New Yorker*, June 14, 1999: 48–68.

Chapter 14

1 Congressional Record, V. 147, Pt. 9, June 26, 2001 to July 16, 2001. June 29, 2001, Congressional Record—Extensions of Remarks p. E1249.

2 Jodi Rudoren, "Holocaust Told in One Word, 6 Million Times," *The New York Times*, January 25, 2014.

3 Personal correspondence of Daniel H. Magilow with Linda Hooper, October 5, 2005.

4 Lydia Kokkola, ed., *Representing the Holcaust in Children's Literature* (London: Routledge, 2003), 3.

5 Deborah H. White, ed., "Learning Through Service: A Tennessee Sampler," http://www.tn.gov/finance/adm/vt/documents/LearningthroughService-ATennesseeSampler.pdf

6 Peter W. Schroeder and Dagmar Schroeder-Hildebrand, *Six Million Paper Clips: The Making of a Children's Holocaust Memorial* (Minneapolis, MN: Kar-Ben Publishing, 2004), 9.

7 "The Beginning" http://www.whitwellmiddleschool.org/?PageName=bc&n=69258

8 Ori Nir, "Bushes 'Touched' by Holocaust Documentary," *Forward*, March 4, 2005.

9 Simone Schweber, "Holocaust education," *International Handbook of Jewish Education* (Springer: Dordrecht, 2011), 475.

10 Henry Petroski, *The Evolution of Useful Things: How Everyday Artifacts—From Forks and Pins to Paper Clips and Zippers—Came to be as They Are* (New York: Vintage, 1994), 60–65.

11 "Utstillinges temaer" Forsvarets museer. http://forsvaretsmuseer.no/Hjemmefrontmuseet/Utstillingene/Utstillingenes-temaer

12 Marc Gellman, "Paper Boats," *Newsweek* (online edition), August 10, 2005. On the dehumanization of the victims, see, for example, Omer Bartov, *Germany's War and the Holocaust: Disputed Histories* (Ithaca, NY: Cornell University Press, 2003), 101–102.

13 A.O. Scott, "Grasping Extraordinary Evil Through the Very Ordinary," *The New York Times*, November 24, 2004.

14 See, for example, Lawrence Langer, *Holocaust Testimonies: The Ruins of Memory* (New Haven, CT: Yale University Press, 1991).

15 "Peoria Holocaust Memorial Button Project," http://www.peoriaholocaustmemorial.org/; "The Butterfly Project, Holocaust Museum Houston," http://www.hmh.org/ed_butterfly1.shtml; "Project6Million," http://www.project6million.org/; "Inspired by 'Paper Clips' Students Collect 6 Million Pennies," http://matzav.com/inspired-by-'paper clips'-students-collect-6-million-pennies

Chapter 15

1   "The New Season/Art," *The New York Times*, September 9, 2001.

2   Norman L. Kleeblatt, "Acknowledgments," in *Mirroring Evil: Nazi Imagery/ Recent Art*, ed. Norman L. Kleeblatt (New Brunswick, NJ: Rutgers University Press, 2001), ix.

3   Joan Rosenbaum, "Director's Preface," in Kleeblatt, vii.

4   Two other major exhibitions included "Witness and Legacy: Contemporary Art About the Holocaust," a traveling exhibition with works by 22 artists designed to commemorate the 50th anniversary of the liberation of Auschwitz and shown at 17 different museum sites throughout the United States between 1995 and 2002, and in 1999, "Absense/Presence: The Artistic Memory of Holocaust and Genocide," which linked artistic representations of the Holocaust with those of other genocides. Steve Feinstein, "Introduction," in *Absence/presence. Essays and Reflections on the Artistic Memory of the Holocaust*, ed. Steve Feinstein (Syracuse, NY: Syracuse University Press, 2005), xxii.

5   Reesa Greenberg, "*Mirroring Evil*, Evil Mirrored: Timing, Trauma, and Temporary Exhibitions" in *Museums After Modernism: Strategies of Engagement*, ed. Griselda Pollock and Joyce Zemans (New York: Wiley, 2007), 104–18.

6   Thane Rosenbaum, "*Mirroring Evil*," *Tikkun* 17, no. 3 (May/June 2002): 69.

7   Eleanor Heartney, "Out of the Bunker," *Art in America* (July 2002): 43.

8   Heartney, 43.

9   Howard Kissel, "Shock Art Hits a Rut," *New York Daily News*, January 11, 2002.

10 Peter Ephross, "Holocaust Art Exhibit is Altered, but Critics Vow to Launch Boycott," *Jewish Telegraphic Agency*, March 7, 2002, 6. Also Barbara Stewart, "Jewish Museum to Add Warning Label on Its Show," *The New York Times*, March 2, 2002.

11 Greenberg, 112–13.

12 Stevenson Swanson, "Jewish Museum's Holocaust Exhibit Igniting Outrage," *Chicago Tribune*, March 17, 2002.

13 Menachem Z. Rosensaft, "Demystifying Nazism, or Trivializing Its Victims? A Debate: How Pseudo-Artists Desecrate the Holocaust," *Forward*, January 18, 2002.

14 Michael Kimmelman, "Evil, the Nazis and Shock Value," *The New York Times*, March 15, 2002.

15 Hilton Kramer, "Jewish Museum Show Full of Vile Crap, Not to Be Forgiven," *New York Observer*, April 1, 2002.

16 Linda Nochlin, *Artforum* 40, no. 10 (Summer, 2002): 167.

17 Nochlin, 167.

18 Dora Apel, "Art," in *The Oxford Handbook of Holocaust Studies*, ed. Peter Hayes and John K. Roth (New York: Oxford University Press, 2010), 463.

19   Nochlin, 207.

20   For a broader discussion of the theory of avant-garde, see Peter Bürger, *Theory of the Avant-Garde*, trans. Michael Shaw (Minneapolis: University of Minnesota Press, 1984).

21   Rudolf Gerz, "Zugzwang (Forced Movement)." Accessed December 8, 2013. http://www.rudolfherz.de/ZUGZWANG.HTML

22   Norman L. Kleeblatt, "Maciej Toporowicz: Fascinating Fascism: Then or Now?" in Kleeblatt, 132.

23   Deborah Solomon, "The Way We Live Now: Questions for Tom Sachs, Designer Death Camp," *The New York Times Magazine*, March 10, 2002.

24   Peter Schjeldahl, "The Hitler Show," *The New Yorker*, April 1, 2002, 87.

25   Kleeblatt, 124.

26   Ernst van Alphen, "Playing the Holocaust," in Kleeblatt, 67.

27   van Alphen, 71.

Chapter 16

1   http://www.buzzfeed.com/stacylambe/15-grindr-profile-pics-taken-at-the-holocaust-memo See also Daniel d'Addario, "Grindr's odd Holocaust fetish," http://www.salon.com/2013/01/30/grindrs_odd_holocaust_fetish/

2   http://grindr-remembers.blogspot.com, accessed December 27, 2013.

3   "EasyJet pulls in-flight magazine over Holocaust fashion shoot," *The Guardian*, November 24, 2009, http://www.theguardian.com/business/2009/nov/24/easyjet-holocaust-fashion

4   For a good overview of various responses in English, see http://www.pbs.org/wgbh/pages/frontline/shows/germans/memorial/reviews.html

5   Thomas A. Kovach and Martin Walser, *The Burden of the Past: Martin Walser on Modern German Identity: Texts, Contexts, Commentary* (Rochester, NY: Camden House, 2008), 102.

6   For the purposes of this chapter, we follow James E. Young's definition of monuments as a subcategory of memorials, whereas memorials can be anything that draw attention to memory/commemoration, such as a day or an event, while monuments are "plastic" (that is, physical) objects. *The Texture of Memory: Holocaust Memorials and Meaning* (New Haven, CT: Yale University Press, 1993), 4.

7   "Berlin opens Holocaust memorial," *BBC News*, May 10, 2005, http://news.bbc.co.uk/2/hi/4531669.stm

8   Young, 27.

9   Young, 6.

10   Young, 30.

11   Young, 45.

12 Caroline Wiedmer, *The Claims of Memory: Representations of the Holocaust in Contemporary Germany and France* (Ithaca, NY: Cornell University Press, 1999), 106.

13 Jane Kramer, "The Politics of Memory," *The New Yorker*, August 14, 1995, 48.

14 Kramer, 49–50.

15 Kramer, 56 and "Reviews of Germany's National 'Memorial to the Murdered Jews of Europe," http://www.pbs.org/wgbh/pages/frontline/shows/germans/memorial/reviews.html

16 Irit Dekel, *Mediation at the Holocaust Memorial in Berlin* (New York: Palgrave Macmillan, 2013), 3.

17 Dekel, 4, 31, 35.

18 Dekel, 26.

19 Marita Sturken, "Pilgrimages, Reenactment, and Souvenirs. Modes of Memory Tourism," in *Rites of Return: Diaspora Poetics and the Politics of Memory*, ed. Marianne Hirsch and Nancy K. Miller (New York: Columbia University Press, 2013), 288.

20 Dekel, 173.

21 Karen E. Till, *The New Berlin: Memory, Politics, Place* (Minneapolis: University of Minnesota Press, 2005), 187.

22 Kramer, 62–63.

23 Eisenman Architects, "Realisierungsentwurf" as cited in Janet Ward, "Monuments of Catastrophe: Holocaust Architecture in Washington and Berlin," in *Berlin–Washington 1800–2000: Capital Cities, Cultural Representation, and National Identities*, ed. Andreas W. Daum and Christof Mauch (New York: Cambridge University Press, 2005), 178.

24 "Stolpersteine," http://www.stolpersteine.eu/en/home/

25 Lois Gilman, "Memory Blocks: Artist Gunter Demnig builds a Holocaust Memorial one stone at a time," October 1, 2007, http://www.smithsonianmag.com/people-places/europe/stolpersteine.html

26 Rabbi Levi Brackman, "Shoah memorial app launched in Germany," Ynetnews.com, October 28, 2013, http://www.ynetnews.com/articles/0,7340,L-4446050,00.html

27 Dekel, 2–6.

Further Reading

Introduction

Adorno, Theodor W. *Prisms*. Cambridge, MA: The MIT Press, 1982.

Applebaum, Diana Muir. "Other Outlooks: Is the Jewish museum boom a good thing?" *Jewish Outlook*. November 1, 2011.

Des Pres, Terrence. "Holocaust Laughter." In *Writing and the Holocaust*, edited by Berel Lang, 216–33. New York: Holmes and Meier, 1988.

Hancock, Ian. "On the interpretation of a word: Porrajmos as Holocaust." http://www.radoc.net/radoc.php?doc=art_e_holocaust_interpretation&lang (accessed July 31, 2014).

Hayes, Peter, and John K. Roth, eds. *The Oxford Handbook of Holocaust Studies*. New York: Oxford University Press, 2010.

"Holocaust" Shoah Resource Center http://www.yadvashem.org/odot_pdf/ Microsoft%20Word%20-%206419.pdf (accessed July 31, 2014).

"Holocaust Survivor Stories Live on in Holograms." Here and Now with Robin Young and Jeremy Hobson, 90.9 WBUR Boston. April 8, 2013. http:// hereandnow.wbur.org/2013/04/08/holocaust-survivor-holograms

"Introduction to the Holocaust." United States Holocaust Memorial Museum, http://www.ushmm.org/wlc/en/article.php?ModuleId=10005143 (accessed July 31, 2014).

Lang, Berel. *Holocaust Representation: Art within the Limits of History and Ethics*. Baltimore, MD: Johns Hopkins University Press, 2000.

Lawson, Tom. *Debates on the Holocaust*. Manchester: Manchester University Press, 2010.

Linenthal, Edward T. *Preserving Memory: The Struggle to Create America's Holocaust Museum*. New York: Penguin, 1995.

Mitchell, W. J. T. "Representation." In *Critical Terms for Literary Study*, edited by Frank Lentricchia and Thomas McLaughlin, 11–22. Chicago: University of Chicago Press, 1995.

Niewyk, Donald. *The Holocaust: Problems and Perspectives of Interpretation*. 4th edition. Stamford, CT: Cengage Learning, 2011.

Niewyk, Donald L., and Francis R. Nicosia. *The Columbia Guide to the Holocaust*. New York: Columbia University Press, 2000.

Petrie, Jon. "The Secular Word HOLOCAUST: Scholarly Myths, History, and 20th century Meanings." *Journal of Genocide Research* 2, no. 1 (2000): 31–63.

Ray, Gene. *Terror and the Sublime in Art and Critical Theory: From Auschwitz to Hiroshima to September 11*. Basingstoke: Palgrave Macmillan, 2005.

Rich, Frank. "Journal: The Holocaust Boom." *The New York Times*. April 7, 1994.

Rosenfeld, Alvin H. *The End of the Holocaust*. Bloomington: Indiana University Press, 2011.

Roskies, David G. *Against the Apocalypse: Responses to Catastrophe in Modern Jewish Culture*. Syracuse, NY: Syracuse University Press, 1999.

Shandler, Jeffrey. *While America Watches: Televising the Holocaust*. New York: Oxford University Press, 1999.

Winter, Jay. "The Generation of Memory: Reflections on the 'Memory Boom' in Contemporary Historical Studies." *Bulletin of the German Historical Institute* 27, no. 3 (2000): 69–92.

Young, James E. *Writing and Rewriting the Holocaust: Narrative and the Consequences of Interpretation*. Bloomington: Indiana University Press, 1990.

Zelizer, Barbie. *Remembering to Forget: Holocaust Memory Through the Camera's Eye*. Chicago: University of Chicago Press, 1998.

Chapter 1

Brink, Cornelia. "Secular Icons: Looking at Photographs from Nazi Concentration Camps." *History & Memory* 12, no. 1 (2000): 135–50.

Dwork, Debórah. *Children With A Star: Jewish Youth in Nazi Europe*. New Haven, CT: Yale University Press, 1991.

Engelking, Barbara, and Jacek Leociak. *The Warsaw Ghetto: A Guide to the Perished City*. New Haven, CT: Yale University Press, 2009.

Hirsch, Marianne. "Nazi Photographs in Post-Holocaust Art: Gender as an Idiom of Memorialization." In *Phototextualities: Intersections of Photography and Narrative*, edited by Alex Hughes and Andrea Noble, 19–40. Albuquerque: University of New Mexico Press, 2003.

Jahns, Joachim. *Der Warschauer Ghettokönig*. Leipzig: Dingsda Verlag, 2009.

Kassow, Samuel. *Who Will Write Our History?: Emanuel Ringelblum, the Warsaw Ghetto, and the Oyneg Shabes Archives*. Bloomington: Indiana University Press, 2007.

Kemp, Martin. *Christ to Coke: How Image Becomes Icon*. New York: Oxford University Press, 2012.

"Nazi Terrorism in Poland is Brought to Light." *The New York Times*. December 26, 1947.

"Nuremberg Trials Project: A Digital Document Collection." Harvard Law School Library. Accessed December 3, 2013. nuremberg.law.harvard.edu

"Photographer at War." *The New York Times*. December 27, 1945.

Porat, Dan. *The Boy: A Holocaust Story*. New York: Hill and Wang, 2010.

Raskin, Richard. *A Child at Gunpoint: A Case Study in the Life of a Photo*. Aarhus: Aarhus University Press, 2004.

Stroop, Jürgen. *The Stroop Report: The Jewish Quarter of Warsaw is No More!* New York: Pantheon Books, 1979.

Zelizer, Barbie. *About to Die: How News Images Move the Public*. New York: Oxford University Press, 2010.

Chapter 2

Bathrick, David. "The Afterlife of Triumph of the Will: The First Twenty-five Years." In *Riefenstahl Screened: An Anthology of New Criticism*, edited by Neil Christian Pages, Mary Rhiel, and Ingeborg Majer-O'Sickey, 73–97. New York: Continuum, 2008.

Bathrick, David, Brad Prager, and Michael David Richardson, eds. *Visualizing the Holocaust: Documents, Aesthetics, Memory*. Rochester, NY: Camden House, 2012.

Carr, Steven Alan. *Hollywood and Anti-Semitism: a Cultural History up to World War II*. Cambridge: Cambridge University Press, 2001.

Douglas, Lawrence. *The Memory of Judgment: Making Law and History in the Trials of the Holocaust*. New Haven, CT: Yale University Press, 2001.

Gladstone, Kay. "Separate Intentions: The Allied Screening of Concentration Camp Documentaries in Defeated Germany in 1945–46: *Death Mills* and *Memory of the Camps*." In *Holocaust and the Moving Image: Representations in Film and Television since 1933*, edited by Toby Haggith and Joanna Newman, 50–64. London: Wallflower Press, 2005.

Kaes, Anton. *From Hitler to Heimat: The Return of History as Film*. Cambridge, M.A.: Harvard University Press, 1989.

Kozlovsky-Golan, Yvonne. *The Shaping of the Holocaust Visual Image by the Nuremberg Trials. The Impact of the Movie Nazi Concentration Camps*. Jerusalem: Yad Vashem, 2006.

Lang, Berel. *Holocaust Representation: Art within the Limits of History and Ethics*. Baltimore, MD: Johns Hopkins University Press, 2000.

Picart, Caroline Joan S., and David A. Frank. *Frames of Evil: the Holocaust as Horror in American Film*. Carbondale: Southern Illinois University Press, 2006.

Pollock, Grisela, and Max Silverman, eds. *Concentrationary Cinema: Aesthetics as Political Resistance in Alain Resnais's "Night and Fog."* New York: Berghahn, 2011.

Salter, Michael. *Nazi War Crimes, U.S. Intelligence and Selective Prosecution at Nuremberg: Controversies Regarding the Role of the Office of Strategic Services*. New York: Routledge-Cavendish, 2007.

Tusa, Ann, and John Tusa. *The Nuremberg Trial*. New York: Skyhorse, 2010.

"War-Crimes Court Sees Horror Films." *The New York Times*. November 30, 1945.

Wilson, Kristi, and Tomas F. Crowder-Taraborrelli, eds. *Film & Genocide*. Madison: University of Wisconsin Press, 2012.

Zelizer, Barbie. *Visual Culture and the Holocaust*. New Brunswick, NJ: Rutgers University Press, 2001.

Chapter 3

Amir, Michlean. "Israel as the Cradle of Yizker-Books." In *Memorial Books of Eastern European Jewry: Essays on the History and Meanings of Yizker Volumes*, edited by Rosemary Horowitz, 28–42. Jefferson, NC: McFarland, 2011.

Bakalczuk-Felin, Mellech, ed. *Yizker-bukh Khelm*. Johannesburg: Khelmer landsmanshaft in Johannesburg, 1954.

Boyarin, Jonathan. "Yizker-bikher." In *The YIVO Encyclopedia of Jews in Eastern Europe*. Accessed July 31, 2013. www.yivoencyclopedia.org/article.aspx/Yizker-bikher

Cesarani, David, and Eric J. Sundquist, eds. *After the Holocaust: Challenging the Myth of Silence*. London: Routledge, 2012.

Diner, Hasia R. *We Remember with Reverence and Love: American Jews and the Myth of Silence after the Holocaust, 1945–1962*. New York: New York University Press, 2009.

Herf, Jeffrey. *Divided Memory: The Nazi Past in the Two Germanys*. Cambridge, MA: Harvard University Press, 1997.

Horowitz, Rosemary, ed. *Memorial Books of Eastern European Jewry: Essays on the History and Meanings of Yizker Volumes*, Jefferson, NC: McFarland, 2011.

Jokusch, Laura. *Collect and Record!: Jewish Holocaust Documentation in Early Postwar Europe*. New York: Oxford University Press, 2012.

Kugelmass, Jack, and Jonathan Boyarin, ed. and trans. *From a Ruined Garden: The Memorial Books of Polish Jewry*. 2nd edition. Bloomington: Indiana University Press, 1998.

Novick, Peter. *The Holocaust in American Life*. New York: Houghton Mifflin, 1999.

Roskies, David G., and Naomi Diamont. *Holocaust Literature: A History and Guide*. Waltham, MA: Brandeis University Press, 2012.

Segev, Tom. *The Seventh Million: Israelis and the Holocaust*. Translated by Haim Watzman. New York: Hill & Wang, 1993.

Shatzky, Jacob. "Yisker bikher." *YIVO Bleter 39* (1955): 339–55. Translated as "Review of Yizker Books 1955" in *Memorial Books of Eastern European Jewry: Essays on the History and Meanings of Yizker Volumes*, edited by Rosemary Horowitz, 68–80. Jefferson, NC: McFarland, 2011.

Yizkor Book Project. JewishGen, Inc. Accessed July 31, 2013. http://www.jewishgen.org/yizkor/

Yizker-bukh Khelm. Edited by Mellech Bakalczuk-Felin. Johannesburg: Khelmer landsmanshaft in Johannesburg, 1954.

Yizkor (Holocaust Memorial) Books, New York Public Library. Accessed July 31, 2013. legacy.www.nypl.org/research/chss/jws/yizkorbooks_intro.cfm

Young, James E. *The Texture of Memory: Holocaust Memorials and Meaning*. New Haven, CT: Yale University Press, 1993.

Chapter 4

Barnouw, David, and Gerrold van der Stroom, eds. *The Diary of Anne Frank: The Revised Critical Edition*. New York: Doubleday, 2003.

Canby, Vincent. "A New 'Anne Frank' Still Stuck in the 50s." *The New York Times*. December 21, 1997.

Croes, Marnix, "The Holocaust in the Netherlands and the Rate of Jewish Survival." *Holocaust and Genocide Studies* 20, no. 3 (2006): 474–99.

Driscoll, Molly. "Michigan school: 'Anne Frank' will stay." *Christian Science Monitor*. May 13, 2013.

Flanzbaum, Helene, ed. *The Americanization of the Holocaust*. Baltimore, MD: The Johns Hopkins University Press, 1999.

Goodrich, Frances, and Albert Hackett. *The Diary of Anne Frank*. New York: Random House, 1956.

Graver, Lawrence. *An Obsession with Anne Frank: Meyer Levin and the Diary*. Berkeley: University of California Press, 1995.

Kirshenblatt-Gimblett, Barbara, and Jeffrey Shandler, eds. *Anne Frank Unbound: Media, Imagination, Memory*. Bloomington: Indiana University Press, 2012.

Levin, Meyer. "Life in the Secret Annex." *The New York Times*. June 15, 1952.

Levin, Meyer. *The Obsession*. New York: Simon and Schuster, 1973.

Lindwer, Willy. *The Last Seven Months of Anne Frank*. New York: Random House, 1991.

Müller, Melissa. *Anne Frank: The Biography*. New York: Metropolitan Books, 2013.

Nashon, Edna. "Anne Frank From Page to Stage." In *Anne Frank Unbound: Media, Imagination, Memory*, edited by Barbara Kirshenblatt-Gimblett and Jeffrey Shandler, 59–92. Bloomington: Indiana University Press, 2012.

Ozick, Cynthia. "Who Owns Anne Frank?" In *Quarrel and Quandry*, 74–102. New York: Knopf, 2000.

Prose, Francine. *Anne Frank: The Book, The Life, The Afterlife*. New York: HarperCollins, 2009.

Rosenfeld, Alvin H. "Anne Frank and the Future of Holocaust Memory." Joseph and Rebecca Meyerhoff Annual Lecture, October 14, 2004. Washington, DC: United States Holocaust Memorial Museum.

Tammes, Peter. "Jewish immigrants in the Netherlands during the Nazi occupation." *Journal of Interdisciplinary History* 37, no. 4 (2007): 543–62.

Wolf, Diane L. *Beyond Anne Frank: Hidden Children and Postwar Families in Holland*. Berkeley: University of California Press, 2007.

Zapruder, Alexandra, ed. *Salvaged Pages: Young Writers' Diaries of the Holocaust*. New Haven, CT: Yale University Press, 2002.

Chapter 5

Bloom, Harold, ed. *Elie Wiesel's Night*. New York: Infobase Publishing, 2010.

Finkielkraut, Alain. *The Imaginary Jew*. Lincoln: University of Nebraska Press, 1994.

Garber, Zev, and Bruce Zuckerman. "Why do we call the Holocaust 'The Holocaust'? An Inquiry into the Psychology of Labels." *Modern Judaism* 9, no. 2 (1989): 197–211.

Katz, Steven T., and Alan Rosen, eds. *Elie Wiesel: Jewish, Literary, and Moral Perspectives*. Bloomington: Indiana University Press, 2013.

Lustiger, Cardinal Jean-Marie. "The Absence of God? The Presence of God? A Meditation in Three Parts on *Night*." *America* 159, no. 15 (November 19, 1988): 402–406. (Reprinted in Elie Wiesel's *Night*, edited by Harold Bloom, 27–33. New York: Infobase Publishing, 2010.)

Rosenfeld, Alvin H. "Améry, Levi, Wiesel: The Futility of Holocaust Testimony." In *Elie Wiesel: Jewish, Literary, and Moral Perspectives*, edited by Steven T. Katz and Alan Rosen, 220–33. Bloomington: Indiana University Press, 2013.

Roskies, David G., and Naomi Diamant. *Holocaust Literature: a History and Guide*. Hanover, NH: Brandeis University Press, 2012.

Rothe, Anne. *Popular Trauma Culture: Selling the Pain of Others in the Mass Media*. New Brunswick, NJ: Rutgers University Press, 2011.

Seidman, Naomi. "Elie Wiesel and the Scandal of Jewish Rage." *Jewish Social Studies*, New Series 3, no. 1 (Autumn, 1996): 1–19.

Shandler, Jeffrey. *Jews, God, and Videotape: Religion and Media in America*. New York: New York University Press, 2009.

Weissman, Gary. *Fantasies of Witnessing: Postwar Efforts to Experience the Holocaust*. Ithaca, NY: Cornell University Press, 2004.

Weissman, Gary. "Questioning Key Texts: a Pedagogical Approach to Teaching Elie Wiesel's Night." In *Teaching the Representation of the Holocaust*, edited by Marianne Hirsch and Irene Kacandes, 324–36. New York: Modern Language Association, 2004.

Wiesel, Elie. "Art and Culture after the Holocaust." In *Auschwitz: Beginning of a New Era?*, edited by Eva Fleischner, 403–16. New York: Ktav, 1977.

Wiesel, Elie. *La Nuit*. Paris: Minuit, 1958.

Wiesel, Elie. *Night*. New York: Bantam Books, 1982.

Wiesel, Eli. *Un di velt hot geshvign*. Buenos Aires: Tsentral-Farband fun poylishe yidn in Argentina, 1956.

Wisse, Ruth R. *The Modern Jewish Canon: A Journey Through Language and Culture*. Chicago: University of Chicago Press, 2000.

Chapter 6

Arendt, Hannah. *Eichmann in Jerusalem: A Report on the Banality of Evil* [1963]. New York: Penguin, 2006.

Bankier, David, and Dan Michman, eds. *Holocaust and Justice: Representation and Historiography of the Holocaust in Post-war Trials*. New York: Berghahn, 2010.

Berkowitz, Roger. "Arendt & Eichmann." *New York Review of Books*. December 19, 2013. In response to Mark Lilla, "Arendt & Eichmann: The New Truth." *New York Review of Books*, November 21, 2013.

Bernstein, Richard J. *Hannah Arendt and the Jewish Question*. Cambridge, MA: The MIT Press, 1996.

Buerkle, Darcy C. "Affect in the Archive: Arendt, Eichmann, and The Specialist." In *Visualizing the Holocaust: Documents, Aesthetics, Memory*, edited by David Bathrick, Brad Prager, and Michael David Richardson, 211–38. Rochester, NY: Camden House, 2012.

Cesarani, David. *Becoming Eichmann: Rethinking the Life, Crimes, and Trial of a "Desk Murderer."* Cambridge, MA: Da Capo Press, 2006.

Douglas, Lawrence. *The Memory of Judgment: Making Law and History in the Trials of the Holocaust*. New Haven, CT: Yale University Press, 2001.

Feldman, Ron H., ed. *Hannah Arendt: the Jew as Pariah: Jewish Identity and Politics in the Modern Age*. New York: Grove Press, 1978.

Felman, Shoshana. *The Juridical Unconscious: Trials and Traumas in the Twentieth Century*. Cambridge, MA: Harvard University Press, 2002.

Lipstadt, Deborah. *The Eichmann Trial*. New York: Schocken, 2011.

McGowan, John. *Hannah Arendt: An Introduction*. Minneapolis: University of Minnesota Press, 1998.

Rabinbach, Anson. "Eichmann in New York: The New York Intellectuals and the Hannah Arendt Controversy." *October* 108 (Spring, 2004): 97–111.

Reichman, Ravit. *The Affective Life of Law: Legal Modernism and the Literary Imagination*. Stanford, CA: Stanford University Press, 2009.

Shandler, Jeffrey. "The Man in the Glass Box." In *Visual Culture and the Holocaust*, edited by Barbie Zelizer, 91–110. New Brunswick, NJ: Rutgers University Press, 1998.

Sontag, Susan. "Reflections on *The Deputy*." In *Against Interpretation and other Essays*, 124–31. New York: Delta, 1966. Originally published as "All the World's a Stage." *Book Week* (*New York Herald Tribune*). March 1, 1964: 1, 12–13.

The Specialist: Portrait of a Modern Criminal, DVD, directed by Eyal Sivan and Rony Brauman, 1999.

Stangneth, Bettina. *Eichmann Before Jerusalem: The Unexamined Life of a Mass Murderer*. New York: Knopf, 2014.

Yablonka, Hanna. *The State of Israel vs. Adolf Eichmann*. New York: Schocken Books, 2004.

Young-Bruehl, Elisabeth. *Hannah Arendt: For Love of the World*. New Haven, CT: Yale University Press, 2004.

Chapter 7

Bentley, Eric. *The Storm over the Deputy: Essays and Articles about Hochhuth's Explosive Drama*. New York: Grove Press, 1964.

Bergen, Doris L. *Twisted Cross: The German Christian Movement in the Third Reich*. Chapel Hill: University of North Carolina Press, 1996.

Brecht, Bertolt. "Alienation Effects in Chinese Acting." In *Brecht on Theatre: The Development of an Aesthetic*, edited and translated by John Willett, 91–99. New York: Hill and Wang, 1964.

Cesarani, David, and Paul A. Levine, eds. *Bystanders to the Holocaust: a Re-Evaluation*. London: Frank Cass, 2002.

Cornwell, John. *Hitler's Pope: The Secret History of Pius XII*. New York: Penguin, 1999.

Dalin, David G., and Joseph Bottum, eds. *The Pius War: Responses to the Critics of Pius XII*. Lanham, MD: Lexington Books, 2010.

Demetz, Peter. *Postwar German Literature: A Critical Introduction*. New York: Pegasus, 1970.

Diner, Hasia R. *We Remember with Reverence and Love: American Jews and the Myth of Silence after the Holocaust, 1945–1962*. New York: New York University Press, 2009.

Ezrahi, Sidra DeKoven. *By Words Alone: The Holocaust in Literature*. Chicago: University of Chicago Press, 1980.

Glenn, Jerry. "Faith, Love, and the Tragic Conflict in Hochhuth's *Der Stellvertreter*." *German Studies Review* 7, no. 3 (October 1984), 481–98.

Goldhagen, Daniel Jonah. *A Moral Reckoning: The Role of the Church in the Holocaust and Its Unfulfilled Duty of Repair.* New York: Random House, 2007.

Hochhuth, Rolf. *The Deputy.* With a Preface by Albert Schweitzer. Baltimore, MD: The Johns Hopkins University Press, 1997.

Huyssen, Andreas. *After the Great Divide: Modernism, Mass Culture, Postmodernism.* Bloomington: Indiana University Press, 1986.

Langer, Lawrence L. *Admitting the Holocaust.* New York: Oxford University Press, 1995.

Marrus, Michael R. "Pius XII and the Holocaust: Ten Essential Themes." In *Pope Pius XII and the Holocaust,* edited by Carol Ann Rittner and John King Roth, 42–55. New York: Continuum, 2002.

Phayer, Michael. *Pius XII, the Holocaust, and the Cold War.* Bloomington: Indiana University Press, 2008.

Plunka, Gene A. *Holocaust Drama: The Theater of Atrocity.* New York: Cambridge University Press, 2009.

Rittner, Carol Ann, and John King Roth, eds. *Pope Pius XII and the Holocaust.* New York: Continuum, 2002.

Spicer, Kevin P. "Catholics." In *The Oxford Handbook of Holocaust Studies,* edited by Peter Hayes and John K. Roth, 233–49. New York: Oxford University Press, 2010.

Steigmann-Gall, Richard. *The Holy Reich: Nazi Conceptions of Christianity, 1919–1945.* New York: Cambridge University Press, 2003.

Taëni, Rainer. *Rolf Hochhuth.* Munich: Edition Text + Kritik, 1977.

"Vietnam in Basel." *Der Spiegel.* October 2, 1963, 84–88.

Ward, Margaret E. *Rolf Hochhuth.* Boston: Twayne Publishers, 1977.

Whitfield, Stephen J. "The Deputy: History, Morality, Art." *Modern Judaism* 30, no. 2 (2010): 153–71.

Zuccotti, Susan. *Under His Very Windows: The Vatican and the Holocaust in Italy.* New Haven, CT: Yale University Press, 2002.

Chapter 8

Canby, Vincent. "The Night Porter is Romantic Pornography." *The New York Times.* October 31, 1974.

De Lauretis, Teresa. "Cavani's *Night Porter:* A Woman's Film?" *Film Quarterly* 30, no. 2 (1976): 35–38.

Donahue, William Collins. *Holocaust as Fiction: Bernhard Schlink's Nazi Novels and Their Films.* New York: Palgrave Macmillan, 2010.

Ebert, Roger. "*The Night Porter.*" *Chicago Sun-Times.* February 10, 1975.

Friedländer, Saul. *Reflections of Nazism: An Essay on Kitsch and Death.* New York: Harper & Row, 1984.

Hake, Sabine. *Screen Nazis: Cinema, History, and Democracy.* Madison: University of Wisconsin Press, 2012.

Hilberg, Raul. *The Destruction of the European Jews.* 3rd edition. New Haven, CT: Yale University Press, 2003.

Hoberman, J. "100 Best Films of the 20th Century by the Village Voice Critics Poll." *Village Voice.* January 4, 2000.

Insdorf, Annette. *Indelible Shadows: Film and the Holocaust*. 3rd edition. New York: Cambridge University Press, 2003.

Kerner, Aaron. *Film and the Holocaust: New Perspectives on Dramas, Documentaries, and Experimental Films*. New York: Continuum, 2011.

"Korno, Monik." [pseud.] *Hayiti kalbato ha-peratit shel kolonel Shults* [I was Colonel Schulz's Private Bitch]. Tel Aviv: Eshet, 1962.

Koven, Mikel. "'The Film you are about to see is Based on Documented Fact': Italian Nazi Sexploitation Cinema." In *Alternative Europe: Eurotrash and Exploitation Cinema from 1945*, edited by Ernest Mathijs and Xavier Mendik, 19–31. London: Wallflower Press, 2004.

Magilow, Daniel H., Elizabeth Bridges, and Kristin T. Vander Lugt, eds. *Nazisploitation!: The Nazi Image in Low-Brow Cinema and Culture*. New York: Continuum, 2012.

Meares, Joel. "How Führer Fav Filmmaker Inspired Depictions of Power." *Wired*. August 30, 2011. http://www.wired.com/magazine/2011/08/pl_prototype_leni/

Pinchevski, Amit, and Roy Brand. "Holocaust perversions: The Stalags pulp fiction and the Eichmann trial." *Critical Studies in Media Communication* 24, no. 5 (2007): 387–407.

Rapaport, Lynn. "Holocaust pornography: Profaning the sacred in *Ilsa, She-Wolf of the SS*." *Shofar: An Interdisciplinary Journal of Jewish Studies* 22, no. 1 (2003): 53–79.

Ravetto, Kriss. *The Unmaking of Fascist Aesthetics*. Minneapolis: University of Minnesota Press, 2001.

Schaefer, Eric. *"Bold! Daring! Shocking! True!"*: *a history of exploitation films, 1919–1959*. Durham, NC: Duke University Press, 1999.

Sciolino, Elaine. "It's a Sadistic Story, and France Wants It." *The New York Times*. January 21, 2013.

Shandler, Jeffery. *While America Watches: Televising the Holocaust*. New York: Oxford University Press, 1999.

Sontag, Susan. "Fascinating Fascism." In *A Susan Sontag Reader*, edited by Elizabeth Hardwick, 305–25. New York: Farrar, Straus and Giroux, 1982.

Chapter 9

American Jewish Committee, "Americans Confront the Holocaust." *International Journal of Political Education* 4, nos. 1 and 2. *Special Double Issue: Reactions to "Holocaust"* (May 1981): 5–20.

Green, Gerald. *Holocaust*. New York: Bantam, 1978.

Imaginary Witness: Hollywood and the Holocaust. Directed by Daniel Anker. USA, 2004.

Insdorf, Annette. *Indelible Shadows: Film and the Holocaust*. New York: Cambridge University Press, 2002.

Kaes, Anton. "The American television series Holocaust is shown in West Germany." In *Yale Companion to Jewish Writing and Thought in German Culture 1096–1996*, edited by Sander L. Gilman and Jack Zipes, 783–89. New Haven, CT: Yale University Press, 1997.

Kansteiner, Wulf. *In Pursuit of German Memory: History, Television and Politics after Auschwitz.* Athens: Ohio University Press, 2006.

Kansteiner, Wulf. "What is the Opposite of Genocide? Philosemitic Television in Germany, 1963–1995." In *Philosemitism in History*, edited by Jonathan Karp and Adam Sutcliffe, 289–313. New York: Cambridge University Press, 2011.

Paletz, David L., ed. *International Journal of Political Education. Special Double Issue: Reactions to "Holocaust"* 4, nos. 1 and 2 (May 1981).

Rosensaft, Menachem Z. "Distorting the Holocaust." *Midstream*, June/July, 1978: 54–56.

Schwarz, Daniel R. *Imagining the Holocaust.* New York: St. Martin's Press, 1999.

Shandler, Jeffrey. *While America Watches: Televising the Holocaust.* New York: Oxford University Press, 1999.

Wiesel, Elie. "Trivializing the Holocaust: Semi-Fact and Semi-Fiction." *The New York Times.* April 16, 1978.

Zielinski, Siegfried. "History as Entertainment and Provocation: The TV Series *Holocaust* in West Germany." In *Germans and Jews since the Holocaust*, edited by Anson Rabinbach and Jack Zipes, 258–86. New York: Holmes & Meier, 1986.

Chapter 10

Felman, Shoshana, and Dori Laub. *Testimony: Crises of Witnessing in Literature, Psychoanalysis, and History.* New York: Routledge, 1992.

Hansen, Miriam. "*Schindler's List* is not *Shoah*: The Second Commandment, Popular Modernism, and Public Memory." *Critical Inquiry* 22 (Winter, 1996): 292–312.

Hirsch, Marianne, and Leo Spitzer. "Gendered Translations: Claude Lanzmann's *Shoah*." In *Gendering War Talk*, edited by Miriam Cook and Angela Woollacott, 3–19. Princeton, NJ: Princeton University Press, 1993.

Langer, Lawrence L. *Admitting the Holocaust: Collected Essays.* New York: Oxford University Press, 1995.

Langer, Lawrence L. *Holocaust Testimonies: The Ruins of Memory.* New Haven, CT: Yale University Press, 1991.

Lanzmann, Claude. *The Patagonian Hare. A Memoir.* Translated by Frank Wynne. New York: Macmillan, 2012.

Lanzmann, Claude. *Shoah: an Oral History of the Holocaust. The Complete Text of the Film.* Preface by Simone de Beauvoir. New York: Pantheon Books, 1985.

Liebman, Stuart, ed. *Claude Lanzmann's* Shoah: *Key Essays.* New York: Oxford University Press, 2007.

Loshitzky, Yosefa, ed. *Spielberg's Holocaust: Critical Perspectives on Schindler's List.* Bloomington: Indiana University Press, 1997.

Zelizer, Barbie, ed. *Visual Culture and the Holocaust.* New Brunswick, NJ: Rutgers University Press, 2001.

Chapter 11

Berger, Alan L. *Children of Job: American Second-Generation Witnesses to the Holocaust*. Albany: State University of New York Press, 1997.

Bukiet, Melvin Jules. *Nothing Makes you Free: Writings by Descendants of Jewish Holocaust Survivors*. New York: Norton, 2002.

Diner, Dan. "Negative Symbiosis: Germans and Jews after Auschwitz." In *Reworking the Past: Hitler, the Holocaust and the Historians' Debate*, edited by Peter Baldwin, 251–61. Boston: Beacon Press, 1990.

Hirsch, Marianne. "Family Pictures: *Maus*, Mourning, and Post-Memory." *Discourse* 15, no. 2. *Special issue: the Emotions, Gender, and the Politics of Subjectivity* (Winter, 1992–93): 3–29.

Hirsch, Marianne. *Family Frames: Photography, Narrative, and Postmemory*. Cambridge, MA: Harvard University Press, 1997.

Hirsch, Marianne. "Surviving Images: Holocaust Photographs and the Work of Postmemory." In *Visual Culture and the Holocaust*, edited by Barbie Zelizer, 215–46. New Brunswick, NJ: Rutgers University Press, 2001.

Horowitz, Sara R. *Voicing the Void: Muteness and Memory in Holocaust Fiction*. Albany: State University of New York Press, 1997.

Huyssen, Andreas. "Of Mice and Mimesis: Reading Spiegelman with Adorno." *New German Critique* 81 (Fall 2000): 65–82.

McGlothlin, Erin. *Second-Generation Holocaust Literature: Legacies of Survival and Perpetration*. Rochester, NY: Camden House, 2006.

Rosen, Alan. "The Language of Survival: English as Metaphor in Spiegelman's Maus." *Prooftexts* 15, no. 3 (September 1995): 249–62.

Spiegelman, Art. Letter to the Editor. *The New York Times Book Review*. December 29, 1991, 4.

Spiegelman, Art. *Maus: A Survivor's Tale*. Vols I and II. New York: Pantheon Books, 1986–1991.

Spiegelman, Art. *MetaMaus*. New York: Pantheon Books, 2011.

Chapter 12

Bartov, Omer. *Erased: Vanishing Traces of Jewish Galicia in Present-Day Ukraine*. Princeton, NJ: Princeton University Press, 2007.

Berenbaum, Michael. *The World Must Know: The History of the Holocaust as Told in the United States Holocaust Memorial Museum*. 2nd edition. Washington, DC: United States Holocaust Memorial Museum, 2006.

Cohen, Boaz. *Israeli Holocaust Research: Birth and Evolution*. Abingdon: Routledge, 2013.

Cole, Tim. *Selling the Holocaust: from Auschwitz to Schindler. How History is Bought, Packaged, and Sold*. London: Routledge, 1999.

Diner, Hasia R. *We Remember with Reverence and Love: American Jews and the Myth of Silence after the Holocaust, 1945–1962*. New York: New York University Press, 2009.

Gershenson, Olga. *The Phantom Holocaust: Soviet Cinema and Jewish Catastrophe*. New Brunswick, NJ: Rutgers University Press, 2013.

Gilbert, Martin. *The Atlas of Jewish History*. New York: William Morrow, 1992.

Hartman, Geoffrey, ed. *Bitburg in Moral and Political Perspective*. Bloomington: Indiana University Press, 1986.

Himka, John-Paul, and Joanna Beata Michlic, eds. *Bringing the Dark Past to Light: the Reception of the Holocaust in Postcommunist Europe*. Lincoln: University of Nebraska Press, 2013.

Jockusch, Laura. *Collect and Record!: Jewish Holocaust Documentation in Early Postwar Europe*. New York: Oxford University Press, 2012.

Lehrer, Erica T. *Jewish Poland Revisited: Heritage Tourism in Unquiet Places*. Bloomington: Indiana University Press, 2013.

Linenthal, Edward T. *Preserving Memory: The Struggle to Create America's Holocaust Museum*. New York: Penguin, 1995.

Marcuse, Harold. "Holocaust Memorials: the Emergence of a Genre." *American Historical Review* 115 (February 2010), 53–89.

Mintz, Alan L. *Popular Culture and the Shaping of Holocaust Memory in America*. Seattle: University of Washington Press, 2001.

Young, James E. "Memorials and Museums." In *The Oxford Handbook of Holocaust Studies*, edited by Peter Hayes and John K. Roth, 490–97. New York: Oxford University Press, 2010.

Young, James E. *The Texture of Memory: Holocaust Memorials and Meaning*. New Haven, CT: Yale University Press, 1993.

Zelizer, Barbie, ed. *Visual Culture and the Holocaust*. New Brunswick, NJ: Rutgers University Press, 2001.

Chapter 13

Eskin, Blake. *A Life in Pieces: The Making and Unmaking of Binjamin Wilkomirski*. New York: Norton, 2002.

Geller, Jay. "The Wilkomirski Case: *Fragments* or Figments?" *American Imago* 59, no. 3 (Fall 2002): 343–65.

Gourevitch, Philip. "The Memory Thief." *New Yorker*. June 14, 1999: 48–68.

Kozol, Jonathan. "Children of the Camps." *The Nation*. October 28, 1996.

Langer, Lawrence L. *Using and Abusing the Holocaust*. Bloomington: Indiana University Press, 2006.

Linenthal, Edward T. *Preserving Memory: The Struggle to Create America's Holocaust Museum*. New York: Penguin, 1995.

Mächler, Stefan. *The Wilkomirski Affair: A Study in Biographical Truth*. New York: Schocken, 2001.

Mächler, Stefan, and Moira Moehler-Woods. "Wilkomirski the Victim: Individual Remembering as Social Interaction and Public Event." *History & Memory* 13, no. 2 (2001): 59–95.

Neale, Timothy D. " '... the credentials that would rescue me': Trauma and the Fraudulent Survivor." *Holocaust and Genocide Studies* 24, no. 3 (2010): 431–48.

Peskin, Harvey. "Holocaust Denial: A Sequel. The Case of Binjamin Wilkomirski's *Fragments*." *The Nation*. April 19, 1999.

"Publisher Drops Holocaust Book." *The New York Times*. November 3, 1999.

Rothe, Anne. *Popular Trauma Culture: Selling the Pain of Others in the Mass Media*. New Brunswick, NJ: Rutgers University Press, 2011.

Salomon, Julie. "Childhood's End." *The New York Times*. January 12, 1997.

Suleiman, Susan Rubin. "Problems of memory and factuality in recent holocaust memoirs: Wilkomirski/Wiesel." *Poetics Today* 21, no. 3 (2000): 543–59.

Wieviorka, Annette. *The Era of the Witness*. Trans. Jared Stark. Ithaca, NY: Cornell University Press, 2006.

Wilkomirski, Binjamin. *Fragments: Memories of a Wartime Childhood*. New York: Schocken Books, 1996.

Chapter 14

"The Beginning." http://www.whitwellmiddleschool.org/?PageName=bc&n=69258 (accessed July 31, 2014).

"The Butterfly Project, Holocaust Museum Houston." http://www.hmh.org/ed_butterfly1.shtml (accessed July 31, 2014).

"Inspired by 'Paper Clips' Students Collect 6 Million Pennies." http://matzav.com/inspired-by-paper-clips-students-collect-6-million-pennies (accessed July 31, 2014).

Kokkola, Lydia, ed. *Representing the Holocaust in Children's Literature*. London: Routledge, 2003.

Langer, Lawrence. *Holocaust Testimonies: The Ruins of Memory*. New Haven, CT: Yale University Press, 1991.

Nir, Ori. "Bushes 'Touched' by Holocaust Documentary." *Forward*. March 4, 2005.

"Peoria Holocaust Memorial Button Project." http://www.peoriaholocaustmemorial.org/ (accessed July 31, 2014).

Petroski, Henry. *The Evolution of Useful Things: How Everyday Artifacts-From Forks and Pins to Paper Clips and Zippers-Came to be as They Are*. New York: Vintage, 1994.

"Project6Million." http://www.project6million.org/ (accessed July 31, 2014).

Schroeder, Peter W., and Dagmar Schroeder-Hildebrand. *Six Million Paper Clips: The Making of a Children's Holocaust Memorial*. Minneapolis, MN: Kar-Ben Publishing, 2004.

Schweber, Simone. "Holocaust education." *In International handbook of Jewish education*. Springer: Dordrecht, 2011, 461–78.

Scott, A.O. "Grasping Extraordinary Evil Through the Very Ordinary." *The New York Times*. November 24, 2004.

White, Deborah H., ed. "Learning Through Service: A Tennessee Sampler." http://www.tn.gov/finance/adm/vt/documents/LearningthroughService-ATennesseeSampler.pdf (accessed July 31, 2014).

Chapter 15

Apel, Dora. "Art." In *The Oxford Handbook of Holocaust Studies*, edited by Peter Hayes and John K. Roth, 461–77. New York: Oxford University Press, 2010.

Bürger, Peter. *Theory of the Avant-Garde.* Translated by Michael Shaw. Minneapolis: University of Minnesota Press, 1984.

Ephross, Peter. "Holocaust Art Exhibit is Altered, but Critics Vow to Launch Boycott." *Jewish Telegraphic Agency*, New York. March 7, 2002.

Feinstein, Steve, ed. *Absence/presence. Essays and Reflections on the Artistic Memory of the Holocaust.* Syracuse, NY: Syracuse University Press, 2005.

Gerz, Rudolf. "Zugzwang (Forced Movement)." http://www.rudolfherz.de/ ZUGZWANG.HTML (accessed December 8, 2013).

Greenberg, Reesa. "*Mirroring Evil*, Evil Mirrored: Timing, Trauma, and Temporary Exhibitions." In *Museums After Modernism*, edited by Griselda Pollock and Joyce Zemans, 104–18. Malden, MA: Wiley-Blackwell, 2007.

Heartney, Eleanor. "Out of the Bunker." *Art in America*, New York. July 2002.

Kimmelman, Michael. "Evil, the Nazis and Shock Value." *The New York Times.* March 15, 2002.

Kissel, Howard. "Shock Art Hits a Rut." *New York Daily News.* January 11, 2002.

Kleeblatt, Norman L., ed. *Mirroring Evil: Nazi Imagery/Recent Art.* New York and New Brunswick, NJ: Rutgers University Press, 2005.

Kramer, Hilton. "Jewish Museum Show Full of Vile Crap, Not to Be Forgiven." *New York Observer.* April 1, 2002.

"The New Season/Art." *The New York Times.* September 9, 2001.

Nochlin, Linda. *Artforum* 40, no. 10 (Summer, 2002): 167–68, 207.

Rosenbaum, Thane. "*Mirroring Evil.*" *Tikkun.* New York, May/June 2002.

Rosensaft, Menachem Z. "Demystifying Nazism, or Trivializing Its Victims? A Debate: How Pseudo-Artists Desecrate the Holocaust." *Forward.* January 18, 2002.

Schjeldahl, Peter. "The Hitler Show." *New Yorker.* April 1, 2002.

Solomon, Deborah. "The Way We Live Now: Questions for Tom Sachs, Designer Death Camp." *The New York Times Magazine.* March 10, 2002.

Stewart, Barbara. "Jewish Museum to Add Warning Label on Its Show." *The New York Times.* March 2, 2002.

Swanson, Stevenson. "Jewish Museum's Holocaust Exhibit Igniting Outrage." *Chicago Tribune.* March 17, 2002.

Chapter 16

Daum, Andreas W., and Christof Mauch, eds. *Berlin–Washington 1800–2000: Capital Cities, Cultural Representation, and National Identities.* New York: Cambridge University Press, 2005.

Dekel, Irit. *Mediation at the Holocaust Memorial in Berlin.* New York: Palgrave Macmillan, 2013.

Friedländer, Saul, ed. *Probing the Limits of Representation. Nazism and the Final Solution.* Cambridge, MA: Harvard University Press, 1992.

Hirsch, Marianne, and Nancy K. Miller, eds. *Rites of Return: Diaspora Poetics and the Politics of Memory.* New York: Columbia University Press, 2011.

Kovach, Thomas A., and Martin Walser. *The Burden of the Past: Martin Walser on Modern German Identity: Texts, Contexts, Commentary.* Rochester, NY: Camden House, 2008.

Kramer, Jane. "The Politics of Memory." *New Yorker*. August 14, 1995: 48–65.

Rapaport, Lynn. *Jews in Germany after the Holocaust: Memory, Identity, and German–Jewish Relations*. New York: Cambridge University Press, 1997.

Sturken, Marita. "Pilgrimages, Reenactment, and Souvenirs. Modes of Memory Tourism." In *Rites of Return: Diaspora Poetics and the Politics of Memory*, edited by Marianne Hirsch and Nancy K. Miller, 280–93. New York: Columbia University Press, 2013.

Till, Karen E. *The New Berlin: Memory, Politics, Place*. Minneapolis: University of Minnesota Press, 2005.

Wiedmer, Caroline. *The Claims of Memory: Representations of the Holocaust in Contemporary Germany and France*. Ithaca, NY: Cornell University Press, 1999.

Young, James E. *The Texture of Memory: Holocaust Memorials and Meaning*. New Haven, CT: Yale University Press, 1993.

Young, James E. *At Memory's Edge: After-Images of the Holocaust in Contemporary Art and Architecture*. New Haven, CT: Yale University Press, 2000.

Young, James E. "Germany's Holocaust Memorial Problem—and Mine." *The Public Historian* 24, no. 4 (Fall 2002): 65–80.

Index

9/11 (event), 154, 156
9/11 (memorial), 44
60 Minutes (television show), 136
20th Century Fox (film studio), 24, 27

Absence/Presence: The Artistic Memory of Holocaust and Genocide (art exhibition), 192n4
Academy Awards (Oscars), 27, 89–90, 108, 176n16
Adorno, Theodor W., 5–6, 67; works by, "Cultural Criticism and Society," 5
Afghanistan, 13
Africa, 83
Allied Forces, 24–29, 106, 123, 182n8
Alltagsgeschichte (history of everyday life), 98
America. *See* United States
American Jewish Committee, 100
American Orthopsychiatric Association (ORTHO), 137
American Revolution, 66
Améry, Jean, 56–57
Amsterdam, 44
Anne Frank House, 44
Anne Frank Project, The (art work), 51
anti-Americanism, 50
Anti-Defamation League, 143, 147, 150
anti-Jewish discrimination, 73; measures, 44; persecution, 40; sentiment, 83; violence, 128
anti-Judaism, 78
anti-Semitism, 34–35, 39, 65–68, 78–79, 95, 107, 116, 128, 130, 145, 149, 151, 166, 169
Arad, Boaz, works by, *Marcel, Marcel* (video), 159
architecture, 126–27, 130–31, 169

archives, 36, 41, 70, 79, 102–104, 127, 138, 168
Arendt, Hannah, 8, 24, 62–71, 79, 149, 181n13; works by, *Eichmann in Jerusalem: A Report on the Banality of Evil*, 8, 24, 62–71; *The Origins of Totalitarianism*, 65–66; *The Human Condition*, 66; *Between Past and Future*, 66; *On Revolution*, 66
Argentina, 37, 53, 67
art, 2, 5–9, 24, 33, 51, 55, 69–70, 75, 106, 130, 152–61, 192n4
art exhibitions, 9, 152–61, 192n4
art galleries, 153–54, 158
Aschrott, Sigmund, 166
Askrad, Berl, 39
Atlanta, GA, 146
Aufbau (newspaper), 65
Auschwitz (extermination camp), 5–6, 19, 53, 59, 67, 73, 76–77, 86, 90, 95–97, 104, 114–15, 117, 129, 134–35, 138, 148, 159, 192n4
Auschwitz trials, 79
Australia, 97
Austria, 24, 87–88, 149, 160, 170
Austria-Hungary, 175n3
avant-garde, 115, 158, 193n20
Axis of Evil, 154

Babi Yar, 95
Basel, 74
Basel City Theater, 74
Bauer, Yehuda, 135
Beckett, Samuel, 118
Belgium, 139
Belzec (extermination camp), 76
Berenbaum, Michael, 126
Bergen-Belsen (concentration camp), 22, 28, 44, 124

Berger, Robert, 95
Berlin, 5, 7, 9–10, 16, 27, 65, 73–74, 77, 94, 124, 162–71
Berlin Wall, 166
Berlinale (film festival), 90
Bernstein, Elitsur, 138
Bernstein, Sidney, 28
Bieber, Justin, 44
Bilderverbot (ban on images), 5
Birkenau (concentration camp), 52
Bitburg, Germany, 123–24, 180n21
Black Gestapo, The (film), 86
Blösche, Josef, 18–19, 175n15
Bogarde, Dirk, 84
Bolshevism. *See* communism
Bomba, Abraham, 105, 186n9
Bonhoeffer, Dietrich, 79
Borchert, Wolfgang, works by, *The Man Outside* (drama), 182n9
Borough Park, New York, 156
Bourke-White, Margaret, 120
"Boy in the Warsaw Ghetto, The" (photograph), 12–20
Boys from Brazil, The (film), 90
Brandenburg Gate, 162, 168
Brass, Tinto, works by, *Salon Kitty* (film), 184n4
Brauman, Rony, works by, *The Specialist* (film), 70. *See also* Sivan, Eyal
Braun, Eva, 159
Brazil, 37
Brecht, Bertolt, 75
British Broadcasting Corporation (BBC), 164
Broadway, 48
Brooklyn, 156
Brooklyn Museum of Art, 155
Buchenwald (concentration camp), 28, 53, 57, 86, 120, 139
Budapest, 112
Buenos Aires, 63
Bundestag, 164, 168
Bush, George W., 147, 154
Bush, Laura, 143

Canada, 37, 44
Canby, Vincent, 85

Catholicism, 53–54, 57, 72–80, 108, 104, 183n36
cattle cars, 77, 127, 144, 146, 148–49. *See also* rail cars
Cavani, Liliana, 82, 84–85, 160; works by, *Il portiere di notte* (*The Night Porter*) (film), 82–91, 160, 184n4
Celan, Paul, 10, works by, "Todesfuge" (Death Fugue) (poem), 10
censorship, 36, 84, 130, 155
Central High School (Little Rock, AR), 44
Chelm (Poland), 32–41
Chełm. *See* Chelm
Chełmno (extermination camp), 102–103, 146
Chernofsky, Phil, works by, *And Every Single One Was Someone* (book), 144
Cherokee, 148
children, 8, 13–15, 17–20, 56–57, 76, 103, 112, 114–15, 117, 119–20, 128, 133–40, 142–51, 156
children's books, 143, 145
Childrens' Holocaust Memorial (Whitwell, TN), 9, 142–51
Chomsky, Marvin, 93
Christian imagery, 4, 14, 147
Christianity, 8, 14, 56–58, 79–80, 95, 97–98, 108, 134, 143, 147
Christmas, 49, 73
churban, 3
Civil Rights movement, 35, 44, 83, 148
Civil War, 97
Cold War, 35, 78, 130, 149
comics, 44, 112, 114–16, 119. *See also* graphic novels
commemorations, 10, 36–40, 123–25, 130–31, 146, 150–51, 165, 167, 170–71, 192n4, 193n6
Commentary (magazine), 65
communism, 4, 15, 35, 45, 50, 78, 130
concentration camps, 7–8, 17, 22–30, 36, 43–44, 48, 54, 64, 76, 82, 84–87, 89, 96, 100, 107, 123–24, 126–30, 134, 142, 146–47, 157, 159, 167. *See also* death camps; extermination camps
concerts, 36

Cort Theater (New York), 42
countermonuments, 165–71
crematoria, 24, 77, 104, 127–29
crimes against humanity, 25, 54, 58, 63, 124
Crusades, 36
Cuba, 37
Curb Your Enthusiasm (sitcom), 59
Cusian, Albert, 18
Czechoslovakia, 19, 28–29, 116, 146

Da Vinci, Leonardo, 5, 158; works by, Mona Lisa, 5, 14, 158–59
Dachau (concentration camp), 73
Dadaism, 158
Danube, 85
Darfur, 13
David, Larry, 59
De La Beckwith, Byron, 148
de Toth, Andre, works by, None Shall Escape (film), 29
Dean, James, 44
death camps, 13, 104, 114, 129, 143, 146, 150, 164. See also concentration camps; extermination camps
Defonseca, Misha, works by, Misha: A Mémoire of the Holocaust Years, 139
Demnig, Gunter, 170
democracy, 45, 88, 124, 126–27
Des Pres, Terence, 6, 9
diaries, 2, 25, 42–51, 58, 118
Diary of Anne Frank, The (drama), 7, 25, 27, 33, 42–43, 45, 47–50, 58, 74
Diary of Anne Frank, The (film), 27, 33, 58
Die Weltwoche (magazine), 135
Dietrich, Marlene, 86
digital technology, 41, 131, 154
Dinur, Yehiel. See Ka-Tzetnik 135633
displaced persons camps (DP camps), 36
diversity, 142–51
documentary theater, 74–75
documents, 1, 75, 79–80, 102, 115, 136, 188n8
Død Snø (Dead Snow) (film), 90

Doody, Alison, 88
Dössekker, Bruno. See Wilkomirski, Binjamin
Dössekker, Kurt, 135
Dössekker, Martha, 135
Doubleday (publishers), 48
Douglas, Michael, 160
dramas, 1–2, 5, 7, 25, 43–51, 58, 72–80, 96, 98, 157, 182n9
drawings, 37, 116, 120
Dubkowska, Dora, 39
Duchamp, Marcel, 158–59
Duke, David, 113

Eastwood, Clint, 160
Ebert, Roger, 85
Eich, Günter, works by, Dreams (radio play), 182n9
Eichmann, Adolf, 33, 149; trial of, 8, 24, 33, 58, 62–71, 74, 79, 83, 87, 96, 104, 125, 135
Einsatzgruppen (mobile killing units), 19, 95, 129
Eisenhower, Dwight D., 26–27
Eisenman, Peter, 162, 164, 168, 170
Ejszyszki (Eishyshok) (Lithuania), murder of Jews in, 127–28
Eliach, Yaffa, 128
Emmanuelle (films), 90
Endlösung der Judenfrage. See Final Solution
Englander, Nathan, works by, What We Talk About When We Talk About Anne Frank, 43
Erhard, Ludwig, 74
Eternal Jew, The (film), 116
Europe, 3, 8, 13, 15, 18, 25, 35, 52, 63–64, 67, 69, 74, 83, 88–90, 94, 96, 100, 103, 109, 114, 124–26, 128–30, 145, 164, 170–71; Central Europe, 37; Eastern Europe, 14, 34–38, 95, 98, 130, 138–39; Western Europe, 25, 66, 97, 130
euthanasia, 73, 129
Evers, Medgar, 148
Evian conference, 128
extermination camps, 15–16, 76, 102–103, 106. See also

concentration camps; death
  camps
eyewitness testimony, 26, 64, 71,
  103–10, 119, 121

fables, 116
fascism, 78, 84, 87–89, 91, 126, 159,
  165, 167
fashion, 159–60, 163–64, 168
fiction, 114, 117, 119–21, 133–40
Fiennes, Ralph, 160
films, 1–2, 5, 7, 10, 18, 23–25, 33,
    45, 48, 50, 56, 58, 65, 69–70,
    72–90, 95–96, 98–99, 103–104,
    109, 127–30, 139, 154, 157,
    175n3, 176n16, 186n6; art,
    87, 89; atrocity, 22–30, 50,
    176n12; documentary, 7,
    22–30, 33, 64, 87, 96, 98,
    103–110, 117, 143–45, 150,
    157, 161, 175n3, 186n4; horror,
    23–24, 86, 89; Nazisploitation,
    9, 84, 86–90; neo-Naziploitation,
    89–90, 186n6; Nazi zombie,
    90; propaganda, 24, 89–90,
    116, 159–60; sadiconazista,
    82, 84–89, 160; science fiction,
    88–89, 186n6
Final Solution, 3, 5, 62–63, 128
Fligelman family, 40
Fligelman-Szteinberg, Miriam, 40
Fondation du Judaïsme Français, 133
Ford, Harrison, 160
Forsyth, Frederick, 90
Fortunoff Video Archive for Holocaust
  Testimonies, 138
Forward, The (newspaper), 156
Foxman, Abraham, 147
France, 23, 28, 30, 34, 48, 53–55,
  57, 128
Frank, Anne, 8, 19, 33, 42–51, 58,
    144–46, 148–49; works by, Anne
    Frank: The Diary of a Young Girl
    (book), 33, 41–49, 58, 133
Frank, Margot, 44, 47
Frank, Otto, 42–43, 46–50
Frankenstein's Army (film), 90
Frankfurt, 44, 79
Frankfurter, Felix, 187n15

Freed, James Ingo, 126, 189n13
Freiburg, 65
French Ministry of Foreign Affairs, 107
French Revolution, 66
Frey, James, 59; works by, A Million
  Little Pieces (book), 59
Friedman, Pavel, works by, "The
  Butterfly," (poem), 146–47
Frisch, Max, works by, Andorra
  (drama), 182n9; The Fire Raisers
  (drama), 182n9
Fryd, Leah, 39
Funny Animals (comics), 115

Gambia, 97
Ganzfried, Daniel, 135
Garbage Pail Kids (toy), 115
gas chambers, 15, 28, 34, 37, 55, 76,
  103–105, 108–10
gender, 1, 85, 94, 107
genocide, 1, 3–5, 7–8, 13, 25, 28, 30,
    34, 48, 64, 73–74, 76–77, 83, 87,
    99, 108, 124, 126–27, 137, 139,
    144–45, 149, 153, 157, 161;
    Armenian, 140; Rwandan, 59, 140
German Atrocity Project, 29
German Christians (movement), 79
German language, 47, 65, 104, 117
Germany, 5, 7–8, 10, 22, 24–29, 36–
    40, 44, 48, 57, 65–66, 69, 73–76,
    78–79, 84, 86, 88–90, 92, 94–99,
    105, 108, 116, 123–30, 133,
    135, 137, 145–46, 148–50, 159,
    164–71, 182n9; East Germany,
    19, 34–35, 105, 108, 116;
    ethnic Germans, 18; Holocaust
    memorials in, 124–25, 128,
    162–71; Nazi Germany, 3–5,
    12–20, 32, 34–35, 44, 73, 76, 78,
    84, 88, 90, 106, 128, 161; West
    Germany, 34–35, 74, 98
Gerz, Jochen and Esther Shalev-Gerz,
    works by, Anti-Fascist Memorial,
    165–66
Gerz, Rudolf, works by, Zugzwang (art
    work), 159
Gestapo (secret police), 25, 63, 124,
    167; Department IVB4 (Jewish
    section), 63

ghettos, 12–20, 38, 66, 103–104, 106–107, 116, 127, 129–30, 134, 146
Gies, Miep, 44
Giftgas (poison gas), 154, 159
Gilman, Benjamin A., 143
Giuliani, Rudolph, 155
Goethe, Johann Wolfgang von, works by, *Faust,* 77
Goodrich, Frances, 42–43, 45, 47, 49–50
Göring, Hermann, 25
Gould, Morton, 93
Grabowski, Laura (Lauren Stratford), works by, *Satan's Underground: The Extraordinary Story of One Woman's Escape* (book), 138
graphic novels, 2, 112–21, 158. *See also* comics
Great Britain, 22, 28–29, 34, 49, 87
Great Synagogue on Tłomackie Street (Warsaw), 16
Green, Gerald, 93
Greenberg, Lucia, 116
Grosjean, Bruno. *See* Wilkomirski, Binjamin
Grosjean, Yvonne, 135–36
Ground Zero, 154
Grynzspan, Zindel, 71
Guevara, Ernesto "Che," 44
Guggenheim Fellowship, 65
Gurs (internment camp), 64
gypsies. *See* Roma and Sinti

Hackett, Albert, 42–43, 45, 47, 49–50
Hannah Arendt (film), 65, 69
Hanover, 65
Hanukkah, 49
Harburg, 165–66
Harpur College, SUNY-Binghamton, 115
Hausner, Gideon, 66, 68
Hebrew University, 70, 138
Heidegger, Martin, 65
Heidelberg, 65
Herodias, 85
Hess, Rudolf, 25

Het Achterhuis (*The Secret Annex*). *See* Frank, Anne
Heydrich, Reinhard, 95
High School for Art and Design, Manhattan, 115
Hikind, Dov, 156
Hilberg, Raul, 67, 83, 103, 135, 139, 181n13, 182n8; works by, *The Destruction of the European Jews*, 67, 83; *Perpetrators, Victims, Bystanders*, 182n8
Himmler, Heinrich, 16, 106
Hirt, August, 77
Hitler, Adolf, 40, 44, 64, 74, 77–78, 84, 88–90, 100, 114, 123, 127, 157, 159, 167, 175n3
Hochhuth, Rolf, works by, *Der Stellvertreter: ein christliches Trauerspiel* (*The Deputy: A Christian Tragic Drama*), 72–80
Hoffmann, Heinrich, 159
Hoheisel, Horst, works by, *Aschrott-Brunnen* (memorial), 166
Hollywood, 29, 45, 89, 93, 107, 109, 175n3
Holocaust, abstraction of, 76, 106; Americanization of, 43, 45, 50–51; as "master moral paradigm," 1, 96; as reflecting the "banality of evil," 66–67; bystanders, 2, 74, 78–80, 93, 95, 99, 102, 104, 106–107, 182n8; clichés about, 6, 9, 41, 86, 100, 153, 157–58; denial of, 7, 83, 114, 147, 176n11; education about, 17, 59, 124, 144, 147–48, 150, 161; emotional aspects of, 10, 13, 24, 28, 39, 41, 55–56, 70–71, 86, 88, 95, 105, 110, 114, 121, 127, 129, 136–37, 139, 161, 169; enablers, 2; false memory of, 137–38, 140; historical accuracy of, 20, 100, 144; impossibility of representing, 67, 104, 108, 117; liberators, 2; as master narrative, 108; moral authority on, 54–55, 75–76, 78, 134–35, 139; moral lessons of, 60; moral questions

about, 69; national myths about, 123–31; perpetrators, 2–3, 19–20, 28, 57, 63–66, 68, 85, 93, 95, 99, 102, 106, 117, 120, 124, 148, 153–54, 167, 175n15; redemptive messages of, 4, 7, 60, 96, 108, 129, 144, 150; refugees, 8, 64, 124, 128–29, 149; second generation, 114, 119–20; silence about, 33–36, 54, 57, 73, 76, 78, 99, 118, 120; singularity of, 6, 54, 58, 108; trivialization of, 92–100, 108–109, 144, 149, 155–56, 160–61; unwritten rules about, 54–55, 60, 134, 147–48, 154–55; use of term, 4, 64; witnesses, 2, 26–27, 36, 54, 56–57, 60, 66, 71, 76–77, 85, 102–10, 137–38, 180n1, 187n15
Holocaust memory, 8–9, 36–37, 39–41, 45, 53–54, 60, 64, 69, 83, 85, 87, 104, 110, 113–21, 125–26, 129–40, 144, 147, 151, 162–63, 193n6; collective, 64, 69, 109, 119–20, 151; commercialization of, 152–61; national, 8, 100, 126, 163–71; public, 100, 109, 165
Holocaust Museum Houston, 151
Holocaust survivors, 2, 8–9, 28, 35–37, 39–41, 44, 52, 54–60, 64, 66, 70–71, 83–84, 86, 97–99, 102–105, 109, 112–21, 124–25, 129, 131, 133–40, 154, 156–57; as children, 133–38, children of, 112–21; idealization of, 116; moral authority of, 135; survivor paradigm, 58–59
Holocaust victims, 2–5, 19–20, 24–28, 30, 37, 39–41, 43–45, 56, 58, 60, 64–66, 73, 76, 85–86, 93–98, 104–107, 123–25, 127–28, 130, 135–38, 142–43, 146–54, 159, 165–68, 170–71, 189n21; children, 8; dehumanization of, 191n12; disabled, 129; as metaphors, 59–60; six million, 4–5, 41, 68–69, 79, 129–30, 144–45, 151, 171; testimony

of, 106–107; victim paradigm, 58–59; "victims-by-proxy," 59
Holocaust: A Postscript (news special), 97
Holocaust: The Story of the Family Weiss (television miniseries), 7–8, 33, 74, 83, 93–100, 105, 120, 125
holograms, 8, 131
holokauston, 3. *See also olah*
Holy See, 77
homosexuals, 4, 167, 169
Hooper, Linda, 144, 146
Horrors of War (film), 90
Hrubieszów (Poland), 38
Hungary, 78, 112, 116

I Was Colonel Schultz's Private Bitch (book), 87
iconic images and texts, 13–21, 25, 51, 54–56, 108–10, 120, 129, 144, 148, 153–54
Ilsa, She Wolf of the SS (film), 86, 88, 90
Inglourious Basterds (film), 90
International Military Tribunal, 25–26, 28, 63
Internet, 7, 23, 41, 138, 163
intolerance, 96, 144–45, 147–48
Iran, 154
Iraq, 154
Iron Curtain, 35
Iron Sky (film), 90
Israel, 3, 5, 10, 35, 38, 53, 63, 65–66, 68–70, 86–87, 97, 103, 125, 129–30, 138, 159; anti-Israeli sentiment, 83; Arab-Israeli conflict, 83
Italy, 48, 54, 76, 78, 83–85, 160
Iwo Jima, 14

Jäckel, Eberhard, 165, 167
Jackson, Robert H. (Justice), 25, 27
Japan, 97
Jaspers, Karl, 65
Jefferson Memorial (Washington, DC), 129
Jehovah's Witnesses, 4
Jerusalem, 3, 36, 62, 69–70, 104, 130

Jesus Christ, 14, 76, 78
Jewish Councils, 66–68
Jewish Museum (Berlin), 163–64, 169–70
Jewish Museum (New York), 152–61
Jewish star, 14. *See also* Star of David
Jewish-Christian dialogue, 95, 98, 147
Jews, 1, 3, 5, 7, 8, 12–13, 15–20, 25, 28, 30, 32–41, 44, 48–51, 54–58, 60, 63, 65–69, 73–74, 76–79, 83, 89–90, 92–100, 102–108, 116, 118, 123–25, 127–32, 136, 143–49, 151, 153, 157–59, 163, 166–71, 173n8, 176n12, 182n8, 187n15, 189n21; acculturation, 95; American, 47, 74, 123, 65, 98, 100, 123–24, 131; as biologically degenerate, 17; collaborators, 39–40; as vermin, 116; assimilation, 95; of Chelm, 32, 38–40; Czechoslovakian, 146; children, 15; collaboration, 1; community organizations, 15; destruction of, 4, 28, 37, 54, 63–64, 66–67, 69, 74, 79, 83, 94–96, 100, 107, 128, 151, 171; Dutch, 178n4; Eastern European, 34, 36, 38, 95; European, 3, 8, 13, 15, 25, 63–64, 66–67, 69, 74, 94, 96, 100, 109, 124, 128, 164, 171; exclusion from public life, 8, 166; folklore of, 38; German, 44, 46–47, 64–65, 68, 94–95, 166, 170; history, 3, 10, 34, 36, 38, 40, 128; Italian, 54; of Kassel, 166; Latin American, 53; Latvian, 132; languages 36; literature 36, 39; leaders, 66, 68, 124, 106, 143; Norwegian, 149; Orthodox, 3, 37–38, 46, 156; persecution of, 3; Polish, 108, 114, 130; prisoners, 104; professors, 65; refugees, 8, 44, 128; resistance, 1, 16, 20, 68; Roman, 73, 76–78; stereotypes, 94; symbols, 144, 147; of Warsaw, 15–16; women, 105, 107
Jim Crow, 148
Johannesburg (South Africa), 38

John Paul II (pope), 97
John the Baptist, 85–86
John XXIII (pope), 78
Judaism, 15, 36–37, 57–58, 131, 146

Ka-Tzetnik 135633 (Yehiel Dinur), 71, 86–87
kabbalah, 56
kaddish, 146
Kafka, Franz, 65
Kaleske, Karl, 18
Karski, Jan, 104, 106–108, 187n15
Karski Report, The (film), 187n15
Kassel, 166
kehile, 39
Kellogg, E.R., 27
khurbn, 3, 36
King Haakon VII, 149
King Herod, 85–86
King, Rev. Martin Luther, Jr., 126
kippah, 146
Kipphardt, Heinar, works by, *Joel Brand* (drama), 182
kitsch, 93, 144
Kleeblatt, Norman L., 153, 1 59–60
Klüger, Ruth, works by, *Weiter leben: eine Jugend (Still Alive: A Holocaust Girlhood Remembered)*, 10
Koch, Ilse, 57, 86
Kohl, Helmut, 123–24, 167–68
Kolbe, Maximilian, 73, 76–77, 79
Kolmeshöhe military cemetery (Bitburg), 123
Königsberg, 65
Konrad, Franz, 18–19
Kosiński, Jerzy, works by, *The Painted Bird* (book), 139
Kraków, 16, 134
Kramer, Josef, 28
Kramer, Stanley, works by, *Judgment at Nuremberg* (film), 176n16
Kristallnacht, 19, 95, 128, 131, 146
Kruger, Diane, 90
Krüger, Friedrich Wilhelm, 16
Krystufek, Elke, 160
Ku Klux Klan, 114, 148

labor camps, 19, 116
Laden, Osama bin, 157
landsmanshaftn (mutual aid societies), 37–38, 41, 125
Lang, Fritz, works by, *Hangmen Also Die* (film), 29
Lanzmann, Claude, 76, 102–10, 117, 186n9, 187n15, 187n16
Latin America, 53
Latvia, 132, 134–35
Laurent, Mélanie, 90
Leipzig (concentration camp), 28
Levi, Primo, 54, 56–57, 60; works by, *Se questo è un uomo* (*Survival in Auschwitz*), 54, 133
Levin, Meyer, 47–49
Lewis, Mike, 22
Libera, Zbigniew, works by, *LEGO Concentration Camp* (art work), 152, 154, 156–57, 160–61
Liberty Park (New York), 44
Libeskind, Daniel, 169–70
Libsker, Ari, works by, *Stalagim* (*Stalags*) (film), 87
Lichtenberg, Bernhard, 73, 76, 79
Lidice (Czechoslovakia), 29
Life (magazine), 68
Lindwer, Willy, 44
literature, 5, 7, 36, 38, 130
Lithuania, 128
London, 46, 149
Louisiana, 114
Love Camp 7 (film), 86
Lucas, George, works by, *Star Wars* (film), 88–89
lunch counter boycotts, 148
Lustiger, Jean Marie (cardinal), 54–56

Maechler, Stefan, 136–37
magazines, 17, 18, 29, 36, 48, 64, 68, 78, 115, 135–36, 160, 163
Majdanek (extermination camp), 38, 129, 134–35
maps, 28, 37, 127
Marburg, 65
marriage, interfaith, 94–95
Mary (mother of Jesus), 14
Mauriac, François, 53, 57
Max Hayman Award, 137

Mead, Margaret, 147
memoirs, 1, 5, 9–10, 33, 38–39, 52–60, 67–68, 105, 133–40, 157, 161
memorial books, Yiddish. *See* yizkor books
Memorial to the Homosexuals Persecuted under the National Socialist Regime, 169
Memorial to the Murdered Jews of Europe (Berlin), 7, 9, 130, 162–71
Memorial to the Sinti and Roma of Europe Murdered under the National Socialist Regime, 169
memorials, 2, 4–5, 7–10, 33, 44, 52, 54, 97, 122–31, 135, 142–51, 155–57, 162–71, 193n6
Mengele, Josef, 77, 86, 90
mezuzah, 146
Michigan, 47
Milan, 78
Miller, Arthur, 69
Milton, John, works by, *Paradise Lost* (epic poem), 77
Mirroring Evil: Nazi Imagery/Recent Art (art exhibition), 9, 152–61
Monroe, Marilyn, 44
Montgomery, AL, 148
Montini, Cardinal (Archbishop of Milan), 78
monuments, 1, 139, 161, 164–71, 193n6
Müller, Filip, 104
Munich, 83, 105, 171
Muranów (district of Warsaw), 15
museums, 2, 4–5, 8, 10, 97, 122–31, 135, 138–39, 144, 146, 151–61, 163–64, 169–71, 174n18
music, 10, 30, 96
Mussolini, Benito, 78

Nation, The (magazine), 65, 133
National Jewish Book Award, 133
National Mall (Washington, DC), 122, 125–27
national narratives, 7–8
National Socialism, 13, 24, 65–69, 73–74, 82–83, 87–91; ideology of, 14–15, 25

nationalism, 129. *See also*
    Nationalsozialistische Deutsche
    Arbeiterpartei (NSDAP, Nazi)
Nationalsozialistische Deutsche
    Arbeiterpartei (NSDAP, Nazi), 1,
    3–5, 8, 13–17, 23–28, 34–35, 40,
    43–44, 46, 54, 56, 60, 63–69,
    74, 77–79, 83–91, 93–95, 97–98,
    104–108, 115–17, 123, 126–28,
    130, 134, 143–44, 149, 160,
    166; collaborators, 67, 135, 148;
    imagery, 153–61; resistance to,
    20, 68, 104, 145; scientists, 149;
    symbols, 147. *See also* National
    Socialism
NATO, 34
Nazi imagery, 87–89, 91, 153–61
Nazi Party. *See* Nationalsozialistische
    Deutsche Arbeiterpartei (NSDAP)
Nazi regime. *See under* Germany, Nazi
*Nazi Supreme Court Trial of the Anti-
    Hitler Plot, Sept. 1944–Jan.
    1945, The* (film), 24
Nazi victims. *See* Holocaust victims
Nazism. *See* National Socialism
Nazisploitation. *See under* films
NBC (television network), 92, 97
necrology, 37–38
neo-Nazis, 125. *See also* skinheads;
    white supremacists
neoclassicism, 126
Netherlands, 43–44, 46–48, 50, 67,
    178n4
Netherlands Institute for War
    Documentation, 46, 50
New York City, 42, 44, 51, 65, 93, 125,
    152–61
New York Daily News, The
    (newspaper), 156
New York Observer, The (newspaper),
    157
New York State, 143
New York Times, The (newspaper), 17,
    23, 48, 85, 93, 113, 123, 126,
    133, 144, 153–54, 157
New Yorker, The (magazine), 64–66,
    136, 158–59, 181n13
newspapers, 29, 53, 64–65, 113, 139,
    155–56

newsreels, 18, 24, 29, 95–96
Nicaragua, 97
Niemöller, Martin, 79
Nobel Peace Prize, 53–54, 58, 124,
    180n21
non-fiction, 112–14
non-Jews, 4, 33–36, 55–58, 90, 94–95,
    127, 168–69
North America, 74, 84, 88
North Carolina, 148
North Korea, 154
Norway, 145, 148–49
Nostra Aetate (In Our Time), 78
novels, 1, 46, 86, 90, 95, 157
Nuit et brouillard (*Night and Fog*) (film),
    29–30
Nuremberg, 36, 89
Nuremberg (film), 24, 176n16
Nuremberg trials, 17, 23–27, 29, 63–64,
    110, 176n11
Nussbaum, Tsvi, 18–19, 175n14

Oberhauser, Josef, 105
Odessa File, The (film), 90
Ofili, Chris, works by, *The Holy Virgin
    Mary* (art work), 155
Ohlendorf, Otto, 95
Ohrdruf (concentration camp), 28, 128
oil crisis, 83
olah, 4. *See also holokauston*
Olympics (Munich), 83
Operation Paperclip (U.S. government
    program), 149
orphanages, 15, 134
orthopsychiatry, 137

Palestine, 35, 37, 129
Paper Clips (film), 143, 145, 147, 150
Paris, 64, 72, 74, 103
Parks, Rosa, 148
Partisan Review (magazine), 65
Pasolini, Pier Paolo, works by, *Salò, o
    le 120 giornate di Sodoma* (*Salò,
    or the 120 Days of Sodom*) (film),
    84, 184n4
Passover, 16
Paul VI (pope), 78–79
pedophilia, 86
Penig (concentration camp), 28

Peoria Holocaust Memorial
    Project, 151
Perkins, Millie, 50
Pfeffer, Fritz, 47
philosemitism, 98
photographs, 1–2, 5, 10, 12–20, 24,
    26–27, 32, 37, 39–40, 51, 103,
    115–18, 120, 127–29, 153–55,
    159–60, 163, 171
Pius XII (pope), 72–80
Plath, Sylvia, 69
poetry, 5–6, 10, 39–40, 67, 130, 133,
    146–47
Poland, 4, 14–15, 28, 37, 39, 53, 73,
    77, 94, 102–104, 106–108, 114,
    116–17, 130, 134, 138–39, 146,
    159–60, 187n15
Pontius Pilate, 76
popular culture, 69, 84, 87, 88, 109,
    146, 155, 160
pornography, 9, 47, 85, 86–88,
    90, 160
Portman, Natalie, 50
postmemory, 120
POW (prisoner of war) camps, 116
Poznań (Posen) (Poland), 106
President's Commission on the
    Holocaust, 52, 97, 125
Presley, Elvis, 44
Princeton University, 65
prisons, 85, 118, 127, 164
Prix Mémoire de la Shoah, 133
Project6Million, 151
propaganda, 18, 24, 26, 89–90, 116,
    158–60
Propaganda Kompanie (propaganda
    company), 18
prostitution, 86
Protestantism, 79, 143, 167
Pulaski, TN, 148
Pulitzer Prize, 49, 112–14
puritanism, 87

Quel maledetto treno blindato (The
    Inglorious Bastards) (film), 90

race science, 128
radio, 36, 46, 48, 138, 182n9
Radio Oranje, 46

rail cars, 134, 142–43, 146, 150. See
    also cattle cars
Ramones, The (band), 124
Rampling, Charlotte, 82, 84
rape, 57, 84
Ravensbrück (concentration camp),
    167
RAW (comics), 115
Reader, The (film), 89
Reagan, Ronald, 123–24, 160, 180n21
Rego Park (Queens, NY), 115
Reitz, Edgar, works by, Heimat
    (television miniseries), 98–99
Riefenstahl, Leni, works by, Triumph
    of the Will (film), 24, 89, 159
Riga, 134
Riverside Park (New York), 125
Roberts, Sandy, 144
Roma and Sinti, 4, 167, 169, 173n8
Romania, 53, 55
Rome, 73, 76–78
Rondel, Israel, 18
Roots (television miniseries), 97
Rosenberg, Ethel, 35
Rosenberg, Julius, 35
Rosenblat, Herman, works by, Angel
    at the Fence: The True Story of a
    Love that Survived (book), 139
Rosensaft, Menachem Z., 156–57
Rosh Hashanah, 95
Rosh, Lea, 165, 167, 170
Rotem, Simcha, 103
Rothenberg, Ellen, 51
Russia, 4, 15, 28
Rwanda, 59, 140

S.S. St. Louis, 128
Sachs, Tom, works by, Giftgas Giftset
    (art work), 159; Prada Death
    Camp (art work), 159
Sachsenhausen (concentration camp),
    167
sadomasochism, 84–87
Safdie, Moshe, 130
Salome, 82, 85–86
Sassen, Willem, 67
Schildkraut, Joseph, 42
Schindler, Alexander (rabbi), 124
Schindler, Oskar, 108

Schindler's List (film), 8, 33, 88, 99, 108–109, 144
Schlink, Bernhard, 89
Schocken Books, 65, 137
Scholem, Gershom, 68
Schreiber, Rachel, 51
Schreibtischtäter (desk perpetrator), 64
Schroeder, Peter, 145
Schroeder-Hildebrand, Dagmar, 145–46
Schutzstaffel (SS), 13, 16–18, 25, 62, 76–77, 82, 84–86, 88, 90, 95, 106, 123–24, 128, 180n21
science fiction, 96
sculptures, 153
Séchas, Alain, works by, *Enfants Gâtés (Spoiled Children)* (art work), 156–57
Second Life, 8, 131
Second Temple, 3
Second Vatican Council, 78
Secret Annex, 43–44, 49
Selleck, Tom, 160
Sensation (art exhibition), 155
sermons, 36
Serrano, Andres, works by, *Piss Christ* (art work), 155
sexual abuse, 59, 137
she'erit hapletah (surviving remnant), 37. *See also* Holocaust survivors
sho'ah. See shoah
shoah, 3–4
Shoah (film), 56, 102–10, 117, 186n3–6, 186n9
Shoah Foundation, 138
shtetl, 38, 40, 127–28
Sicherheitsdienst (security police), 18–19
Siemiątek, Artur Dąb, 18, 175n14
Sighet (Romania), 55
Signal Mountain, TN, 148
Sinatra, Frank, 160
Sivan, Eyal, works by, *The Specialist* (film), 70. *See also* Brauman, Rony
Six Million Paper Clips: The Making of a Children's Holocaust Memorial (book), 145
Six-Day War, 83, 125

skinheads, 158. *See also* neo-Nazis; white supremacists
Skokie, IL, 125
Slovakia, 78
smartphone apps, 163, 171
Smith, David, 145
Sobibór (extermination camp), 38, 95
socialism, 4, 34
Sonderkommando, 104
songbooks, 36
Sontag, Susan, 69–70, 75, 84–85, 88, 91
South Africa, 37–38
South America, 83
Soviet Union (USSR), 15, 19, 23, 34–35, 38, 78, 129–30, 149
Spain, 48
Specialist, The (film), 70
speeches, 36, 106, 126, 159
Spiegelman, Anja, 114–18
Spiegelman, Art, 112–19, 158; works by, *Maus*, 70, 112–21, 158; *MetaMaus*, 115, 118
Spiegelman, Richieu, 115–17
Spiegelman, Vladek, 114–19
Spielberg, Steven, 8, 88, 99, 108–109, 138, 144; works by, *Indiana Jones and the Last Crusade* (film), 88; *Schindler's List* (film), 8, 33, 88, 99, 108–109, 144
Srebnik, Simon, 103
Stalag fiction, 87
Stalin, Joseph, 78
Stalingrad, 78
Stalinism, 65
Star of David, 77, 129, 146. *See also* Jewish star
Stern, Günther, 65
Sternberg, Josef von, works by, *The Blue Angel* (film), 86
Steven Spielberg Jewish Film Archive, 70
Stevens, George C., 27, 50; works by, *Nazi Concentration Camps* (film), 23–30, 50, 64, 109–10; *The Nazi Plan* (film), 24, 176n12
Stier, Walter, 105, 108, 187n16
Stih, Renate and Frieder Schnock, works by, Places of

Remembrance: Memorial to the Deported Jewish Citizens of the Bayerische Viertel, 166
Stolpersteine (memorial project), 160
Strasberg, Susan, 42, 49
Streep, Meryl, 92, 94
Strigler, Mordecai, 36
Stroop, Jürgen, 16–18
Stroop Report, 16, 18–19
Suchomel, Franz, 104, 108, 187n16
Sudetenland, 18
Suhrkamp Verlag (publisher), 137
suicide, 57, 115–16, 118
Sukowa, Barbara, 65
Survivor (television program), 59
Sutzkever, Abraham, 36
swastikas, 117, 127, 144–45, 147, 158
Sweden, 115
Switzerland, 74, 134–36, 138
synagogues, 16, 36, 39, 93–94, 125
Szrojt, Rivka, 39

Tablet, The (magazine), 78
Talmud, 56
Tarantino, Quentin, works by, *Inglourious Basterds* (film), 90
television, 7–8, 23, 25, 45, 48, 59, 64, 69, 74, 83, 92–100, 104–105, 125, 134, 136, 138, 165, 167
television commercials, 160
television programs, miniseries, 7–8, 33, 74, 83, 92–100, 104–105, 125; newsmagazines, 136; reality, 59, 134; science fiction, 96; sitcoms, 59
Ten Commandments, 6
Tennessee, 9, 142–51
testimonies, 1, 26, 37, 55–56, 60, 64, 70–71, 87, 103–10, 118–21, 129, 133–34, 136, 138–40, 150, 161
Theater De L'Athenee, 72
Theresienstadt (concentration camp), 92, 146
Third Reich, 87, 98
Times Square (New York), 90
Tisha B'Av, 3
tolerance, 45, 47, 126, 142–48, 151
Tom and Jerry (animated series), 116
Tony Award, 49

Topography of Terror (museum), 124
Toporowicz, Maciej, works by, *Obsession* (art work), 159–60
Torah, 37–38
torture, 27, 84, 129
Totem and Taboo (blog), 163
toys, 160–61
trauma, 6, 9, 59, 69, 105, 108, 112, 114, 119–20, 130, 134–38, 154, 157, 161
Treaty of Versailles, 24
Treblinka (extermination camp), 15, 16, 76, 104–105, 108
trials, 8, 17–18, 23–26, 29, 33, 58, 62–71, 74, 79–80, 83, 87, 96, 104, 110, 125, 135, 175n15, 180n1
Trotta, Margarethe von, 65, 69; works by, *Hannah Arendt* (film), 65, 69
True Glory, The (film), 22
Turkey, 97

U.S. Department of Agriculture (Washington, DC), 126
Uklański, Piotr, works by, *The Nazis* (art work), 160
Ukraine, 15
Umsiedlung. See resettlement
Union of American Hebrew Congregations, 123–24
Union of Polish Jews of Argentina, 53
United States, 3, 8, 23–27, 29, 34–35, 37–39, 43–45, 47–48, 54, 58–59, 64–65, 69, 74, 83–87, 92–100, 103, 115, 123–31, 136–39, 142–51; Congress, 126; history of, 64–65, 148; House of Representatives, 143, 150; national self-identification of, 125, 129, 131; South, 143, 147–48
United States Army Signal Corps, 27
United States Holocaust Memorial Council, 123, 126
United States Holocaust Memorial Museum (Washington, DC) (USHMM), 4, 5, 8, 10, 97, 122–31, 135, 138, 144, 146, 156, 170
United States Naval Reserve, 27

University of Chicago, 65
University of Southern California (USC), 131, 138
Urbach (Thuringia), 19

Vaaler, Johan, 148
van Alphen, Ernst, 161
van Pels family, 47
van Pels, Auguste, 47
Varnhagen, Rahel, 65
Vatican, 72–75, 77–79, 182n8
Vergangenheitsbewältigung (coming to terms with the past), 164
Verhoeven, Paul, works by, *Zwartboek (Black Book)* (film), 89
video, 70, 94, 138, 153, 159–60, 168
Vienna, 84
Vietnam, 13
Vietnam War, 83
Village Voice, The (newspaper), 124, 139
Visconti, Luchino, works by, *La caduta degli dei (The Damned)* (film), 160, 184n4

Wacky Packages (toy), 115
Waffen-SS, 16, 123
Wall Street Journal, The (newspaper), 155
Walser, Martin, 164
Waltz, Christoph, 90
Wannsee Conference, 95
Wannsee Villa, 5
war crimes, 17–18, 23, 25, 28, 57, 63–64, 90, 97, 105
Warsaw, 10, 12, 15, 94, 106, 126
Warsaw Ghetto, 12–20, 104, 106–107
Warsaw Ghetto Uprising, 15–16, 103
Warsaw Pact, 34–35
Washington, DC, 10, 122–31, 145, 188n8
Washington Monument (Washington, DC), 129
Watergate, 83
websites, 17, 41, 145, 147, 163–64
Weimar, 28, 56–57
Weiss, Peter, works by, *Die Ermittlung (The Investigation)* (drama), 182n9

Weizsäcker, Ernst von, 77
Wertmüller, Lina, works by, *Pasqualino Settebellezze (Seven Beauties)* (film), 184n4
Westerbork (transit camp), 43
white supremacists, 147–48. *See also* neo-Nazis; skinheads
Whitwell, TN, 142–51
Whitwell Middle School, 143–51
Wiesel, Elie, 8, 52–60, 93, 98, 105, 124–25, 133, 150; works by, *Night*, 52–60, 105, 133; *Un di velt hot geshvign*, 53, 55, 57–58; *La Nuit*, 53–54, 57
Wilder, Billy, 24, 175n3; works by, *Death Mills* (film), 24, 29; *The Seven-Year Itch*, 175n3; *Some Like it Hot*, 175n3
Wilkomirska, Wanda, 138
Wilkomirski Affair, 134–40
Wilkomirski, Binjamin (Bruno Grosjean, Bruno Dössekker), 9, 132–40; works by, *Bruchstücke: Aus einer Kindheit 1939–1948 (Fragments: Memories of a Wartime Childhood)*, 9, 132–40
Winfrey, Oprah, 59–60
Winslet, Kate, 89
Witness and Legacy: Contemporary Art about the Holocaust (art exhibition), 192n4
women, 8, 13, 17–18, 20, 28, 39, 55, 93, 103, 105, 107–108
Women's Liberation, 83
Woods, James, 94
World Jewish Congress, 123
World Trade Center, 154, 157
World War II, 33–34, 36–38, 54–55, 57, 63, 74, 83–84, 87–89, 113, 123–24, 128, 130, 132, 142, 145–46, 148, 171, 178n4

Yad Vashem, 3–4, 10, 37, 129–31, 138
Yale University, 138
Yiddish, 3, 9, 32, 34–36, 38, 40–41, 53, 55, 57–58, 104
yisker-bukh. See yizkor books

Yizker-bukh Khelm (Yizkor Book Chelm)
    (memorial book), 32–41
yizker-bukh. See yizkor books
yizkor books, 9, 32–41, 55, 125
Yom Kippur, 56, 95
Yom Kippur War, 83

Zeilinwarger, Levi, 18, 175n14
Zionism, 35, 39, 65–66, 69, 94–95,
    129
Zurich, 132, 135
Zygielbojm, Faviel, 39
Zyklon-B, 159